HEALTH CARE AND THE OLDER CITIZEN
Economic, Demographic, and Financial Aspects

C. Carl Pegels, Ph.D.

Professor of Management Science and Systems
School of Management
State University of New York at Buffalo
Buffalo, New York

AN ASPEN PUBLICATION®
Aspen Publishers, Inc.
1988

Rockville, Maryland
Royal Tunbridge Wells

Library of Congress Cataloging-in-Publication Data

Pegels, C. Carl.
Health care and the older citizen:
economic, demographic, and financial aspects/C. Carl Pegels.
p. m.
"AN Aspen publication."
Includes bibliographies and index.
ISBN: 0-87189-771-7
1. Aged--Medical care--United States.
2. Community health services for the aged--United States.
I. Title. [DNLM: 1. Delivery of Health Care--United States.
2. Health Services for the Aged--United States. WT 30 P419h]
RA564.8.P44   1988   362.1'897'00973--dc19
DNLM/DLC
for Library of Congress
88-6179
CIP

Editorial Services: Marsha Davies

Library of Congress Catalog Card Number: 88-6179
ISBN: 0-87189-771-7

Printed in the United States of America

1 2 3 4 5

Table of Contents

Preface

Health care for older citizens is becoming an increasingly important area for several reasons. The first reason is the growth in numbers of older citizens. They will continue to increase to about 12% of the population by the turn of the century, but between then and 2020 the percentage of elderly will increase to 20% of the total population. The second reason is the increase in the average age of the elderly. The older age groups, especially those over 80 years of age, will increase most rapidly. From a health care point of view this is especially important because the older the individual the more health care he or she consumes. The third reason is the increase in technology in health care. Health care technology has exploded in recent years and will continue to grow rapidly. Most of this new technology benefits the elderly patient but simultaneously also increases the cost of caring for that older patient.

Based on the above we shall see increasing amounts of the total health care dollar being expended on older citizens. Whereas it is estimated that the elderly now utilize about one-third of all health care resources; by the year 2020 they will utilize more than one-half of all available health care resources.

The problem that needs to be addressed is how health care for the elderly is to be financed now and in the future. In this book we attempt to find answers to the problems that arise because of the issues presented above. The most promising solution to the health care financing problem may lie in the increasing affluence of the older population. Unfortunately, health care costs do not affect each individual equally. As a matter of fact health care costs on an individual basis vary widely. Because of this wide variation the issue of financing health care costs now, by the turn of the century, and in the year 2020 should be addressed so that plans can be drawn up now to ensure an orderly health care delivery process and financing system.

This book also attempts to address the multidimensional aspects of health care in general, but especially health care for the older citizen. These multidimensional aspects range from nursing homes to home care, from acute care hospitals to ambulatory care facilities, from health maintenance organizations to preferred provider organizations, from Medicare to Medicaid, from medigap insurance to long-term care insurance, from hospice to family care, from prescription drugs to hearing aids, and so on.

The background information for the book comes from a variety of sources too numerous to mention here. I do appreciate the cooperation of all contributors. I also want to express my thanks to my wife, Patricia, for providing moral support during the preparation of this book. I also want to thank Valerie Limpert for an outstanding job of typing and proofreading the several versions of this manuscript.

C. Carl Pegels
June 1988

Chapter 1

Income Status and Health Care for the Elderly

INTRODUCTION

According to the Census Bureau, in 1985 there were almost five Americans of working age to provide support for each person over 65. It is estimated that by 2030 that ratio will be three Americans of working age for each person over 65 (Northrup 1987). The clamor already being raised is who is going to pay the costs of feeding, housing, and health care of all those elderly people?

There is little question that the elderly will become more numerous, both in absolute numbers and in proportion to the total population. The most rapid increase will occur in the first two decades of the next century. After that, it will gradually stabilize at slightly below 20 percent unless there are dramatic breakthroughs in the aging process. The question then becomes: Will the economy be able to provide housing and health care as well as other necessities to a population consisting of 20 percent elderly and 80 percent under 65 years? The answer I believe is an unqualified positive one.

The 65-and-over population after the turn of the century will be considerably better off on average than the current 65-and-over population. Large numbers of the elderly will be so well off that they will actually be paying more in taxes on income than they will be consuming in public funds. The important point, however, is that the burden of caring for the elderly will not be nearly as heavy as assumed by many of today's policy planners and analysts. As a result, even a population composed of 20 percent 65 and over need not be a burden at all to the rest of the population.

In light of this projection, it is imperative that appropriate legislation be introduced now to provide adequate services, housing, and health care to all of the elderly. This legislation should be as self-financing as possible. This may not be entirely possible now, but it may very well be in the future. Very few of the elderly want to be a burden to the younger generation. As the elderly population becomes more affluent in the future, it will be able to take care of

1

most of its needs. Until that time, however, general tax funding should support those elderly who grew up during a period of much lower affluence and were therefore unable to accumulate sufficient assets to provide for themselves in their later years.

KEY ISSUES

In the following sections, we address the issues of the income status of the elderly, the high cost of their health care, and the long-term problem of care they pose.

Income Status of the Elderly

During the five-year period between 1979 and 1984, the average income of elderly families increased by 18 percent and that of elderly individuals increased by 34 percent after adjusting for the effects of inflation (U.S. Congress, Senate 1986, 54–56). Elderly families are defined as two or more people, at least one of which is a person 65 or older. Elderly individuals are people who are 65 or older and living alone or with nonrelatives.

The income status of the elderly has improved for two reasons: (1) general increases in Social Security benefits through cost-of-living adjustments and (2) improvements in employer-sponsored pension programs. As a result, a smaller proportion of the nation's elderly were in poverty in 1984 than in the late 1960s. The poverty rate for the elderly declined from 25.3 percent in 1969 to 12.4 percent in 1984. The 1984 percentage assumes a poverty threshold of $4,979 in income for individuals 65 and older and $6,282 in income for two-person households headed by a person 65 or older (Gordon 1986).

The improved economic status of the elderly results from a shift in retirement income support. The shift is from a reliance on individual resources to a reliance on public programs. Prior to the mid-1960s, the elderly depended to a greater extent on income from earnings, families, or charities. Since then, public programs—such as Social Security, Medicare, and Supplemental Social Security—have become critical to the retirement income status of the elderly (U.S. Congress, General Accounting Office 1986a, 19).

Because of this improved economic status, the number of elderly in the labor force has dropped dramatically. In 1950, nearly one-half of all men 65 and over were in the labor force; by 1980, the proportion had dropped to only 20 percent. Women age 65 and over also decreased their participation in the labor force, from 10 percent in 1950 to about 7 percent in 1985 (U.S. Congress, General Accounting Office 1986b, 14).

Table 1-1 Annual Income of the Elderly, 1984

	Range of Income	
Percentiles	Couples	Individuals
0–20	Less than $10,000	Less than $4,200
20–39	$10,100–$14,449	$4,200– $5,799
40–59	$14,450–$20,099	$5,800– $8,049
60–79	$20,100–$30,099	$8,050–$13,699
80–100	$30,100 and up	$13,700 and up

Thus, it is not surprising that men also have been retiring earlier. Labor force participation rates for men at age 60 to 64 declined from 80 percent in 1960 to 57 percent in 1984. For the 55–59 age group, labor force participation for men declined from 92 percent in 1960 to 81 percent in 1983 (Manton and Liu 1984).

Income distribution levels among the elderly vary widely. In 1984, 20 percent of elderly couples had annual incomes of $30,100 or more, and 20 percent of elderly individuals had annual incomes of $13,700 or more. At the lower end, 20 percent of elderly couples had annual incomes of $10,100 or less, and 20 percent of elderly individuals had annual incomes of $4,200 or less. The detailed distribution of incomes is shown in Table 1-1.

The above disparity in annual incomes is expected to become even wider in the future. The higher-income elderly will see their incomes rise from assets, earnings, and employer-sponsored retirement income programs. The lower-income elderly will see their income levels remain relatively stable.

As noted earlier, there is currently a substantial reliance among the low-income elderly on Social Security payments as a source of income. However, the upper-income elderly derive most of their income from assets and employer-sponsored pensions. Table 1-2 shows the sources of income for the elderly by income groupings.

Table 1-2 Sources of Income by Income Groups

Income Group in Percentiles	Percent from Public Programs	
	Couples	Individuals
0–20	86	93
20–39	70	89
40–59	56	77
60–79	37	53
80–100	18	22

Source: Current Population Survey, Congressional Budget Office, March 1985.

In 1984, elderly women in poverty numbered 2.4 million, or 71 percent of the elderly poor. Although women outnumber men in the 65-and-over population, the poverty rate for women far exceeds that for men. In 1984, women comprised 59 percent of the elderly population; the poverty rate for elderly women was 15.0 percent, while for men it was only 8.7 percent (U.S. Congress, House 1986, 77–78). Elderly women's low-income status was the result of low participation in the labor force. They were thus less likely to be participating in employer-sponsored pension plans.

The poverty rate for the black elderly is substantially higher than for the white elderly. In 1984, the poverty rate among black elderly was about 32 percent, compared with only about 11 percent among white elderly. The median income of black elderly was only 60 percent of the median income of white elderly (Chen 1985, 664).

The low income status of the black elderly can be attributed to their lower-income, and usually jobs of shorter tenure, held during their younger years. Employer-sponsored pension plans for the majority of black elderly have been minimal or nonexistent.

The very old, those 85 and over, have a high poverty rate: about 21 percent in 1984. The elderly 85 and over had only 80 percent of the median income of the 64–84 age group. And 70 percent of the 85-and-over group consisted of women.

The reason the very old have lower incomes can be attributed to the fact that they had lower incomes when working. Any assets they might have accumulated have probably been used up or wasted away by inflation. As a result, for many of the very old, Social Security payments are the only source of income.

High Cost of Medical Care for the Elderly

In 1984, the majority of the elderly were in good health, according to the National Health Interview Survey conducted by the Department of Health and Human Services. In this survey, the health status of the elderly was defined in terms of three factors: (1) perceived health status, (2) days confined to bed due to illness, and (3) limitations of activity (Kovar 1986, 5).

Despite this apparently good health status, the elderly are relatively high health care consumers in terms of hospital care, physician services, and other medical services. Moreover, for the elderly population health care utilization increases with age. Those elderly in the 75-and-over age group are higher health care consumers than those in the 65-to-74 age group.

Health care expenditures for the elderly have also increased more rapidly for the elderly population, rising from $43 billion in 1977 to about $120 billion in

1984. In 1984, people age 65 and over accounted for one-third of all personal health care expenditures nationally (Waldo and Lazenby 1984).

Medicare pays almost half of the health care costs of the elderly. Medicare consists of the Hospital Insurance Program (Part A) and the Supplementary Medical Insurance Program (Part B). In the latter program, the elderly pay premiums to cover part of its overall expenditures.

Medicaid provides health care coverage to low-income elderly, most of whom are also enrolled in Medicare. State and federal Medicaid expenditures for the elderly exceeded $15 billion in 1984. This figure amounted to about 13 percent of all health care expenditures for the elderly (Waldo and Lazenby 1984).

Considerable sums are paid directly by the elderly for health care. Many medical and health services are not covered by Medicare. These include dental care, prescription drugs, eyeglasses, hearing aids, routine or preventive medical care, and long-term care. Medicare also requires the beneficiary to pay considerable co-insurance and deductibles. In 1987, the average Medicare enrollee's personal health care expenditure amounted to about $700. This average figure is deceiving, however, since some elderly have personal health care bills in the thousands of dollars.

To cope with these high personal health care expenditures, in 1984 over 20 million, or 80 percent, of the elderly were covered by either private supplemental insurance (about 18 million) or Medicaid (about 2 million), in addition to Medicare. Private supplemental insurance plans, called Medigap policies, are, as one would expect, quite expensive. In 1984, premium costs for Medigap policies averaged about $350 per person per year. Medigap policies providing more comprehensive coverage had considerably higher annual premium costs (Gordon 1986).

The five million elderly who do not have supplemental health care coverage in addition to Medicare are also those with the greatest health care needs. They are usually older and, because of the lack of coverage, are likely to avoid the use of health care services if at all possible.

Long-Term Care for the Elderly

Long-term care is an area of health care that public programs of health insurance have avoided because of the high costs involved. The only public program that covers long-term care is Medicaid. But Medicaid is available only to the financially destitute; to become eligible, one must first become financially destitute.

Long-term care is dominated by institutional care, but it can also include home care. Essentially, it consists of services provided to the chronically impaired and disabled. The classical notion of institutional care is the nursing home, which is not a homogenous institution. Some nursing homes provide an extensive array of medical, nursing, and rehabilitative services; while others provide only custodial and nursing care. The cost of institutionalization is high, ranging from about $18,000 per year and up. Medicare coverage for this type of institutional service is available only following hospitalization, and then only for a limited period. As a result, nearly all long-term institutionalization must be paid for by the person who is institutionalized, by relatives, or, if the person is financially destitute, by Medicaid.

As the elderly population increases, and as the very old as a proportion of the elderly increases, the need for institutionalization will continue to grow. In 1985, approximately 16 percent of the elderly age 85 and over were in nursing homes, compared with only 2 percent of the elderly between 65 and 74 (Manton and Liu 1984). Most of the elderly with chronic impairments remain in the home environment where they are cared for by a close relative. Usually, the elderly in nursing homes are there because they have no close relatives or they suffer from certain disabilities, such as Alzheimer's disease.

The cost of much of the long-term care provided in the home setting is difficult to determine. Home care is funded from many sources in addition to private pay. In addition, the home care provided by relatives is difficult to cost out. Usually, such care is not considered a cost if no payment transfer is made. However, when relatives are not available, the disabled elderly usually are institutionalized, and the real cost becomes evident, and can become enormous. Nursing home expenditures are quite well documented. In 1985, over $35 billion was spent on nursing home care. By 1990 these expenditures are projected to grow to $55 billion (U.S. Congress, General Accounting Office 1986a).

The major financing mechanism for nursing home costs is Medicaid. In 1985, federal, state, and local Medicaid expenditures for nursing homes amounted to nearly $15 billion. In contrast, in the same year, Medicare's share of nursing home expenditures amounted to only $0.6 billion. Thus, over half of nursing home expenditures come from the nursing home residents themselves or from their relatives. Currently, private insurance coverage for nursing home care is insignificant. However, given the high cost of nursing home care, and even though the premiums would be quite high and probably not affordable by those on limited incomes, the potential for long-term care insurance is promising.

Medicaid expenditures for nursing homes are a considerable budget item for the states. As a result, there are constant efforts to determine how the state's share of Medicaid can be reduced. The two most common ways of holding down Medicaid expenditures for nursing homes is by strict control and constant tightening of reimbursements to nursing homes and by controlling the number of nursing home beds available in the community. Because of tight reimbursement policies by the state Medicaid administration, most nursing homes try to avoid having to take Medicaid patients and instead prefer private pay patients. The overall result of such policies is that there is a scarcity of nursing home beds for Medicaid patients and an abundance of space for private pay patients. About half the states spend over 50 percent of their Medicaid budgets on nursing home care. Hence, it is not surprising that there is concern about the prospect of high long-term care expenditures. With the elderly population increasing, there is little relief in sight for state Medicaid budgets. They will in fact continue to increase for the foreseeable future.

It thus is clear that something must be done to provide a more rational financing scheme for health care for the elderly. This is especially important for chronic long-term care.

THE HARVARD PLAN

A recent study by the Harvard Medicare Project concluded that Medicare coverage needs to be expanded to provide more adequate treatment of chronic illness (Division of Health Policy Research 1986). One of the major problems associated with this conclusion is that public costs would rise significantly if the study's recommendations were adopted.

In effect, the Harvard study proposed that Medicare

- pay for home health care and outpatient mental health care for the chronically ill,
- provide comprehensive coverage of nursing home care,
- cover the costs of care coordination and gatekeeping (the gatekeepers would determine eligibility for services to prevent unnecessary use of long-term care), and
- finance long-term care in the same general way as for other Medicare costs but phase in this financing burden over a ten-year period.

The major advantage of this proposal is that, if adopted, Medicare would become a realistic national health insurance plan for the elderly. At present, Medicare is only a partial-coverage health benefits insurance plan.

Unfortunately, the Harvard proposal will probably not be adopted for fear of its high public cost. Yet much of the projected cost is already, or will be, incurred in any event. Older people will continue to enter nursing homes or receive chronic illness care at home, and the care will be paid for by the people themselves or by Medicaid, Medicare, or some other public or private financing mechanism. What the Harvard plan proposes is to finance it all under Medicare and thus coordinate the entire range of chronic care activities.

Financing of the Harvard plan is feasible in a variety of ways. Those elderly who can afford it could be asked to pay for the entire actuarial cost themselves.

Those who cannot afford it could be covered through funding under the general budget. Provided that the gatekeeping activities are well-organized, copayments are extensive for those who can afford them, and health care coordination is thorough, the Harvard plan could be a model health care mechanism as America enters the 21st century.

REFERENCES

Chen, Y.P. "Economic Status of the Aging." In *Handbook of Aging and the Social Sciences*, 2nd ed., edited by R.H. Binstock and E. Shanas. New York: Van Nostrand Reinhold Co., 1985.

Division of Health Policy Research. *Medicare Coming of Age: A Proposal for Reform*. Cambridge, Mass.: Division of Health Policy Research, Harvard University, March 1986.

Gordon, N. "Statement Before the House Subcommittee on Health and Environment." Washington, D.C.: Committee on Energy and Commerce, Congressional Budget Office, 26 March 1986.

Kovar, M.G. "Aging in the Eighties. Preliminary data from the Supplement on Aging to the National Health Interview Survey, United States, January–June 1984." In *Advance Data*, National Center for Health Statistics, HHS, no. 115, 1 May 1986.

Manton, K.G., and Liu, K. "The Future Growth of the Long Term Care Population: Projections Based on the 1977 National Nursing Home Survey and the 1982 Long Term Care Survey." Paper presented at the Third National Leadership Conference on Long Term Care Issues, Washington, D.C., 7–9 March 1984.

Northrup, B. "Gray Matters. An Aging Population Grows Younger and Shatters Stereotypes of What Is Old." *Wall Street Journal*, 24 April 1987.

U.S. Congress. General Accounting Office. *An Aging Society, Meeting the Needs of the Elderly While Responding to Rising Federal Costs*. GAO/HRD 86–135. Washington, D.C.: U.S. GPO, 1986a.

———. *Retirement Before Age 65: Trends, Costs, and National Issues*. GAO/HRD 86–80. Washington, D.C.: U.S. GPO, 1986b.

U.S. Congress. House. *Background Material and Data on Programs Within the Jurisdiction of the Committee on Ways and Means*. 99th Cong., 2d sess., 1986.

U.S. Congress. Senate. Special Committee on Aging. *Aging America: Trends and Projects*. 99th Cong., 2d sess., 1986.

Waldo, D.R., and Lazenby, H.C. "Demographic Characteristics and Health Care Use and Expenditures by the Aged in the U.S.: 1977–1984." *Health Care Financing Review* 6 (Fall 1984):1–29.

Chapter 2

Historical Development of Health Care

INTRODUCTION

This chapter traces the historical development of health care for the aged and analyzes the process by which the elderly became a separate demographic group. A considerable portion of the chapter is devoted to long-term care and the nursing home. Nursing home care consumes the largest portion of the health care dollar devoted to health care for the aged—this despite the fact that only about five percent of those 65 and over are residents of nursing homes.

The chapter also explores alternative forms of long-term care, such as home health care and day health care. These forms of health care can be either alternatives to nursing home care or supplemental services that help the elderly enhance the quality of their lives.

HISTORICAL PATTERNS

Conditions Prior to 1900

Historical analysis reveals that the concept of government-financed long-term care evolved not necessarily and solely for the care of the aged, but rather for paupers who were unable to care for themselves. When the family could or would no longer care for their poorest members, they became the government's responsibility by default, not necessarily by design. This governmental responsibility ranged from providing financial assistance to families and individuals to financing institutional relief programs, such as almshouses, hospitals, workhouses, orphanages, and prisons. Families received government assistance for the care of a disabled or senile relative, even for the building of a separate cell or enclosure for a mentally ill person. This type of support system, developed during the colonial period, made no distinction between poverty due to physical disability and poverty resulting from economic distress.

In the 17th and 18th centuries, paupers were auctioned to persons who were willing to undertake their support at the lowest cost to the community. Among those auctioned were children, the disabled, the handicapped, the feebleminded, and the insane. Others were contracted to work in return for their care. It was not until after the American Revolution that the almshouse was considered the most suitable and least costly way to take care of people in need. The 1843 Poor Law of England supported the concept of the almshouse as a means of assisting the poor.

In Britain, the view of the long-term care institutions as a method of caring for the needy continued to gain acceptance during the 19th century, despite the inhumane conditions prevailing in such institutions. The British almshouse has been described by Cohen:

> The Almshouse became the place of refuge for the impoverished, the insane, the feebleminded, the blind, the vagrant, and the sick, whether they were aged and abandoned, or so marginal as to be unable to make their way home. The almshouse pressed those who could work into servitude, for it often had an associated workhouse. Poorhouses were operated cheaply on low appropriations, often no more than ten cents a day per resident, by persons who had to take out their own income from whatever they could save from the meager appropriations. (Cohen 1974, 13)

In the Colonies, at a time when the formation of the state was barely underway, there were few voluntary organizations. The towns and counties gave financial support to those that existed. Not until 1854 did the government begin to accept the responsibility of caring for the disadvantaged and aged. In that year, a bill for federal financing of the indigent insane was passed; this was the first federal action dealing with public welfare. However, President Franklin Pierce vetoed the measure, maintaining that the federal government should not be involved in welfare programs.

With continued U.S. industrial development, the growing trend toward urbanization, and widespread unemployment, the almshouse continued to be the principal method of dealing with society's castoffs. Harsh treatments in such institutions continued and in fact was a matter of public policy, as noted in the New York State Department of Public Charities Report of 1875: "Care has been taken not to diminish the terrors of this last resort of poverty, 'the almshouse,' because it has been deemed better that a few should test the minimum rate at which existence can be preserved than that they would brave the shame of pauperism to gain admission to it" (Cohen 1974, 14).

By 1867, 16 states had developed state boards of charities, which began to inspect state welfare institutions and eventually assumed supervision of private institutions that received public funds. Ultimately, these state boards of charities developed standards of care for hospitals for the aged, for nursing homes, and for other welfare agencies.

Improvements in the Twentieth Century

Social reform characterized the 20-year period following the turn of the century. Public health dispensaries, hospitals for the indigent as well as the affluent, and convalescent and rest homes were established. A few states and cities attempted to improve the almshouse by developing systems of institutional classification, segregation of inmates and patients, and general program improvements.

As might be expected, welfare policy changed drastically during the Great Depression of the 1930s. Americans who once had frowned on public assistance now found themselves demanding it. In 1933, 25 million people depended on relief for their sustenance. The growing need for assistance brought a turnabout in opinions concerning government involvement in public welfare programs. The shift in attitudes was soon reflected in governmental policy.

The most important legislative action was the Social Security Act of 1935. Under this act, two systems were created: (1) a national retirement income system designed to provide income in lieu of wages to workers or their dependents when the worker retired or became disabled, and (2) a system of federal grants to assist the states in providing financial support to the aged, to dependent children, to the blind, and to the disabled. Early versions of the Social Security Act contained specific provisions against federal financial assistance to any kind of institutional setting. This prohibition reflected general attitudes of distaste for the traditional almshouse.

Formation of the Elderly As a Separate Demographic Group

In 1985, over 27 million people in the United States, almost 12 percent of the total population, were over 65. This population group is larger than the entire population of the most heavily populated state. However, this group has not always been that large. In 1900, the elderly amounted to 3.1 million, or about 4 percent of the population. By the year 2000 the group of elderly is expected to grow to over 30 million people, or over 12 percent of the population.

What sets this population group apart from the rest? There are three important factors: (1) political strength, (2) retirement, and (3) a relatively high need for and consumption of health care services.

The political strength of the elderly is evidenced by the increasing amount of attention paid to them by politicians. The educated elderly have proven to be politically influential because they have been able to organize themselves politically and get out the vote. As their numbers and their educational levels increase, their political power will also increase. Their governmental benefits are bound to increase, too, although there is a limit on the resources that society as a whole will be willing to spend on the elderly.

About 100 years ago, Bismark selected 65 as the pension age for Germans. This decision is probably responsible for eventually setting off the elderly as a separate demographic group. In 1935, the United States Congress adopted 65 as the mandatory retirement age, making U.S. workers eligible for benefits under the new Social Security system. Since that time, American society and industry have accepted 65 as the mandatory retirement age and have based many rules and plans on that chronological turning point.

In 1978, Congress extended a person's right to work to age 70, and in 1985 it abolished the age limit entirely. It was reasoned that the old mandatory retirement age had been set arbitrarily and that, though age 65 might once have been a reasonable age for retirement, it could no longer be justified, especially since the average person's life expectancy now extended a considerable period of time beyond 65. Moreover, although we do not fully understand the aging process, it is known that people age at different rates and do not abruptly lose their ability or capability to work.

According to studies undertaken by federal agencies and in academia, there is no indication that older workers are by definition poor workers. In fact, many studies reveal that older workers are superior in some instances. For a variety of reasons, older workers are usually more satisfied with their jobs than are younger workers; they have more realistic goals and expectations than their younger colleagues. Furthermore, older workers usually have settled into routine and stable lifestyles and are therefore likely to be steady, punctual employees with good attendance records.

The retirement syndrome, characterized by anxiety and depression, describes the physical and psychological consequences of mandatory retirement. Persons who develop this condition often complain of headaches and gastrointestinal problems, sleep more than they need to, and become irritable, nervous, and lethargic. Studies also indicate a correlation between mandatory retirement and the death rate. Early studies showed the mortality rate to be 30 percent higher than average for those who were forced into retirement at age 65. A forced change in lifestyle, caused by early retirement, can have a deleterious health effect, a possibility considered by many, especially those in the field of gerontology, to be a legitimate concern.

Pension plans and insurance packages are currently geared to a retirement age of 65. However, workers who can choose early retirement (such as firefighters, police officers, and federal employees) quite often do so. They can then collect their retirement checks, and proceed to find new jobs that are less demanding.

However, forced early retirement puts an economic burden on the American people. Those in the work force are particularly hard hit because that population segment becomes proportionately smaller compared with the growing retired population. The labor force must in effect support those who are retired and, for the most part, nonproductive.

The current pressure for earlier retirement is due to concern about unemployment and comes primarily from younger workers and from employers who feel that rigid seniority and tenure rules give them very little flexibility. Contrary to popular belief, the pressure does not emanate from the older workers.

Abolishing the mandatory retirement age is a positive step. A still better solution would be to allow the older worker to withdraw gradually from the labor force, for example, at reduced levels of pay. This would encourage people to work as long as possible but not beyond their limits.

The Growth of Private Nursing Home Care

It has been estimated that in the early 20th century there were over 1,000 nursing homes in the United States. These homes were sponsored and supported largely by churches, fraternal organizations, social organizations, and philanthropic groups. Applicants for admission had to comply with requirements with respect to physical condition, age, and property and residence mandates. In some instances, membership in the sponsoring organization was also required. Some homes accepted only men, others only women, although many admitted both sexes. Nearly half made no financial demands, while others required weekly or monthly charges. Sometimes applicants had to pay an entrance fee ranging from about $500 to thousands of dollars. In some homes, the residents were expected to "lend their services" for small duties around the home.

A clause in the Social Security Act established the groundwork for the present nursing home industry. As reported by Jacoby,

> The little-noticed Social Security provision encouraged the conversion of private housing into profit making boarding homes for the elderly— the forerunner of today's nursing home industry. In the thirties, few planners foresaw the massive social needs that would arise when families began to slough off the responsibility for older relatives at the same time that medical advances were keeping unprecedented numbers of people alive into their 70s and 80s. And no one asked whether profit-making institutions were best designed to meet those needs. (Jacoby 1974)

Long-term institutional care changed little between the early 1900s and the 1930s. But it has grown phenomenally since the 1930s. A 1939 Bureau of the Census study estimated that at that time there were 1,200 facilities in the United States with 25,000 beds. A 1954 inventory of all types of nursing homes and related facilities reported a total of 300,000 beds in 8,000 homes. The bulk of the growth reflected major postwar development of proprietary nursing homes to meet a significant backlogged demand. The demand continued unabated well into the late 1960s and early 1970s. By 1980 there were approximately 23,000 homes with a total capacity of approximately 1.4 million beds (Bureau of the Census 1985).

GOVERNMENT INVOLVEMENT IN CARE FOR THE ELDERLY

Since World War II, a variety of explicit public policy enactments and events have been directed toward the issue of long-term care for the aged. The following chronology of major executive and legislative decisions shows the extent and direction of national policy on this issue (Cohen 1974, 16–18):

- 1948 The Federal Security Agency (predecessory to the Department of Health, Education, and Welfare) sets up a task force on aging.
- 1950 Oscar Ewing, director of the Federal Security Agency, calls the first National Conference on Aging.
- 1953 Federal participation in financial assistance given to indigent persons in private institutions is authorized. The prohibition against payment in public institutions continues. States seeking federal participation in covering the cost of payments made to persons in private institutions are required to establish standards for such institutions.
- 1954 The Hill-Burton Program, for the first time, is given authority to aid, through direct grants, public and other nonprofit sponsors in constructing and equipping nursing homes and related facilities.
- 1958 The Small Business Administration is authorized through the Small Business Act and the Small Business Investment Act to provide loans to nursing homes.
- 1959 The National Housing Act is amended to provide for mortgage insurance to private lenders to facilitate construction or rehabilitation of qualified proprietary nursing homes. (Subsequently this was extended to provide the same kinds of benefits to nonprofit facilities.)
- 1950s Improvements in Social Security benefits include significant increases and extensions of benefits to the disabled and improvements in the earned income limitation provisions.

- 1960 Congress passes the Federal Assistance for the Aged Act to provide a program of federal financial assistance to the states to furnish care for the indigent and the medically indigent for a wide variety of institutional and noninstitutional programs. Activities for the White House Conference on Aging are initiated throughout the United States at local and state levels.
- 1961 The White House Conference on Aging is held.
- 1965 Title 18 of the Social Security Act (Medicare) is passed, providing for, among other things, payment of posthospital care in extended care facilities.
- 1965 Title 19, the Medical Assistance title, is passed, requiring states to include in their vendor payment programs inpatient and outpatient hospital services, laboratory and x-ray services, skilled nursing home care, and physicians' services. Amendments to the Social Security Act provide grants to the states to aid in meeting the cost of care for persons 65 and over who are receiving the equivalent of skilled nursing care and active treatment in state hospitals for the mentally ill.
- 1965 The Older Americans Act is passed, setting forth congressional policy concerning older Americans, defining the responsibilities of the state and federal governments, and providing for demonstration projects, research, and training programs.
- 1968 Congress authorizes the president to call a White House Conference on Aging.
- 1968 Intermediate care facilities are recognized as another type of facility that qualifies for federal participation in payments to indigent persons.
- 1968 The Social Security Act is amended to strengthen the enforcement activities of the individual states in regard to nursing homes. The amendment provides that no federal matching funds be paid to any nursing home that does not fully meet state requirements for licensure. In connection with the medical assistance program for skilled nursing home care, the act is amended to provide that states require a medical evaluation of each patient's needs prior to admission, followed by regular and periodic inspection (by an independent review team consisting of physicians and other health and social service personnel) of care being given to medical assistance patients in nursing homes.
- 1969 President Nixon calls the White House Conference on Aging and initiates planning activities.

- 1971   The White House Conference on Aging is held. The Secretary of Health, Education, and Welfare appoints a special assistant on nursing homes to deal with related problems. The president makes an address concerning nursing homes and federal actions designed to assist in correcting problems and abuses.
- 1972   Congress passes the Nutrition Bill for the Elderly, authorizing an expenditure of $100 million during fiscal 1973 and $150 million during fiscal 1974 to improve the nutrition of elderly Americans.
- 1973   Older Americans Act amendments provide $543.6 million for fiscal years 1973–1975, provide "such sums as necessary" for various federal programs, shift the Administration on Aging from HEW's Social and Rehabilitation section to the Office of HEW Secretary, establish a National Clearinghouse for Information on Aging, create a Federal Council on Aging, authorize grants for training and research in the field of aging, and authorize funds for the establishment of gerontology centers and for special transportation research projects.
- 1973   Social Security Act amendments extend Supplementary Security Income (SSI) coverage and increase benefits, alter the distribution of Social Security payments to increase old age and survivors' payments and disability and hospital insurance, and extend Medicaid coverage to SSI recipients.
- 1974   Actions by Congress increase nutrition funding, authorize $35 million in grants to states for transportation programs for the elderly, and expand the authority of the National Institute of Arthritis, Metabolism, and Digestive Diseases to "advance the attack on arthritis."
- 1975   The Health Services Program requires that new and existing mental health centers seeking financial aid provide specialized services to the elderly; authorizes grants to establish, operate, or expand programs providing health care at home (priority areas are those with large numbers of elderly); and broadens Supplementary Security Income eligibility.
- 1977   The Food Stamp Program is changed to allow some recipients to receive stamps without paying for them.
- 1978   Older Americans Act amendments authorize funding for home-delivered meals programs and expand the purpose of the act to include provision of "a continuation of care" for the "vulnerable elderly."
- 1978   Congress increases retirement age from 65 to 70 years.
- 1984–1986   A prospective payment system (PPS)—also known as the diagnostic related groups (DRG) system—is introduced for hospital patients covered by Medicare.

- 1985   Congress abolishes retirement age except for those in special job and professional categories.

THE NEXT STEP IN LONG-TERM CARE

Although demand for nursing home care is still quite extensive and many communities report virtually no vacancies in their nursing homes, there are indications that nursing home bed growth will at least level out to a rate that reflects the growth of the elderly population. The reason for this reduced growth is the increasing demand for home and day health care. Although home and day care is not always a possibility for those elderly ill who require skilled nursing facility care, it is frequently adequate for many elderly now in health-related facilities. Thus, the next few decades will see the development of programs that offer combinations of nursing home care, home care, and day care for the elderly ill. The appropriate care will be determined by assessment and placement programs.

Home and day health care programs will have a much greater likelihood of success if the elderly who can benefit from these types of care have a human support system of family, relatives, and friends on whom they can depend. In fact, there are indications that these kinds of human support systems will become more prevalent in the future. Neugarten and Havighurst (1976) note that the last two decades have seen an increase in the percentage of older people who are married and living with spouses. In addition, the intergenerational family structure is expanding, with the four- and five-generation family becoming the norm. Furthermore, because of the 1950–1960 baby boom, by the turn of the century the older person will have more surviving children on average than does the senior citizen living now.

All of these changes assume, of course, that family members will be willing to provide emotional and physical support to their elderly parents and/or grandparents. A whole range of smaller studies have in fact shown that the family has remained a strong and supportive institution for older people. It is safe to assume that this will also hold true for the future.

Another factor that supports the growth of home and day health care is the development of senior citizen housing. High quality senior citizen housing provides the elderly with opportunities to socialize more easily and to support each other, emotionally and physically. Provisions of home and day health care services to the elderly in a senior citizen housing project also results in considerable economies of scale by eliminating a great deal of travel time for health care providers.

CONCLUSION

Since World War II, our nation has shown increasing concern over the provision of adequate long-term care for the elderly. Historical acceptance of the nursing home as an appropriate method of providing care and the growth in the proportion of people over 65 have combined to make the proprietary nursing home the major dispensary of long-term care services. Spurred on by various legislative enactments (such as the Social Security Act), the nursing home industry has grown at a phenomenal pace.

In recent years, there has also been a phenomenal growth in home health care. Although home health care is intended for all ages, the elderly are the major utilizers, and also the major beneficiaries, of this new form of care. Home health care in many cases has become an alternative to nursing home and hospital care. The home health care alternative provides a welcome option to many elderly people who, without it, would probably end up in a nursing home.

All of this has led to more and more questions about the cost and quality of services provided to the elderly. Our society continues to look for better ways of caring for the elderly frail, including further improvements and increased quality in the various forms of home health care, day health care, and, of course, the traditional nursing home.

REFERENCES

Bureau of the Census. *National Master Facility Inventory*. Washington, D.C.: U.S. GPO, 1985.

Cohen, E.S. "An Overview of Long-Term Care Facilities." In *A Social Work Guide for Long-Term Care Facilities*, edited by Elaine M. Brody. Washington, D.C.: National Institute of Mental Health, U.S. GPO, 1974.

Jacoby, S. "Waiting for the End: On Nursing Homes." *New York Times Magazine*, 31 March 1974.

Neugarten, B.L., and Havighurst, R.J. "Aging and the Future." In *Social Policy, Social Ethics, and the Aging Society*. Washington, D.C.: Division of Advanced Productivity, Research, and Technology, RANN-Research Applications Directorate, National Science Foundation, 1976.

Chapter 3

Demographics of Older Americans

INTRODUCTION

The older population has been changing significantly in the past 85 years, and over the next 50 years it will continue to change. This change is especially important because it will significantly impact on the health care resources required to serve the growing elderly segment of the American population.

In the first section of this chapter, we take a close look at how the older population is changing, especially at the specific age-sex groups that are anticipated to change significantly. We also review retirement preferences, income levels, health problems, and family assistance.

The second section deals with the statistical impact of people living longer. As a result of this phenomenon, certain age-sex groups are increasing rapidly and will significantly impact on the cost of health care in general. Indeed, the additional health care costs for the elderly will be so substantial that they will affect the financing of the entire health care system.

In the third section, we review the geographic distribution of older Americans. Older Americans are not distributed evenly across the fifty states; percentages range from a high of 17.5 percent of 65 and older in Florida to a low of 3.0 percent of 65 and older in Alaska.

Finally, a close look is taken at one of the larger states, New York State. Specific statistical data on the 60-and-older population in that state are evaluated and analyzed to provide the reader with an appreciation of some of the differences in demographics that exist at the micro level.

THE CHANGING OLDER POPULATION

Basic Patterns

At the beginning of this century, persons 60 and over represented one of every 16 persons. In the mid-1980s, the 60-and-over population represented one of every 6 people. By the year 2030, the ratio is projected to be over one in four persons, or 27 percent of the population (Fowles 1983).

Yet, *older persons* is a relative term. To the teenager, someone over 30 years of age is older; to the 65-year-old, an older person is someone over 75 years of age. In the present discussion, we define the older person as someone 60 years of age and over, unless otherwise specified.

Moreover, older persons are by no means a homogeneous group. Older persons in the 60–69 age group are different from those in the 70–79 age group, who in turn differ from those in the 80–84 age group and those 85 years of age and older.

Although the majority of older Americans are reasonably well-off economically and health-wise, there are significant numbers of the elderly who experience a diminished ability to function independently, due to poor health, low income, lack of transportation, lack of social interaction, or other deficiencies in their environment.

The size of the 60-and-over population has increased more than 7 times since 1900. However, the population of those 75 and over has increased by 11 times, and the population of those over 85 has increased by 16 times since the turn of the century. The 85-and-older age group now comprises 1 in every 16 older people. By the year 2030, it is projected that the 85-and-older age group will represent 1 in every 11 older people.

The majority of older people, and especially the very old, are women. At the beginning of the 20th century, men actually outnumbered women. But improvements in health care and health standards have changed that dramatically. In 1980, older women outnumbered men by about 6 million, and they are projected to outnumber men by about 12 million by the year 2030.

Home ownership is quite common among the elderly. About 70 percent of all households, headed by someone 65 or older, own their own homes. About 85 percent of these homeowners have no mortgage obligations.

Since 1960, the number of persons 60 and over living alone has increased two and one-half times as fast as the overall growth in the 60-and-over population. This may be explained by the greater mobility of the population in general, but it is also likely to be due to increased affluence that allows people to live more independently in their own private households.

In terms of education, the elderly have also changed. Among the elderly, the number of school years completed has increased from 8.3 years in 1960 to 11.1 years in the mid-1980s. This higher educational level coincides with the increased preference for independent living and thus helps to explain the high level of independent living by the elderly.

Retirement preferences are also changing. Fowles (1983) reports that in 1982 only about 57 percent of men in the 60–64 age group were working or looking for work. Among males 65 and older, workers or those looking for work decreased to about 18 percent of that age group.

In 1981, the median income for families headed by persons 65 years and older was $14,335; the median income for individuals 65 and over and living alone or with nonrelatives was $7,710. These income levels were about half the income levels reported by younger families and individuals. However, family size was not considered in these results, and the expenditures of the younger families and individuals was in fact considerably higher. In any event, these average figures must be used with caution; many older people have incomes well-below the average, while others have incomes well-above.

The majority of the older population are healthy. But with age, the probability of health impairment increases. About 9 percent of the noninstitutionalized elderly 65 and over are limited in their activities by chronic conditions and require assistance. When we break these figures down by age group, we find that 5 percent of the 65–74 age group, 12 percent of the 75–84 age group, and 31 percent of those 85 years and over are afflicted by health and mobility impairments.

A similar situation prevails in nursing home utilization. In 1977, about 5 percent of the elderly 65 and over resided in nursing homes (Fowles 1983). When we break this down by age groups, we find that 1 percent of the 65–74 age group, 7 percent of the 75–84 age group, and 22 percent of those 85 years of age and older resided in nursing homes.

Health problems afflicting the elderly vary widely. However, higher rates of impairment were found for hypertension, visual impairments, arthritis, rheumatism, and periodontal disease. Incidences of mental disease were also higher for the elderly.

Family assistance is an important factor in keeping the lives of many of the elderly reasonably manageable and satisfactory. A 1975 survey reported that 80 percent of people 65 years and older had living children. Of those with children, only 27 percent lived more than one-half hour away from their children. Thus, children form a powerful and necessary support system for many of the elderly (Fowles 1983). At the same time, it should be noted that these survey data are quite old; given the high mobility of the American population in general, these statistics will undoubtedly deteriorate over time.

In any event, based on these findings, it is clear that society as a whole will have to accept a growing responsibility to provide community and other services to those elderly who do not have access to necessary support services.

People Are Living Longer

Demographic changes have an important impact on a country's population in terms of health status, use of health services, and health care expenditures. For example, those 65 years of age and over comprise about 12 percent of the population, but they are responsible for over 30 percent of total health care expenditures. As the elderly population increases, and as the very old within the elderly population increases at a rate even faster than the elderly as a whole, the impact on future health care expenditures will become dramatic (Rice and Feldman 1983).

As increasing numbers of younger people move into the older age group, termination of life of all people, and especially the aged, will be further delayed by dramatic decreases in mortality rates for vascular diseases, heart diseases, and accidents. Correspondingly, the older age groups will grow increasingly larger, and other health problems will increase. Thus, the net effect over the next 50 years is going to be a substantial increase in health care expenditures. In particular, more people will be needed to serve the growing number of people requiring health care.

Specific increases in population figures are shown in Table 3-1. For example, the 65-and-over population is projected to increase from 11.1 percent in 1980 to 20.5 percent in 2040. Among females, the 65-and-over population is projected to increase from 13.1 percent in 1980 to 23.5 percent in 2040. However, the most startling increases are projected for the 75–84 and 85-and-over age groups: the 75–84 age group will increase from 2.6 percent to 7.5 percent of the population; the 85-and-over group will increase from 0.5 to 4.0 percent, an eight-fold increase. Increases in the 65–74 age group will be more modest, at least as measured as a percentage of total population.

Since the very old are the highest utilizers of health care resources, these projected increases are especially relevant for health care planners. They must begin to plan now so that the requisite resources can be made available to meet the mushrooming demands that these population segments will impose on our health care system in the years to come.

The area of the total health care complex that will be especially tested in the future is the nursing home component. To be sure, physician visits and hospital visits will also increase; but, by far, the biggest impact will be in terms of nursing home utilization.

Projected nursing home utilization is shown in Table 3-2. The nursing home population is projected to increase from 1,511,000 in 1980 to 5,227,000 in 2040, a three-and-a-half-fold increase. The biggest jump will occur between 2020 and 2040. Most of the projected increases will be the result of increased numbers of people over 75, especially of people over 85 years of age. In fact, for women over 85 years, the nursing home population is projected to increase from 456,000 in 1980 to 2,359,000 in 2040. For the 75–84 age group, the projected increase for both men and women is from 525,000 in 1980 to 1,631,000 in 2040.

Clearly, many of us will live to an older age than our forefathers. And, if we live long enough, the probability of spending our very old years in a nursing home will be very high.

Table 3-1 Projected Number of Persons by Age and Sex, 1960–2040

Age and Sex	1960		1980		2000		2020		2040	
	Number	Percent of All Ages	Number	Percent of All Ages	Number	Percent of All Ages	Number	Percent of All Ages	Number	Percent of All Ages
Total										
All Ages	183.2	100.0	237.7	100.0	273.9	100.0	306.9	100.0	328.5	100.0
65 and over	16.7	9.1	25.9	11.1	36.3	13.3	52.7	17.2	67.3	20.5
65–74	11.1	6.1	15.6	6.7	18.3	6.7	30.1	9.8	29.4	9.0
75–84	4.7	2.6	7.7	3.3	12.5	4.6	14.9	4.9	24.6	7.5
85 and over	0.9	0.5	2.6	1.1	5.4	2.0	7.7	2.5	13.3	4.0
Male										
All Ages	90.5	100.0	114.1	100.0	133.8	100.0	149.5	100.0	158.8	100.0
65 and over	7.6	8.4	10.4	9.1	14.4	10.8	21.8	14.6	27.3	17.2
65–74	5.2	5.7	6.8	6.0	8.3	6.2	13.8	9.2	13.6	8.6
75–84	2.0	2.2	2.8	2.5	4.7	3.5	5.9	4.0	9.9	6.2
85 and over	0.4	0.4	0.8	0.7	1.5	1.1	2.1	1.4	3.9	2.5
Female										
All Ages	92.7	100.0	118.6	100.0	140.1	100.0	157.4	100.0	169.7	100.0
65 and over	9.1	9.8	15.5	13.1	21.8	15.6	30.9	19.6	39.9	23.5
65–74	5.9	6.4	8.8	7.4	10.1	7.2	16.3	10.4	15.9	9.4
75–84	2.6	2.8	4.9	4.1	7.8	5.6	9.0	5.7	14.7	8.7
85 and over	0.6	0.6	1.8	1.5	4.0	2.9	5.5	3.5	9.4	5.5

Note: All numbers are in millions; 1960 and 1980 are actual numbers.

Source: *Actuarial Study No. 85,* Office of the Actuary, Social Security Administration, July 1981.

Table 3-2 Projected Nursing Home Residents by Age and Sex, 1980–2040

Age and Sex	1980	2000	2020	2040
Total				
All Ages	1,511	2,542	3,371	5,227
65 and over	1,315	2,316	3,129	4,979
65–74	227	265	434	425
75–84	525	850	1,006	1,631
85 and over	563	1,201	1,689	2,903
Male				
All Ages	422	641	865	1,304
65 and over	328	534	750	1,185
65–74	87	105	175	172
75–84	135	225	280	469
85 and over	107	204	295	544
Female				
All Ages	1,090	1,901	2,506	3,924
65 and over	987	1,783	2,380	3,794
65–74	140	160	259	252
75–84	391	625	726	1,182
85 and over	456	997	1,395	2,359

Note: Figures are in thousands; 1980 figures are actual.

Source: *Projections of Nursing Home Residents*, National Center for Health Statistics, Office of Analysis and Epidemiology, 1982.

GEOGRAPHIC DISTRIBUTION OF OLDER AMERICANS

In 1983, the 65-and-older population numbered 27.4 million people (Bureau of the Census 1984); this group represented 11.7 of the U.S. population. Women constituted 16.4 million of the 27.4 million elderly, or 60 percent; men constituted 11.0 million of the 27.4 million, or 40 percent. Among the elderly 85 years and older, women constituted 71 percent and men only 29 percent.

In 1983, about half of the 65-and-older population lived in seven states. California and New York each had over two million elderly; while Florida, Illinois, Ohio, Pennsylvania, and Texas each had over one million (American Association of Retired Persons 1984). The highest percentage of those 65 and over were in Florida, where they constituted over 17 percent of the population. High percentages of 65-and-over populations (around 14 percent) were also found in Arkansas, Rhode Island, Iowa, Pennsylvania, South Dakota, and Missouri.

States with low elderly population levels in 1983 are shown in Table 3-3. The lowest percentages were 3.0 percent in Alaska, 7.6 percent in Utah and 7.9 percent in Wyoming. States with high elderly population levels in 1983 are

Table 3-3 States with Low-Percentage Elderly Population Levels

State	1983 Numbers	1983 Percentage
Alaska	14	3.0
Utah	123	7.6
Wyoming	40	7.9
Colorado	270	8.6
Hawaii	89	8.7
Nevada	81	9.1
New Mexico	130	9.3
Texas	1,470	9.4
Louisiana	426	9.6
Georgia	563	9.8
South Carolina	321	9.8

Note: Numbers are in thousands.

Source: Current Population Reports, 1983, Bureau of the Census, U.S. Department of Commerce, 1984.

shown in Table 3-4. As noted, the highest percentage was in Florida, with 17.5 percent.

In 1983, for 28.4 percent of families headed by a person 65 or older, income levels exceeded $25,000 per year. Only 5.8 percent of individuals living alone reported income levels over $25,000. At the lower end of the scale, 23.0 percent of families headed by someone 65 years or older reported annual incomes under $10,000. Among individuals living alone, 29.7 percent reported annual income levels under $5,000.

Thus, on average, America's elderly are reasonably well-off. However, the range of annual incomes includes substantial numbers of elderly with very low income levels.

OLDER AMERICANS IN NEW YORK STATE

As an illustration of the demographics of a large American state, we present in this section some statistics on older Americans in New York State, based on the 1980 U.S. Census (New York State Office for the Aging 1983).

In 1980, New York's population was about 17.5 million. Of this total, 17.1 percent were over 60 years of age, and 12.3 percent were over 65 years of age. Among those 60 and older, the 60–64 age group constituted 28.0 percent, the 65–74 age group constituted 43.1 percent, the 75–84 age group constituted 22.5 percent, and the 85-and-older age group constituted 6.4 percent. Since the 1970

Table 3-4 States with High-Percentage Elderly Population Levels

State	1983 Numbers	1983 Percentage
Florida	1,867	17.5
Arkansas	329	14.1
Iowa	404	13.9
Pennsylvania	1,639	13.8
Missouri	674	13.6
South Dakota	95	13.6
Nebraska	213	13.3
Massachusetts	763	13.2
Kansas	319	13.2
Maine	149	13.0

Note: Numbers are in thousands.

Source: Current Population Reports, 1983, Bureau of the Census, U.S. Department of Commerce, 1984.

census, New York's population had decreased by 3.8 percent, but its 60-and-older age group had increased by 6.3 percent, with those 85 and older showing a 44.1 percent increase. On the basis of household income, it was found that of those 60 and over, 11.0 percent lived below the poverty level; whereas, of those under 60, 13.9 percent lived below the poverty level.

The distribution of those 60 years and older varied widely across counties. In one small rural county, 23.9 percent of the population was 60 years or over; in another county, the proportion was only 11.5 percent. In one of the largest counties, an urban county, those 60 years and over constituted 20.5 percent, well over the state average of 17.1 percent. Table 3-5 shows the counties in New York State with those 60 years and over constituting more than 20 percent of the population.

CONCLUSION

Over the next 50 years, Americans who are 65 years or older will increase to 20 percent of the population, from the present level of a little under 12 percent. Within this older age group, there will be a growing very-old age group, those 85 years and older. It is this latter group, in particular, that will have a significant impact on the nation's health care costs.

At present, 22 percent of those 85 years and older are institutionalized in nursing homes. This utilization statistic is not likely to change. The 85-and-older age group, which is anticipated to increase eight-fold, will therefore create a

Table 3-5 New York State Counties with Large 60-and-Over Populations

County	1980 Number	1980 Percentage
Hamilton	1,202	23.9
Montgomery	12,463	22.9
Greene	9,199	22.5
Columbia	12,662	21.3
Fulton	11,358	20.6
Sullivan	13,395	20.6
Queens	388,449	20.5
Schenectady	30,236	20.2
Yates	4,340	20.2
New York State	3,001,774	17.1

Note: Numbers are in thousands.

Source: Older New Yorkers, New York State Office for the Aging, April 1983.

virtual explosion in nursing home demand. These very old Americans will constitute a negative saver group; that is, they will need to support their institutionalization from past savings. And when those savings are depleted, the rest of the population, via the government, will have to support their institutionalization. If our standard of living does not decline, especially if it increases somewhat, this should not be an insuperable problem. However, health care planners must begin now to ensure that, as the demand for nursing home care grows, the necessary financing will be available.

REFERENCES

American Association of Retired Persons. *A Profile of Older Americans, 1984.* Washington, D.C.: American Association of Retired Persons, 1984.

Bureau of the Census. *Current Population Reports, 1983.* Washington, D.C.: U.S. Department of Commerce, 1984.

Fowles, D. "The Changing Older Population." In *Aging Magazine.* Washington, D.C.: U.S. GPO, May/June 1983:6–11.

New York State Office for the Aging. *Older New Yorkers.* Albany, N.Y.: New York State Office for the Aging, 1983.

Rice, D.P., and Feldman, J.J. "Living Longer in the United States: Demographic Changes and Health Needs of the Elderly." *Milbank Memorial Fund Quarterly/Health and Society* 61, no. 3 (1983):362–396.

Chapter 4

Health Care and Its Costs

INTRODUCTION

In the 1970s and 1980s the rapid increases in health care costs became a topic of major public concern. The rise in health care costs has been attributed not only to the health care industry, but also to the growing number of elderly. A close examination of how various facets of the health care system relate to rising health care costs reveals both the impact of the older population on health care costs and the impact of rising health care costs on the elderly.

In the period between fiscal year 1970 and fiscal year 1985, total health care expenditures rose at a rate of 12 to 15 percent per year, reaching $425 billion or $1,721 per person in 1985, as shown in Table 4-1. Put another way, in 1985 health care expenditures amounted to 10.7 percent of the gross national product (GNP). Between 1980 and 1985, health care expenditures increased 71.3 percent, from $249.0 billion to $425.0 billion (Waldo, Levit, and Lazenby 1986).

A large portion of medical care costs for the elderly is paid from public funds, as shown in Table 4-2. One source of public money is Medicare, which was established in 1966 to give the elderly some relief from the financial burden of high medical bills. In fiscal 1981 the Medicare program paid 44 percent of the elderly's medical bills, or approximately $38 billion (U.S. Congress 1982).

PUBLIC HEALTH EXPENDITURE SUPPORT

The Medicare program was not created to provide total coverage of all medical care costs for the aged. Actually, Medicare is very similar to private health insurance, with an emphasis on coverage of hospital care and physicians' services; it covers 74 percent of hospital care expense and 54 percent of the cost of physicians' services. However, nursing home care is covered only if it is required after a hospital stay. In 1985, Medicare provided only about 6.7 percent of

Table 4-1 National Health Expenditure Summary

Year	Billions	Percent Growth	Percent of GNP	Per Capita National Health Expenditures
1950	$ 12.7		4.4	$ 82
1960	26.9	11.8	5.3	146
1970	74.7	77.7	7.5	358
1971	83.3	11.5	7.7	394
1972	93.5	12.2	7.9	438
1973	103.2	10.4	7.8	478
1974	116.4	14.0	8.1	535
1975	132.7	14.0	8.6	604
1976	149.7	12.8	8.7	674
1977	169.2	13.0	8.8	755
1978	189.3	11.9	8.7	836
1979	215.0	13.6	8.9	938
1980	249.0	15.8	9.5	1,075
1981	286.6	15.0	9.7	1,225
1982	322.4	12.5	10.5	1,365
1983	355.4	10.2	10.7	1,500
1984	387.4	9.0	10.3	1,631
1985	425.0	9.7	10.7	1,721

Source: Health Care Financing Review, Vol. 5, No. 3, p. 7, Health Care Financing Administration, Department of Health and Human Services, Spring 1984; *Health Care Financing Review*, Vol. 8, No. 1, p. 13, Health Care Financing Administration, Department of Health and Human Services, Fall 1986.

Table 4-2 Per Capita Health Care Expenditures for the Aged, Fiscal Year 1981

Source of Funds	Hospital	Physician	Other	Total
Medicare	$1,022 (74%)	$318 (54%)	$ 82 (7%)	$1,422 (45%)
Medicaid	$ 55 (4%)	$ 18 (3%)	$ 363 (31%)	$ 436 (14%)
Other public programs	$ 111 (8%)	$ 6 (1%)	$ 47 (4%)	$ 164 (5%)
Private sources	$ 193 (14%)	$247 (42%)	$ 678 (58%)	$1,118 (36%)
Totals	$1,381 (44%)	$589 (19%)	$1,170 (37%)	$3,140 (100%)

Type of Care (spanning Hospital, Physician, Other)

Source: Developments in Aging, Senate Report 98-13, Committee on Aging, U.S. Senate, 98th Congress, First Session, 1982.

nursing home care expenditures. As with most private health insurance coverage, costs of routine physical examinations, dental care, and vision care are excluded. In 1981, Medicaid provided the elderly with $11.4 billion in health care; this constituted 14 percent of all health care costs incurred by the elderly.

In addition to Medicare and Medicaid, several other public sources of funds are available. The Veterans Administration provides health care for eligible veterans and their dependents, while the Department of Defense provides health care to retired military persons and dependents. Mental hospital care for some elderly is financed by state funds.

When all government program health care expenditures are added together, they amount to about 64.3 percent of the medical costs paid by the elderly. Private health insurance provides 6.6 percentage points of the remaining 35.7 percent. In 1981 the balance of 29.1 percent, or $914, came from family aid (U.S. Congress 1982).

It is interesting to note that, before 1966, only 25 percent of total health care expenditures were paid for by government funds. Since that time, government expenditures have risen almost 18 percent annually, and private spending has risen by about 10 percent annually (National Center for Health Statistics 1983). During the same period, per capita expenditures for the aged increased 13 percent annually, while direct or "out-of-pocket" payments by the elderly increased 6 percent annually (if insurance premiums paid by the elderly are included in "out-of-pocket" expenses, the figure is 6.6 percent). In the same period, per capita income for the aged went up 10 percent a year. Therefore, "out-of-pocket" expenses as a percentage of average income declined from 15 to 11 percent (Gibson and Fisher 1979).

There are essentially two reasons why the government has had to assume an ever-increasing share of health care expenses for the aged: (1) decline of family support and (2) increase in the number of elderly women.

Decline in Family Support

The decline in family support has to date been moderate. Most persons 65 and over still live in families. Although the proportions of older men and women living in families differ greatly, the number of older men and women living in families is about the same: 7.6 million men versus 7.5 million women. In 1980, about 84 percent of all elderly men lived in families, and 76 percent maintained their own families. Among elderly women, however, only 59 percent still lived in families; in 1982, only 40 percent still had spouses, as shown in Table 4-3 (National Center for Health Statistics 1983).

In addition, a large proportion of older persons maintain their own households, alone or with nonrelatives. Most older women who live alone are widows. As

Table 4-3 Percentage of Persons 65 Years and Over, by Marital Status and Sex, 1982

	Percent	
Marital Status	*Male*	*Female*
Single	4.4	5.6
Married	80.0	40.2
Widowed	12.4	50.4
Other	3.2	3.8

Source: Statistical Abstract of the U.S., 104th ed., Bureau of the Census, U.S. Government Printing Office, 1984.

Table 4-4 Percentage of Persons 65 Years and Over, by Marital Status, for Both Sexes, 1984

	Percent		
Marital Status	*Total*	*Live Alone*	*Live with Others*
Single	6.3	13.8	2.9
Married	54.0	0.3	78.9
Widowed	35.0	77.2	15.4
Other	4.7	8.7	2.8

Source: Division of Health Interview Statistics, Data from Nursing Home Interview Survey, Supplement on Aging, National Center for Health Statistics, U.S. Government Printing Office, 1984.

shown in Table 4-4, in 1984, 35 percent of all people 65 years and over were widowed, but 77.2 percent of those living alone were widowed, and only 15.4 percent of those living with others were widowed (National Center for Health Statistics 1984).

In recent years, the husband-wife dyad has been declining because of higher divorce rates. If this trend continues, the proportion of elderly living without traditional family support will increase even more sharply, necessitating even broader public financing of health care costs.

Increase in the Number of Elderly Women

The number of women 65 and over has increased faster than the number of men in the same age group. Specifically, since 1970 the annual increase for women has been 22 percent, as compared with 10 percent for men. Interestingly, the number of elderly men and women were about equal at the beginning of this century. At present, elderly women outnumber elderly men by about 5 million—16.1 million women to 10.8 million men (Bureau of the Census 1984).

At age 65, life expectancy is about 14.6 years for white men but 18.7 years for white women. As a result, in 1982, there were 149 elderly women for 100 elderly men, and the gap continues to grow with age. Put another way, of the 1.2 million older people who died in 1976 at a rate of 54 per 1,000, 67 were men and 46 were women (Bureau of the Census 1984). Assuming that mortality trends do not change in the future, 82 percent of female babies will live to the age of 65, as compared with only 68 percent of male babies.

CAUSES OF RISING HEALTH CARE EXPENDITURES

Growing Numbers of Elderly

Since 1900, the elderly population has increased nearly 800 percent (a nine-fold increase), while the total population has increased only about 200 percent. Since 1970, the number of elderly has increased 25 percent, from 20 million to about 25 million. In 1900, the proportion of elderly to the total population was 4.1 percent (see Table 4-5). This proportion rose to 12.0 percent in 1985.

The declining death rate has been another cause of growing health care costs. In 1965, the death rate for the elderly was 60 persons per 1,000, as compared with 54 persons per 1,000 in 1975 (Bureau of the Census 1984). During the five-year period, 1979–1984, death rates for the elderly have decreased by 6 percent (National Center for Health Statistics 1987).

Table 4-5 Older Population Statistics in the Last Quarter of the 20th Century

Year	Number (in Millions)	Percent of Total	Men (in Millions) White	Black	Women (in Millions) White	Black	Number of Women to 100 Men
1979	25.13	11.2	9.17	.85	13.62	1.23	148
1980	25.54	11.3	9.31	.84	13.84	1.25	149
1981	26.26	11.5	9.55	.86	14.24	1.28	149
1982	26.82	11.6	9.74	.87	14.54	1.31	149
1983	27.47	11.7	9.99	.90	14.84	1.35	149
1984	27.96	11.8	10.17	.92	15.08	1.37	148
1985	28.53	12.0	10.39	.94	15.35	1.40	148
2000	35.04	13.1	13.7		21.3		155

Sources: *Statistical Abstract of the U.S.*, 104th ed., Bureau of the Census, U.S. Government Printing Office, 1984; *Health Statistics on Older Persons, U.S. 1986*, Vital Health Statistics, Series 3, No. 25, National Center for Health Statistics, U.S. Government Printing Office, 1987.

It is projected that by 2020 the elderly may constitute as much as 20 percent of the total population. At that point, the median age of the population will be 37, as compared with 29 in 1980. Not only is the total number of persons age 65 and over increasing, the number of very old is increasing even more rapidly. For example, from 1950 to 1975 the total U.S. population rose by less than 50 percent. However, in that same period, the number of persons age 75 to 84 doubled, and the number of those 85 years and over more than tripled. It is anticipated that the number of those 85 and over will increase by an additional 80 percent by the year 2000.

Average life expectancy has also increased. In 1900, average life expectancy for Americans at birth was 47.3 years. In 1984, it was 74.7 years. The average white man at age 65 can expect to live 14.6 additional years, and the average white woman can expect 18.7 additional years, as shown in Table 4-6. Most of this increase is due to the decline in infant mortality and the improvement in elderly mortality. Another factor, though not as significant, is immigration.

Increased Need for Health Care

Because older persons tend to suffer from chronic conditions, many elderly are limited in their activities or are hospitalized more frequently and for longer periods. People age 65 to 69 require about 3,000 days of short-stay hospital care per year per 1,000 persons. People in their late 70s require 4,700 days per 1,000 persons, while those over 85 require 8,300 days per 1,000 persons (Gibson and Fisher 1979).

Table 4-6 Expected Number of Years Remaining at Age 65 by Race and Sex, for Selected Years, 1950–1984

Year	White		Black and Other	
	Male	*Female*	*Male*	*Female*
1950	12.8	15.0	12.8	14.5
1974	13.4	17.6	13.4	16.7
1975	13.7	18.1	13.7	17.5
1976	13.7	18.1	13.8	17.6
1979	14.4	18.8	13.5	17.3
1980	14.2	18.5	13.5	17.3
1984	14.6	18.7	13.5	17.2

Sources: Statistical Abstract of the U.S., 104th ed., Bureau of the Census, U.S. Government Printing Office, 1984; *Health Statistics on Older Persons, U.S. 1986*, Vital Health Statistics, Series 3, No. 25, National Center for Health Statistics, U.S. Government Printing Office, 1987.

In the period between 1960 and 1980, the proportion of elderly living in institutions increased 25 percent, from 4 percent (1960) to 5 percent (1980). However, the use of nursing home services increases with age. Generally, the elderly require about 16,000 days of nursing home care per year per 1,000 persons; however, those 85 and over require 86,400 days per 1,000 persons per year. Between 1965–1966 and 1975–1976, the surgical rate for the aged increased 44 percent. Physician visits are also higher for the elderly than for the younger population, mainly because of the chronic nature of the elderly's conditions (Gornick 1976). However, there has been no significant rise in the rate of physician visits for the elderly: between 1965 and 1975, the average was 6.6 visits per year; in 1981, the average was 6.3 visits per year (U.S. Congress 1982). One reason for this constancy is that the decrease in physician visits to the nonpoor cancelled the increase in visits to the poor elderly.

Many people believe that the tremendous rise in health care expenditures, especially the government's share, is due simply to the increased use of medical care by the aged. This is true to some extent. But there are other factors involved. First of all, medical science and technology has advanced a great deal, enabling the elderly to take advantage of more complex and more expensive procedures and medications. Also, medical care has grown more intensified, with physicians using every possible means to treat patients, even the dying. Finally, there are simply not many inexpensive long-term care facilities.

Inflation

Inflation has been the major factor responsible for the increase in health care expenditures between 1965 and 1982, as shown in Table 4-7. During that period, total expenditures rose at an annual rate of over 10 percent. Price changes accounted for a large percentage of the total change, ranging from a low of 43 percent to a high of 78 percent during the period.

The annual growth rate has not been uniform among the various components of national health care expenditures. Hospital costs generally have risen at a higher rate than other cost components. For instance, in 1976 the hospital room rate rose by 16 percent, as compared with an increase of 8 percent for all nonmedical items (Somers 1978). This phenomenal increase in room rates slowed to 13 percent by the beginning of 1977. During the fiscal year ending March 1985, $166.7 billion was spent on hospital care. Also by March 1985, $82.8 billion had been spent for physician services, and nursing home expenditures reached $35.2 billion (Waldo, Levit, and Lazenby 1986). Other types of personal health care spending—such as for dental treatment, drugs and eyeglasses—also showed increases.

Table 4-7 Causes of Increases in Personal Health Care Expenditures for Selected
Periods, 1950–1982

	Causes of Increases			
Fiscal Year Period	*Changes in Prices*	*Changes in Composition of Services*	*Changes in Population*	*Total*
1965–1971	50%	41%	9%	100%
1971–1974	43%	49%	8%	100%
1974–1976	78%	16%	6%	100%
1976–1977	64%	28%	8%	100%
1977–1978	69%	22%	9%	100%
1978–1981	72%	21%	7%	100%
1981–1982	78%	14%	8%	100%

Source: Health U.S., National Center for Health Statistics, U.S. Government Printing Office, 1983.

AMERICAN ASSEMBLY STATEMENT ON HEALTH CARE COSTS

During the period November 13–16, 1986, the 72nd American Assembly on Health Care and Its Costs convened at Arden House, Harriman, New York. At the close of their discussions the assembly's statement on health care costs was revised (The 72nd American Assembly 1986). The statement, reprinted below in its entirety, represents a general agreement. However, no one was asked to sign it and it should be understood that not everyone agreed with all of it.*

The twentieth century vision of American citizenship embraces participation by all in the benefits of our wealthy society. Over time, health care has become a part of this vision. Indeed, medical progress has come to be an emblem of American innovation and success. As the Thirty-seventh American Assembly on *The Health of Americans* proclaimed in 1970, ''Access to adequate health care for all in the United States must be recognized as a basic right.''

In the ensuing sixteen years, American society has changed in ways that challenge this vision. As a nation, we spend faster than we earn. As a people we are growing older; more of us live alone than before. Our work force now includes more part-time, low-paid, and other workers with marginal health care coverage. Technology creates new

---

*The statement is reprinted with permission of the American Assembly, Barnard College, Columbia University, 1987.

possibilities as well as unanticipated risks. These forces also are re-shaping the American health care system.

The Thirty-seventh Assembly observed a crisis in health care that could be solved "only by a national commitment to prompt action of a sweeping nature." The nation has addressed many of the problems articulated by that Assembly through development of new technologies, the training of more physicians and the implementation of innovative forms of delivery. However, the most profound difficulties—cost, quality, and access—persist. Indeed, they are in some ways linked to what we have achieved.

Health care costs have continued to rise despite two decades of growing concern and efforts by private and public actors to reduce both annual increases and aggregate costs. New approaches to cost containment have emerged from these policies. Increasingly, public and private purchasers have focused on price and utilization control as the central mechanisms of control. Powerful payers gained discounts on behalf of large pools of consumers. This price-centered policy rests on the assumption that more efficient production and distribution of health care will result.

As each purchaser scrutinizes the aggregate cost of care for the population it covers, medical care is now treated as a commodity. The result is a profound challenge to our historic system of implicit cross-subsidization. Traditionally cross-subsidized products of the health care system included: the provision of care to the poor, support of medical education, and the sustenance of an environment where medical research and technology could flourish. These are now threatened and may be lost. Our past failure to solve the cost problem forces us to face these and perhaps more perplexing problems in the future.

Health care for the uninsured is particularly problematic in a price-centered world. With eroding public and private commitment to care for the medically indigent, where fewer people are covered less adequately, the importance of historic cross-subsidies is put in higher relief. Some institutions, long devoted to the care of disproportionate numbers of poor and near-poor patients, may not survive. The vision of a medically just society is at risk as a result of recasting medical care as a price-distributed commodity.

This change has, however, heightened concern for efficiency and quality of care. Unfortunately, we lack adequate systematic and scientific means for both providers and consumers to evaluate quality of care.

In addition, profound organizational change characterizes our environment. Institutions that traditionally have been devoted to the delivery and finance of care are in flux. The magnitude of change is evidenced by the growth of alternative providers; the decline in inpatient utilization, the reduction of the importance of the hospital to the medical care system; the reconfiguration of the relationship among physicians, hospitals, and payers; the melding of identities between finance and delivery illustrated by health maintenance organizations (HMOs) owned by health insurance companies, and preferred provider organizations (PPOs) owned by physicians and/or hospitals, and insurance companies owned by hospitals; and the significant market presence and general acceptance of for-profit providers. These changes are simultaneously celebrated and decried. They hold potential for increased efficiency, effectiveness, and improvement in the quality of care. We are mindful, however, of the potential problems. The pursuit of lower cost may have produced incentives for insurers to avoid some risks and for providers to avoid some patients (the most poor and, ironically, the most sick).

As we contemplate the future, it is important to note one characteristic of the American system of health care. Unlike other western democracies, we never nationalized health coverage. This reflects both the American ambivalence about the role of government and the value we place on mixing private and public action. Our past reflects the coexistence of voluntary, public, and for-profit hospitals; a system of charitable, private, cooperative and government financing; and attempts by hospitals, employers, unions, physicians, payers and government to control the future of health care. In addition, state and local governments have become active participants in the search for innovations; they have demonstrated new capacities and introduced a wide range of reforms. It is unproductive to characterize the past as one that has been dominated by either government or private initiative; it is misleading to cast the contemporary dilemma as a stark choice between public or private, "regulation" or "competition." Americans appear comfortable with their pluralistic approach to solving problems.

This uniquely American way of solving problems will continue to characterize our approach to health care, because there is no clear consensus on the relative importance of health care in the package of individual rights enjoyed by every American. We do agree, however, that not all the health care provided is necessary (meaning that some Americans receive more services than they need) and all that is necessary is not provided (meaning that some Americans do not receive adequate care). We agree that not providing care for those who need it should be unacceptable in a rich society committed to decent and humane life for all its people.

The participants of the Seventy-second American Assembly make the following recommendations for national action:

1. Making quality health care available to all members of our society remains a national goal. However, there are limited resources to be spent on health care in our society. For some of our spending, we are not receiving results in health status improvement or maintenance that are worth their cost. The efficiency is not optimal in delivery of individual and aggregate services. There are difficult questions of individuals' claim to societal resources. Health care expenditures must be evaluated within the context of the full spectrum of societal goals. We strongly urge a higher profile of national discourse on the level and distribution of health care spending. There should be a strong public and private effort to reduce the long-term rate of growth in health care spending, and consideration should be given to measuring success in this endeavor against the rate of change in some external indicator.

2. The Assembly believes that the nation must take action to secure access for all Americans to basic medical, surgical, and preventive services. The Assembly calls on the federal government to seek preventive services. The Assembly calls on the federal government to seek this objective by passing legislation that would:

   - Reform Medicaid eligibility and set federal standards of participation for all individuals with incomes under the federal poverty line;

   - Assure that non-Medical eligible individuals who are uninsured receive coverage for basic health care services and specify the benefits to be included in the plan;

   - Set maximum copayment requirements;

   - Require all employers not offering basic health insurance to provide coverage to their employees, with special consideration given to the problems of small employers, marginal employers, and employers of part-time workers; and

   - Establish a mechanism analogous to unemployment insurance to assure that individuals do not lose health insurance coverage during temporary spells of unemployment.

   The Assembly strongly believes that states should have flexibility in implementing these recommendations.

The Assembly recognizes that its proposal would involve a commitment of additional federal and/or state funds to expand the Medicaid population and subsidize certain employers and others who on their own cannot obtain health care benefits. The Assembly recommends that consideration be given to financing this greater effort through a variety of mechanisms including:

- General revenues;
- Earmarking taxes on alcohol and cigarettes;
- Value added taxes; and
- Savings resulting from improved efficiency.

3. We support the broadly increasing efforts to promote health and prevent disease, including expanding coverage of screening and preventive care, enforcement and expansion of existing legislation on environmental standards and accident prevention. Research to define which programs pay off in real health impact is especially needed. Education of the public through the schools, workplace, and media is essential to support responsible behavior, such as smoking cessation and seat belt use.

4. The Assembly believes that there is too much emphasis on institutionally based services for long-term care. Mechanisms should be developed to shift the emphasis of chronic and long-term care toward formal home care and community-based services. Family support systems that in the past were available to provide long-term care are insufficient to meet today's needs.

   Medicare beneficiaries often have little knowledge of benefits with respect to long-term care. More information should be provided regarding the limits of the Medicare benefits package. Steps should be taken to expand access by exploring public and private options for financing services, such as:

   - Creating a contributory program within the Medicare system;
   - Community-based care with case-managed systems;
   - Reverse annuity mortgages; and/or
   - Social Health Maintenance Organizations (SHMOs).

5. This Assembly urges public officials and the legal, medical and insurance professions to take steps to reduce the incidence of malpractice, to introduce new forms of dispute resolution and injury compensation, and to pass more uniform laws among the states.

6. Much attention has been given to health improvements attributable to new technology. Some have clearly saved money;

many have required substantial additional expenditures. To balance progress and cost containment, we recommend that states monitor the diffusion of new equipment and procedures. Federal support should be expanded for assessing technology and promoting information and consensus on appropriate uses of technology.

The rapid pace of technology development in the past has been a function of a combination of the profit motive and readily available payment for capital intensive innovative services. New payment arrangements (per admission, per capita) will continue to reward cost saving technologies and development. Those public and private agencies devoted to technology assessment should give special attention to the pace at which new technology is harvested from basic and clinical research.

7. The nation has exhibited a firm commitment to the discovery and application of new knowledge through support of basic science and technology. The Assembly endorses this historic commitment and affirms the importance of continued federal support of basic biomedical research.

8. The Assembly believes that there is a national oversupply and maldistribution of hospital beds and number of physicians. The Assembly urges states to develop appropriate mechanisms to address these problems with the objectives of improving efficiency, equity, and access to care.

9. We recognize the right of patients to refuse medical treatments they find disproportionately burdensome. Providers should be relieved of liability in such instances.

10. The Assembly encourages the collection and analysis of data by states consistent with national guidelines in the areas of morbidity, mortality, utilization, quality of care, and expenditures. Researchers, businesses, unions, and the public should be encouraged to use these data. There should be disclosure requirements on information necessary to assess quality and the cost of care. These efforts must assure the protection of patients' confidentiality.

11. It is increasingly important that we develop a national analytic capacity to monitor the changes occurring in the medical care system. Basic research around the question of medical practice, with particular emphasis on indicators related to quality and access of care, should be undertaken.

12. Physician services have been an important factor in the increasing cost of medical care. The Assembly recognizes the lack of

information currently available about controlling the costs of physician services. More attention and further study should be given to innovative and equitable forms of financing.

CONCLUSION

There is little doubt that rising health care costs will remain an important area of concern for legislators, administrators, and policy makers. Since the elderly as a group are the highest per capita health care consumers, it is also clear that their health care consumption will continue to be analyzed and evaluated.

Unfortunately, it is unlikely that health care consumption can be reduced. If anything, total health care expenditures for the elderly will increase, because the number of elderly in the total population is growing. In addition, as the many unmet health care needs of the elderly are in the future underwritten by public financing, the per capita health care costs of this group will increase further.

In short, barring some major scientific breakthrough that results in reduced health care needs and increased health, there is only one direction for health care expenditures to go in the next several years—up.

REFERENCES

Bureau of the Census. *Statistical Abstract of the U.S., 1983*, 104th ed. Washington, D.C.: U.S. GPO, 1984.

Freeland, M.S., and Schendler, C.E., "Health Spending in the 1980s: Integration of Clinical Practice Patterns with Management." *Health Care Financing Review* 5 (Spring 1984):7.

Gibson, R.M., and Fisher, C.R. "Age Difference in Health Care Spending Fiscal Year 1977." *Social Security Bulletin* 42-1. Washington, D.C.: U.S. GPO, 1979:3–16.

Gornick, M. "Ten Years of Medicare: Impact on the Covered Population." *Social Security Bulletin* 39 (July 1976):3–21.

National Center for Health Statistics. *Health U.S.* Washington, D.C.: U.S. GPO, 1983.

———. *Data from Nursing Home Interview Survey,* Supplement on Aging. Washington, D.C.: U.S. GPO, 1984.

———. "Health Statistics on Older Persons, U.S., 1986." *Vital Health Statistics*, 3rd ser., no. 25. Washington, D.C.: U.S. GPO, 1987.

Seventy-Second American Assembly. *Health Care and Its Costs.* Harriman, N.Y.: Arden House, 1986.

Somers, A.R. "The High Cost of Health Care for the Elderly: Diagnosis, Prognosis, and Some Suggestions for Therapy." *Journal of Health Politics, Policy and Law* (Summer 1978):163–180.

U.S. Congress. Senate. Committee on Aging. *Development in Aging.* 98th Cong., 1st sess., 1982. S. Rept. 98-13.

Waldo, D.R., Levit, K.R., and Lazenby, H. "National Health Expenditures 1985." *Health Care Financing Review* 8 (Fall 1986):13.

Chapter 5

Controlling Health Care Costs

INTRODUCTION

The public is getting upset about the high cost of health care. In this chapter, we first examine the implications of a recent survey of attitudes about health care costs. We next attempt to determine whether health care deregulation is the solution to rising health care costs. For example, it has been proposed that Medicare should be abolished and that the elderly should be provided with equivalent funds with which to purchase private health insurance.

During the year following the introduction of the prospective payment system for Medicare recipients, the cost of health care, especially the cost of hospital care, rose more slowly than it had done in several years. Will this trend continue? We examine this question in turn.

We next address the issue of whether home care is a good cost-cutting option. Finally, we take a look at the impact that retirees' health insurance premiums are having on a number of large corporations. Corporations that in recent years have contracted out their health insurance programs are in fact being seriously affected by the relatively high financial burden they now carry for their retirees' health insurance premiums.

THE PUBLIC VIEW OF HEALTH CARE COSTS

In September 1984, some rather intriguing results were obtained in a *Business Week* survey of 1,211 people who were of voting age and likely to vote. The poll was conducted by Louis Harris and Associates, and the overall results are statistically accurate within three percentage points in either direction (*Business Week*/Harris Poll 1984).

The survey showed that people were negative toward the American health care system, especially as it relates to prices charged by physicians, hospitals, nursing homes and pharmacies. In particular, hospital charges were considered to be too high, with 70 percent claiming they are "somewhat" or "very unreasonable."

The general feeling among the survey respondents was that health care providers are free to charge whatever they want for their services. Over 75 percent felt that lack of competition among doctors, hospitals, and nursing homes is a major cause of health care inflation.

There was strong support among the respondents for bringing health care costs under control. Support was indicated for a wide variety of measures to do this, from price control and prospective payment systems (PPS) to health maintenance organizations. In fact, there was strong support to expand PPS to the entire health care system.

The respondents also showed strong support for preferred provider organizations (PPOs), in which only certain doctors and hospitals are utilized by a group of insured individuals, thereby assuring reduced costs for each member of the group.

In light of this survey, it is clear that the health care industry must begin to police its pricing policies. If the industry cannot control its own prices, the public may well demand that the government step in and control those prices for them.

SOME BASIC QUESTIONS

Is Health Care Deregulation the Answer?

An interesting proposal has been made by Wohl (1983, 30). He proposes to abolish Medicare and turn the Medicare budget over to the Medicare recipients so that they can buy their own private health insurance policies and thus obtain more value for the money that is now expended for them through Medicare.

Although the proposal sounds revolutionary, it should not be dismissed out of hand. Wohl points out that the 1984 federal budget for health care entitlement programs was nearly $70 billion. If this amount were divided among the 35 million beneficiaries, it would provide $2,000 per year for each beneficiary to purchase private health insurance. Of course, the kind of health insurance policy available for $2,000 per person per year may not be sufficiently comprehensive for the older person. Still, even at present, Medicare covers only about 40 percent of the average elderly patient's health care bill. Thus, under Wohl's proposal, if an elderly person could afford to pay an equivalent additional amount of $2,000 toward a private health insurance policy, considerable coverage could be obtained, except possibly for the very old.

The potential benefit of Medicare abolition would be the development of more private sector competition in all health care sectors—among physicians, hospitals, nursing homes, home care organizations, health maintenance organizations, and health insurance companies. Medicare currently provides large amounts to guarantee financing of hospital care. To be sure, the prospective payment system (PPS) for Medicare-reimbursed hospital care has temporarily arrested the rapid increase in Medicare expenditures. The arrest is, however, only temporary; indeed, costs have already picked up again since the introduction of PPS.

Wohl argues that perpetuation of Medicare in its present form means continued, and probably increasing, government control of health care, the extension of price supports that artificially drive up costs, and continued immunity from market forces. According to Wohl, in 1984 only 66 percent of hospital beds were filled. Those empty beds incur costs and are paid for indirectly and in part by Medicare dollars. A dismantled Medicare bureaucracy would save literally billions of dollars in administrative costs and would provide a truly functioning marketplace without the waste that is currently being institutionalized.

Although Medicare recipients may feel that they would be the major losers if Medicare were abolished and replaced with a payment system that required them to buy health insurance, they would in fact benefit from such action. The current health industry structure of hospitals, physicians, and nursing homes would be the losers. That this is well-realized is shown by the fact that the biggest opponents of deregulation of Medicare are the hospital associations and the American Medical Association.

Medicare can be viewed as a system of price supports under which health care costs will continue to increase and the rate of health care inflation will continue to outpace the consumer price index. Clearly, in view of the nearly 12 percent of Gross National Product that we are now spending on health care, we must look seriously for ways to slow this growth. The most efficient means of doing that is through the marketplace. As prices escalate, the elderly, especially those on marginal incomes, will be worse off. We owe it to them to find a better way to control run-away health care cost increases. Deregulation may well be the answer.

Are Hospital Costs Rising More Slowly?

With the adoption of the prospective payment system in 1983 for Medicare-reimbursed hospital patients, there was hope that hospital costs would finally stop rising at their double digit rates. Evidence reported in 1984 reinforced that hope, in that it showed clearly a slower rise in hospital costs (Waldholz 1984). In Iowa, the Blue Cross and Blue Shield plan actually reduced its premiums for the first time in its 40-year history. Other insurers reported relatively small increases in health insurance premiums because of lower costs of hospitalization.

The slowed hospital cost increases in 1984 were attributed largely to concerns by health care providers to hold down health care costs. Patients, doctors, and hospitals were all looking for ways to reduce health care costs. In some cases, less expensive care outside of the hospital was substituted for hospital treatment. In other instances, treatments were curtailed or avoided altogether.

Another reason for the slower growth of health care costs is the requirement by employers that employees pay a larger portion of their health care costs. Waldholz reports that Evanston Hospital, north of Chicago, persuaded its orthopedic surgeons to discharge artificial hip implant patients in eight days, half the previous time. The cost of a typical heart bypass operation was reduced from $6,000 to $3,500. At other hospitals, a brain tumor typically meant a six-week hospital stay; with available home health care, the brain tumor patient was now discharged in a few days and then cared for at home at only a fraction of the cost of hospitalized care (Waldholz 1984). This experience suggests a viable formula for controlling health care costs, at least for keeping the rate of increase to a reasonable level.

However, a report by Stipp (1987) indicates that the recent slowing of the growth of hospital costs is misleading. He predicts that costs will skyrocket about 1990 if we do not impose painful health care "rationing," as is now practiced in Great Britain. Stipp's report was based on a study by medical economist William B. Schwartz of the Tufts University School of Medicine. Schwartz argues that sharp increases in hospital costs will continue unless access to expensive high technology medicine is limited. The British already control their health care costs by limiting access to certain high technology health care procedures. Clearly, the main factor behind rapidly increasing health care costs remains the growing population of the elderly who are extensive utilizers of health care. However, the current availability of high technology and the further introduction of new and expensive technology is likely to fuel an even bigger explosion in health care expenditures unless access to the plethora of new procedures and new technology is controlled. An example of restricting access to high technology might be in the use of high-technology heart surgery, which could remain available for a younger individual but would not be utilized for an older patient with multiple diseases.

The real problem with rationing health care is, of course, posed by the question, Who is going to do the rationing? To some extent, health maintenance organizations (HMOs) might take it upon themselves to perform this function. Since the major economic justification for HMOs is their ability to reduce hospital utilization, high technology and expensive procedures could in many instances be avoided and lower-cost medication therapy utilized instead. Indeed, to a large extent, the British are already doing this.

The difficulty with introducing health care rationing in the United States stems from the abundance of physicians and hospitals. In these circumstances, it would be difficult to impose rationing. In Great Britain, rationing is frequently done out of necessity, in that the system just does not have the capacity to accommodate all those that present themselves. In those circumstances, rationing is a lot easier and a lot less likely to be challenged.

Is Home Care a Good Cost Cutting Option?

Home care alternatives, especially for respiratory care, are proliferating (Bunch 1984). Especially in the area of home ventilator care, the savings from keeping a patient at home instead of in the hospital are astounding. Home care alternatives for home ventilator systems are quite feasible because the patient's family members can be trained to service the equipment and assist the patient. In such situations, the cost for a normal month at home begins to approximate one day's worth of hospital care.

The most revolutionary home care device for respiratory patients is the oxygen walker system. First manufactured by Linde, the oxygen walker system developed out of a cooperative effort between Linde and top pulmonologists in New York in the late 1960s. In some cases, the oxygen walker system even allows patients to resume work.

The oxygen concentrator has also played a major role in reducing the cost of caring for respiratory patients. The oxygen concentrator uses room air to produce concentrated oxygen. Especially for patients on continuous oxygen therapy, it has been a boon. In fact, for patients who use a high volume of gas each month, their costs are nearly cut in half.

The concept of using home ventilation for respiratory patients is not new, but it is now being more actively supported by both the medical community and third party reimbursement agencies because of its much lower costs. In addition, it provides considerably more freedom to the individual undergoing the therapy.

The success in respiratory therapy on a home care basis is opening the way to other types of therapy that can be provided at home, such as nutritional therapy, certain chemotherapies, fluids therapy, and antibiotic therapy. Whereas many of these therapies in the past were given in the hospital setting, they can now be safely provided in a home care environment. Particularly for those therapies that are not totally reimbursed by third parties, the savings of such home therapy can be substantial. Family members can usually be trained to deliver the bulk of the day-to-day care the patient needs, thus saving not only the cost of the hospital stays but also the cost of routine home nursing care.

THE IMPACT OF RETIREES' HEALTH CARE COSTS ON AMERICAN COMPANIES

It has been a practice of many large corporations to extend health care coverage to their retirees. This practice dates back many years. It was instituted at a time when health care insurance premiums were relatively low and when the number of active workers by far exceeded the number of retirees. However, now, with the restructuring of many older smokestack industries and with the increasing mechanization of industry, the number of active employees is declining while the number of retirees remains largely unchanged.

The above situation became evident in an extreme form when Kaiser Steel missed a quarter-million dollar weekly premium payment for its 4,300 retired employees. At the time, Kaiser was in financial distress and had only 200 active employees left on its payroll (Nielsen 1987). In stopping weekly premium payments for its retirees' health insurance, Kaiser assumed it could avoid the heavy financial burden generated by health insurance premiums that amounted to about $13 million per year. The retirees, through the United Steel Workers, sued for reinstatement of the insurance. In light of precedence, they will probably win their case, and Kaiser Steel will have to find ways to pay the premiums, at least until it goes bankrupt.

The Kaiser Steel case is an extreme case, but numerous American corporations are saddled with a similar burden. The large steel firms and automobile companies are particularly hard hit and are likely to remain so for a number of years, at least until the presently large contingent of retirees dies off and is replaced by fewer current employees.

Nielsen reports that Bethlehem Steel has 37,500 active employees and 70,000 retirees. American Telephone and Telegraph has 97,500 retirees, about half of whom are too young for Medicare (Medicare covers part of hospitalization costs, and the balance is covered by the company-paid health insurance). In 1985, General Motors spent $837 million in premiums for their 285,000 retirees (Nielsen 1987).

Legally, these large corporations cannot extricate themselves from the liabilities they incurred in decisions made many years ago. There are, however, ways by which these corporations can reduce their obligations. One way is to require that their retirees join health maintenance organizations or preferred provider organizations. In this way, the corporations could directly control health care costs to some extent.

In any event, control of these costs is becoming absolutely essential for many of these larger corporations. Unless these costs are controlled, some of these corporations will not be able to compete effectively. As a result, some will be weakened financially and drift toward bankruptcy. Bankrupt organizations can no longer pay health insurance premiums. Thus, retiree groups would be well-advised to check closely the financial condition of the corporation that is paying their health insurance premiums. Under certain conditions, the retirees as a group may even want to grant the corporation certain concessions to ensure its continued viability and strength.

CONCLUSION

Health care costs can be controlled if society demands that they be controlled. Over the short term, that is not likely to happen. To be sure, many people are upset about the high cost of health care. But as long as the rising cost does not directly affect them seriously, they are unlikely to insist that drastic action be taken to control health care costs. The fact is that the American population is still insulated from assuming directly the financial burden of health care costs. Most health care in the United States is paid by third party payers. In addition, the health insurance premiums for most people are paid by other entities. For these reasons, the high cost of health care has not impacted directly on the American consumer.

However, this condition may change as employers increasingly shift health care costs from the company to the individual. As this practice becomes more prevalent, the American citizen will become more concerned and will start demanding some form of control. The form this control will take will probably involve increasing numbers of health maintenance organizations and preferred provider organizations. It may also involve some rationing of health care, especially for elective treatments, and especially for older Americans. Since these trends are already developing in Great Britain, it is difficult to imagine that they will not also develop in the United States.

REFERENCES

Bunch, D. "Home Care: The Best Cost Cutting Option." *AAR Times* 8 (August 1984):32–33.

Business Week/Harris Poll. "Americans Prescribe Radical Surgery." *Business Week*, 15 October 1984, 148.

Nielsen, J. "Sick Retirees Could Kill Your Company." *Fortune*, 2 March 1987, 98–99.

Stipp, D. "Easing of Hospital Cost Misleading." *Wall Street Journal*, 9 January 1987.

Waldholz, M. "New Views about Care in Hospitals Lead to Slower Rise in Health Costs." *Wall Street Journal*, 8 October 1984.

Wohl, S. "Deregulate to Cure Health-Care Paralysis." *Wall Street Journal*, 9 October 1983.

Chapter 6

Information, Referral, Support, and Ombudsman Services

INTRODUCTION

Local government, especially in the more urban areas, is becoming increasingly aware of its responsibilities to provide or arrange for a variety of support services tailored to the needs of the elderly. Recognition of this responsibility has usually resulted in the creation of an office or department in the local government devoted to and responsible for the needs of the elderly. Usually these divisions are known as offices for the aging, departments of senior services, and so on.

There are many factors to be evaluated in determining what services are needed by older people. It has been estimated that about one-quarter of the elderly live alone, that about one-quarter have incomes at or below the poverty level, and that well over one-third have one or more activity-limiting conditions. Frequently these three factors overlap. In such situations, the affected elderly are in particular need of assistance.

Although many elderly with activity-limiting conditions are able to sustain a minimum daily living standard, there are many others who require assistance in one or more areas, such as meal preparation, housekeeping, and shopping. Others require assistance with transportation, medical treatment, social activities, and so forth. Still others are completely homebound and need home health care services. This chapter reviews these various services that are available to the elderly.

COMMUNITY ORGANIZATIONS

Community support services are designed to help older persons remain in their customary environments, usually their own homes and neighborhoods. The overall goal is to minimize their chances of relocation and to defer various levels of dependency, especially institutionalization, for as long as possible.

Community support services include all those services that may be required to complement a comprehensive system of health-social services. For example, community organizations can promote the use of existing programs and provide opportunities for the elderly to enhance the quality of their lives. They can generate activity programs and coordinate services offered by various government, charitable, and profit-motivated organizations. They can inform individuals about appropriate types of assistance and make referrals as needed. They may try to identify hard-to-reach persons and help them gain access to needed services. Finally, in conjunction with other support efforts, they can facilitate the provision of appropriate transportation for the elderly.

The senior citizen center provides a setting for organized activities and recreation and serves as a meeting place for the elderly. It usually offers a wide range of services, such as nutritional programs and shuttle services; makes arrangements for medical examinations; and provides counseling regarding personal and legal problems, the aging process, and civil rights. To augment its programs, the senior citizen center establishes certain working relationships with other agencies.

The multipurpose center is an extension of the senior citizen center concept. The multipurpose center offers a complete range of services at a central location and provides limited services at surrounding satellite centers. Although the idea was designed to apply to the elderly, it has the potential for application to all age groups in the community.

A strategically placed multipurpose center can reduce fragmentation of services. However, the multipurpose concept is often difficult to implement because of the variety of organizations currently providing their own services. Most of these organizations are reluctant to yield control. In such cases, communities must coordinate the efforts of the various organizations in a manner consistent with the operational requirements of the multipurpose center and with the needs of the people it serves.

AN INVENTORY OF FEDERAL GOVERNMENT SERVICES

The broad range of services available to the older person under federal government sponsorship include health services, social services, income maintenance, social supports, housing, transportation, and volunteer support services. The following description of these services is provided by the National Institutes of Mental Health (1981).

1. Health Services (1981).
   - *Medicare (Title 18)*. This federal program provides coverage for specified health care services for persons 65 and over and for eligible disabled persons. It covers hospital and posthospital skilled nursing home care and home health services. Subject to premiums, it covers physicians' and other specified outpatient services. Subject to certain limitations, it also covers psychiatric treatment.
   - *Medicaid (Title 19)*. Medicaid grants to states cover 50 to 83 percent of the costs of medical care for eligible low-income families and individuals. Within federal guidelines, the states establish eligibility, determine the scope of benefits, and administer the program. Under federal requirements, provision is made for inclusion of optional mental health benefits in psychiatric hospitals for persons over 65. Most Medicaid eligibles 65 and over are also covered under Medicare. In such cases, most state Medicaid agencies pay for Medicare premiums, deductibles, and coinsurance; Medicare makes the primary payment for medical service.
2. Social Services (Older Americans Act)
   - *State and community programs on aging*. Federal formula grants are made to the states to develop comprehensive and coordinated systems of social service for persons 60 and over. This federal support covers the entire range of services: transportation and escort, outreach, health-related, preventive (homemaker, home health, chore, friendly visiting, telephone reassurance, protective, housing), legal, nutrition, employment, recreational, information and referral, and other services determined to be necessary for the welfare of older persons.
   - *Multipurpose senior centers*. State and area agencies on aging may award grants for acquiring, altering, or renovating existing facilities or for the construction of a new facility to serve as a multipurpose center, that is, a community facility for provision of health, social, nutritional, educational, and recreational activities for persons 60 and over. State agencies can use Title III-B Social Services funds to construct such centers in areas where no suitable structures are available. States can also use Title III-B money to cover personnel and operating costs of senior centers.
   - *Nutrition services*. Formula grants are awarded through state and area agencies on aging to public and private nonprofit agencies to establish the means to provide low-cost group meals and home-delivered meals for persons 60 years and over and their spouses of any age. Each project is required to provide meals in a congregate setting and to offer other supportive services, including nutrition, education, and outreach.

- *Community service employment for older Americans.* The secretary of labor may contract with public and private nonprofit agencies to develop and administer part-time employment in public service activities for low-income persons 55 or older.
- *Demonstration projects.* Federal project grants are awarded to public agencies or nonprofit private organizations to develop projects designed to demonstrate new or improved methods of providing needed services to older people, focusing especially on housing, transportation, education, preretirement counseling, and special services for older handicapped persons.

3. Income Maintenance

- *Supplemental Security Income (SSI).* This program provides monthly cash payments to persons with limited or no income who are aged, blind, or disabled. It is a federally funded, needs-tested income maintenance program. Most states supplement federal payments.
- *Food stamps.* Low-income families and individuals are eligible to receive monthly food stamp allotments, varying with income and household size. The elderly may exchange food stamps for home-delivered meals. Elderly and certain disabled persons may also use food stamps in specified congregate programs.

4. Social Supports. Under Title 20, providing social services for low-income persons and public assistance recipients, federal formula grants are made to state welfare agencies to establish and operate social service programs for individuals meeting state income limitations. Services for the elderly may include information and referral, home health care, day care, transportation, and mental health services.

5. Housing

- *Community development block grants.* The U.S. Department of Housing and Urban Development (HUD) provides formula grants to urban communities, based on poverty population and other economic and population factors, for a variety of community development activities, including construction of senior citizen centers.
- *Housing assistance payments.* HUD provides funds to assist low-income persons and families who cannot afford decent and sanitary housing in the private sector. Rent supplements cover the difference between the community's fair market rent values down to 15–25 percent of the tenant's adjusted income.
- *Section 202 housing program for the elderly.* Federal loans are made by HUD for the construction of multifamily rental housing for the elderly 62 and over. Tenants may qualify for rent supplements under the Section 8 program.

- *Low-rent public housing.* Local housing authorities receive federal loans from HUD to aid in the purchase, rehabilitation, leasing, or construction of multifamily housing for low-income families, individuals 62 and over, and handicapped persons. Housing designed for the elderly may have congregate dining rooms and other special features. Rents may not be more than 25 percent of the family's income.

- *Mortgage insurance on rental housing for the elderly.* HUD insures against loss on mortgages for construction and rehabilitation of multi-family rental housing for those elderly, 62 or over, and disabled who are above the low- or moderate-income level.

- *Rural rental housing loans.* The Farmers Home Administration (FmHA) in the Department of Agriculture makes direct and guaranteed insured loans to construct, improve, or repair rental or cooperative housing in rural areas for low-income persons, including senior citizens 62 or over. Multifamily housing may have congregate dining and other congregate facilities.

- *Rural rental assistance.* FmHA provides rental assistance payments to low-income families in FmHA-financed multifamily housing who would otherwise have to pay more than 25 percent of their income for rent.

- *Rural home repair program.* FmHA makes loans and grants to low-income homeowners 62 or over to repair or rehabilitate their homes to remove dangers to their health and safety.

6. Transportation
  - *Reduced fares.* Mass transportation companies that receive federal funds from the Department of Transportation (DOT) for either capital or operating expenses can charge elderly and handicapped persons no more than half-fare during off-peak hours.

  - *Capital and operating assistance grants.* DOT awards grants to local public agencies under Section 3 of the Urban Mass Transportation Act for the acquisition and construction of mass transit vehicles; under Section 5, for capital and operating expenses; and under Section 9, for planning. These grants may be used for special services for the elderly.

  - *Capital assistance grants for use by public agencies and private nonprofit groups.* Under Section 16(B)(1) of the Urban Mass Transportation Act, up to 2 percent of the annual allotment for capital assistance grants may be set aside by local public agencies for the acquisition of transit vehicles, equipment, and facilities. Grants may be used to meet special transportation needs of the elderly. The remaining 2 percent funding limitation also applies to private nonprofit agencies under Section 16(B)(2), which stipulates that 2 percent of the annual allotment for capital assistance grants may be set aside for private nonprofit groups to provide mass transportation services for elderly persons.

7. Volunteer Support Programs

- *Volunteers in Service to America.* The ACTION program provides volunteer service opportunities for persons 18 or older in urban and rural poverty areas and in Indian reservations, for persons with migrant families, and for persons in federally assisted institutions for the mentally ill and mentally retarded. Most older VISTA volunteers serve part-time.

- *Senior Companion Program.* ACTION awards grants to public and private nonprofit agencies to create volunteer service opportunities for low-income persons 60 and over who wish to render supportive service to adults, usually senior adults. The volunteers receive a modest payment.

- *Retired Senior Volunteer Program (RSVP).* Federal grants are made to public or private nonprofit agencies to establish or expand volunteer activities for the elderly. Compensation for out-of-pocket expenses incidental to their services is provided.

- *Foster Grandparent Program.* Federal grants are awarded to public and private nonprofit agencies to create volunteer service opportunities for low-income persons, age 60 and older, to render supportive services to children. The volunteers receive a modest payment.

COMPONENTS OF HEALTH AND SOCIAL SERVICES

The broad range of health and social services can also be categorized as maintenance services, personal care services, supportive medical services, medical services, and personal planning. The following descriptive outline is based on Brody's guidelines (Brody 1974):

1. *Maintenance Services*
   - Income maintenance is available through public assistance, Social Security, veterans benefits, unemployment compensation, Workmen's Compensation, and food stamps.
   - Personal maintenance
     a. Public assistance is available under Titles 1 or 16 of the Social Security Act (Old Age Assistance). States are authorized to provide homemaker services as part of social services to the aged.
     b. The Older Americans Act provides assistance under Title 3. Grants are made to homemaker and nutrition programs, including Meals-on-Wheels.

    c. The Veterans Administration provides special support to handicapped veterans and their dependent survivors. This support can be used to purchase homemaker services.

2. *Personal Care*

- Medicare includes personal care as a reimbursable item only when furnished through a home health agency primarily engaged in delivering skilled nursing care, on a part-time intermittent basis. Reimbursement is provided only if it can be demonstrated that personal care is needed and that the patient is severely limited in function. The physician must regularly certify that the patient is sick enough to need the service and that the patient's condition demands only part-time intermittent care.
- In several states, Medicare provides reimbursement for medical assistance programs, such as personal health care services.
- In some states, public assistance provides personal care services through a "special-need" grant as an addition to the income maintenance grant.
- Local public health services may include personal care as part of their home health programs. Hospital-based home health programs and neighborhood health centers may also offer personal care services, although they usually depend on Medicare or Medicaid for reimbursement. Private health insurance policies rarely cover such services.

3. *Supportive Medical Services.* As part of home health care, supportive medical services include nursing, physical therapy, occupational therapy, and speech therapy.

- Medicare provides reimbursement under the same conditions as required for personal care (see Item 2 above).
- In some states, Medicaid reimburses coordinated home care programs, particularly when they are extensions of hospital service.
- State rehabilitation agencies may provide vendor payments for supportive medical services if they are part of a plan to make the client self-sufficient. These services are provided under a state-federal matching funds program.

4. *Medical Services.* Medical services for the aged are financed largely under Title 18 (Medicare) and Title 19 (Medicaid) of the Social Security Act. Medicaid is commonly available only for very low income groups.

- Hospital insurance (Medicare) is provided through Part A of Title 18. It provides protection for covered services to any person 65 or over who is entitled to Social Security or railroad retirement benefits. Hospital insurance benefits are paid to participating hospitals, to extended care facilities (skilled nursing homes), and to related providers of health care to cover the reasonable cost of medically necessary services furnished to individuals entitled under the hospital insurance program. The program pays a large part of the cost of hospital care during each benefit period. The benefit period begins with the first day of hospitalization and ends 60 days after discharge from a hospital or extended care facility (ECF). Hospital insurance also pays part of the cost of care (during the benefit period) in a participating ECF when admission follows a hospital stay of at least 3 days. In addition, the program covers home health visits in the 12-month period following discharge from a hospital or ECF.

- Supplementary medical insurance (SMI) is a voluntary medical insurance program financed by monthly premiums from enrollees and a matching payment from federal general revenues. It provides payment for 80 percent of the reasonable charges for physicians' services, outpatient hospital services, medical supplies and services, home health services, outpatient physical therapy, and other health care services. Its coverage includes home health visits, diagnostic tests, x-rays, radium and radio-active isotope therapy, ambulance services, prosthetic devices, and the rental of durable medical equipment. An annual deductible must be met before benefits begin. Thereafter, Medicare pays 80 percent of the charge for covered services. The beneficiary is responsible for the deductible and for 20 percent of the cost of covered services. Application for the program is made through the local Social Security office within three months after the 65th birthday, or within three years of the first opportunity to sign up for medical insurance.

- Medicaid coverage varies by state, both as to eligibility and extent of benefits. Those aged receiving or eligible for categorical assistance are eligible for the medical program provided under Title 19. The elderly with marginal incomes above public assistance eligibility limits are often provided with the same amount or with a reduced amount of benefits. The usual arrangement for the medically and categorically needy is for the state to buy in on their behalf for Part B of Title 18 and to supplementally fund the co-pay aspects of Parts A and B.

- Health maintenance organizations and health insurance companies provide coverage for that portion of health care not covered under Medicare.

5. *Personal Planning and Other Services.* Counseling offered by social workers, family agencies, mental health centers, home health care agencies, vocational rehabilitation agencies, and protective services for adults unable (or unwilling) to manage their own affairs falls under the auspices of a multitude of government and charitable programs. The range and quality of these services vary widely, representing what is available in the community. Information, referral, transportation, and outreach services are similarly diverse. Usually, funding for such services is available under

such service-granting mechanisms as the Office of Economic Opportunity (OEO), the Department of Health and Human Services (HHS), or the Older Americans Act (OAA) or under service sections of Titles 1, 16, and 19 of the Social Security Act.

A TYPICAL LOCAL GOVERNMENT OFFICE FOR THE AGING

Local government offices for the aging perform important functions in transmitting information and referring clients, both to their own programs and to those offered by other agencies. Major agencies to which clients are referred include the county department of social services, Legal Aid Bureau, Legal Counseling for the Elderly, planning and community services, the United Way, the In-Home Support Services Corporation, Meals-on-Wheels, and Catholic Charities. The services range from counseling to home-delivered meals. The primary targets of a local office for the aging are persons over 60 who are isolated, have a low income level, or have physical or mental functional impairments and are considered to be at high risk for institutionalization.

Offices for the aging offer many programs and services to the older segment of the population. In a typical office for the aging in a large urban area in the northeastern United States, these programs and services could include any or all of the following:

- *Transportation*—maintaining and updating a system of escort service for older persons
- *Information and referral*—providing current information on services available to older persons
- *Multiservice senior centers*—providing aid to senior citizen centers, including help in offering a broader range of services
- *Nutritional services*—providing a balanced home-delivered meal to those elderly unable to cook for themselves
- *In-home services*—providing homemaker and home health aide services to those ineligible under Medicaid, Title 20, or for private services
- *Legal services*—providing legal counseling services
- *Personal contacts*—providing personal contact, escort, and chore services to alleviate loneliness and isolation
- *Complimentary cards*—to assist the elderly by stretching the purchasing power of their limited income
- *Outreach*—seeking out and identifying hard-to-reach individuals so that they can gain access to services

- *Protective services*—assisting elderly persons who are unable to protect their own interests or meet their own needs and who have no one willing or able to help
- *Safety*—helping to protect the elderly from crime
- *Institutionally related services*—providing, for example, day care and respite services
- *Employment*—developing jobs and providing employment opportunities
- *RSVP*—providing administrative support to the Retired Senior Volunteer Program
- *Education*—increasing community awareness through educational services
- *Recreation*—providing opportunities for recreational activities
- *Housing improvement programs*—for example, contracting with Catholic Charities to operate a housing improvement service

Each of the above programs and services is designed to meet the needs of a particular part of the elderly population. In each case, the effort is implemented in compliance with applicable federal, state, and local laws.

INFORMATION AND REFERRAL SERVICES:
A DEMONSTRATION PROJECT

An extensive HEW-supported demonstration project designed to offer information and referral services was established in the state of Wisconsin during the mid-1970s. The demonstration project included a subsequent evaluation of the effectiveness of the services provided. The reported results covered the period beginning October 1, 1973, and ending September 30, 1974 (Long 1977).

The demonstration project provided two basic services—information-giving and referral. Information-giving was defined as providing information about services and programs. It included some effort to obtain background information on potential clients in order to determine their eligibility for the services of a specific provider. Referral was defined as making an appointment with the appropriate service provider by the information and referral center on behalf of the caller.

The demonstration project provided these services by telephone through a dozen information and referral centers. The bulk of the activities of the centers involved information-giving. Although referral services (including the making of appointments) were offered, less than one percent of the callers accepted referral appointments. Of those who accepted referral appointments, 82 percent contacted the recommended facility. Of those receiving information, 71 percent contacted the recommended facility. Callers who accepted referral appointments required about ten minutes more staff time than those who were given only information. About 61 percent of all calls were handled within ten minutes, with 60 percent completed during the initial contact. Over 87 percent of all callers were helped within one day of their contact with an information and referral center.

Once the centers had become known in the communities and the center staffs had been trained, the overall cost of providing basic information and referral services amounted to less than five dollars per call (in 1973–1974 dollars). Almost 90 percent of those who contacted a recommended service or program were sent elsewhere for help with their problems.

These statistics clearly indicate the value and need of the services that can be provided to the elderly by an information and referral service.

THE LONG-TERM CARE OMBUDSMAN PROGRAM

The Long-Term Care Ombudsman Program, mandated under the Older Americans Act as amended in 1978, is a coordinated system of state and local advocacy services that are designed to be responsive to the complaints and problems of older residents of long-term care facilities. Any state office for the aging is authorized to establish and administer a long-term care ombudsman program, using one percent of the annual funds allotted to it under Title III-B (Social Services) of the Older Americans Act.

The purpose of the program is to organize community-based assistance to permit complaints about the quality of care and life in skilled nursing homes, health-related facilities, and residential care facilities for adults to be received, investigated, and resolved through joint state and local efforts.

The typical long-term care ombudsman program consists of state-level staff who provide community organization, training, coordination, ongoing support, and technical assistance to local programs. The state staff also assist the state office for the aging in developing legislative positions and advocating the development of state regulations and policies beneficial to long-term care residents and their families.

The program provides access for the ombudsman to long-term care facilities. It supports a reporting system to collect and analyze data relating to complaints and conditions in long-term care facilities, including procedures to protect the confidentiality of such records and the identity of the complainant or resident.

For example, in New York State, the Long-Term Care Ombudsman Program developed three major thrusts in achieving the objectives of the program.

1. The local long-term care ombudsman programs are the forefront of the state's advocacy efforts on behalf of patients/residents and their families. Substate programs, designated by the state office for the aging, are de-

veloped through the cooperation and interaction of area agencies on aging, public and private community organizations, and concerned citizens. These combined groups are responsible for coordinating the program at the local level and for mobilizing the resources of the community in support of the institutionalized elderly. Volunteers are recruited and trained as citizen ombudsmen to assist in the protection of patients/residents rights and to serve as advocates in resolving complaints.

2. The state office for the aging's capacity to administer the Long-Term Care Ombudsman Program is expanded by the development of a network of regional ombudsmen who are assigned to function in areas analogous to those of the area offices of health systems management. Their responsibilities include assisting in the development of designated substate long-term care ombudsman programs in cooperation with the area agency and other community agencies; receiving, investigating, and resolving complaints; stimulating community interest and concern for the institutionalized elderly; and organizing consumer advocacy and friendly visitor groups.

3. The state office for the aging has taken the lead in organizing an Inter-Agency Coordinating Council for Long-Term Care Patient Advocacy. This council is comprised of representatives from eight state agencies that have statutory or monitoring responsibilities for the institutionalized elderly. The purpose of the council is to promote the coordination of separate state agency activities to ensure that appropriate care is provided to older residents of long-term care facilities; to identify issues that affect large groups of institutionalized persons; and to secure policy, regulatory, and legislative changes necessary to improve the quality of life and care.

In New York State, consumers are urged to contact first the appropriate facility staff and administration with their problems. If no resolution occurs, they should contact the designated local ombudsman program or, if none exists, the state ombudsman staff. Assistance with resolving a problem is given by local or state ombudsmen; or, if more appropriate, a referral to the Office of Health Systems Management or the state Department of Social Services can be facilitated. These latter offices can take action on problems or complaints related to violations of state regulations.

CONCLUSION

It is now widely accepted that society has an obligation to help support the elderly. Assistance is best offered as a preventive service that provides information and referral as well as support. The isolation of elderly persons as a result of retirement or lack of regular social contact often leads to declining health, which, in turn, can lead to other problems. It is in such cases that information, referral, and support services become increasingly important to the elderly.

Support programs provided by community and senior citizen centers offer the elderly sources of information and local sites for social gatherings. Other agencies supported by federal, state, and local governments can complement these centers by facilitating programs designed to enable older persons to achieve or maintain independence and self-sufficiency.

REFERENCES

Brody, S.J. "Long Term Care in the Community." In *A Social Work Guide for Long-Term Care Facilities*, edited by Elaine M. Brody. Washington, D.C.: National Institutes of Mental Health, U.S. Government Printing Office, 1974, 46–62.

Long, N. *Information and Referral Services: Research Findings*, vol. 1, DHEW Publication no. (OHDS) 77–16251. Washington, D.C.: Office of Human Development, Administration on Aging, 1977.

National Institutes of Mental Health. *A Resource Guide for Mental Health and Support Services for the Elderly*. U.S. Department of Health and Human Services, 1981.

New York State Office for the Aging. *Long Term Care Ombudsman Program*. Albany, N.Y.: New York State Office for the Aging, 1983.

Chapter 7

Institutional versus Noninstitutional Care

INTRODUCTION

With the advent of Medicare and Medicaid in the mid-1960s, a solution to the problem of how we could care for the ill, the disabled, and the infirm elderly appeared to be at hand. The solution: put them in a nursing home where they will be cared for by a professional and dedicated staff. Unfortunately, the solution was not all that simple. Financing mechanisms such as Medicare and especially Medicaid resulted in a proliferation of nursing homes, some of which were very good but many of which were bad to very bad. Some of these homes were likened by some to warehouses for the infirm elderly.

The poor conditions in many nursing homes were often the result of a lack of management or a lack of staff dedication. In many cases, however, they were the result of cost-cutting by local government administrators of the Medicaid mechanism. The lack of quality control, the lack of health care and utilization review, and the lack of adequate physician supervision also led to instances of abuse and poor health care. It was not surprising therefore that, by the mid-1970s there was an outcry against nursing home practices and against nursing homes in general, this despite the existence of many nursing homes in which high quality, professional, and dedicated care was provided.

The result was a public and professional clamor for deinstitutionalization. But how do you institutionalize? Do you send people back home? What about those who have no home? Will their children take them in? What type of health care will be provided if they can be placed in a home setting? These and many other relevant questions were not easily answered. In time, the pressures for deinstitutionalization were gradually replaced by a movement to prevent institutionalization and to develop support organizations that could provide a variety of services to the elderly to enable them to remain at home as long as possible. The result was a proliferation of both nonprofit and for-profit support organizations that could provide a wide range of services—meal services, transportation services, home health care services, maintenance services, and so on—all intended to keep the infirm elderly out of institutions as long as possible.

By the mid-1980s, 20 years after the appearance of Medicare and Medicaid, institutionalized care in nursing homes and hospitals was being supplemented by home health care and support services in serving the infirm and disabled elderly. An important result of this expanded system of care is that many homebound elderly who previously had no access to home health care are now able to receive it. The addition of a home health care system has of course also contributed to rising health care costs. But these rising costs are also providing improved access to health care for many infirm and disabled elderly who need it.

DETERMINING THE APPROPRIATE HEALTH CARE SETTING

The ill or impaired elderly can be cared for basically in three types of settings: in acute care hospitals for acute care problems, in nursing homes for continuing care problems, and in a home environment. Which of these is the appropriate setting will depend on a variety of factors, including the condition of the patient, the availability of home support for the patient, and the availability and practices of health care facilities in the community.

Acute care hospitals are generally the most expensive care settings, followed by nursing homes, and then by home health care. Thus, from a cost perspective, home health care is usually the most desirable. However, to be feasible and effective, home health care requires a strong family support system. Also, if home health care becomes intensive, based on the needs of the patient, a skilled nursing facility may actually be a lower-cost setting.

The fact remains, however, that most elderly persons would prefer to live outside the institutional setting of a hospital or nursing home. Indeed, in most urban areas home health care has made tremendous strides. Unfortunately, not all communities have well-developed home care alternatives to institutional care.

Once it is determined that a person is incapable of living at home without some form of additional support, the question of an appropriate alternative care setting will depend upon the existence of social support (generally family or close friends), the adequacy of financial resources, and the availability of noninstitutional health and social services. Unfortunately, many of the elderly are poor or have no spouse or children to assist them. Or their families may refuse or be unable to assist them due to distance, lack of living facilities, inadequate family structure, or financial limitations. In any event, if there is no social support available from family or friends, the alternative will be a nursing home, in which long-term care services may be heavily subsidized by the government.

The establishment of mechanisms to curb inappropriate placement in institutionalized facilities poses a dilemma. Within the growing elderly population, those 75 and over, who are most likely to have chronic conditions, are the fastest growing segment. This growing subpopulation will put increasing pressure not only on institutionalized facilities but also on alternative forms of care, principally home care.

THE EXTRA-MURAL HOSPITAL: THE NEW BRUNSWICK EXAMPLE*

Current projections indicate that 15 percent of the U.S. population 65 and older will be functionally disabled and need some form of long-term care by 1990. The total cost of that care will amount to over $100 billion.

One solution to the dilemma posed by these statistics may well be represented by the approach taken by the small Canadian province of New Brunswick. Since 1981, an organization called the extra-mural hospital has functioned in the province. This way of delivering home health care is analogous to the delivery of health care in the acute care hospital. The major difference is the absence of the physical hospital building. Except for this, the extra-mural hospital functions much as an acute care hospital, with its own affiliated physicians, its own nursing staff, and its own ancillary health services staff.

Background

The term *extra-mural hospital* originated in Auckland, New Zealand, where an organization of this type has been in operation for over 25 years. One may think of an extra-mural hospital as a hospital without walls. It is intended to provide a total health care program similar to that in an established hospital, up to the point where the specialized knowledge and equipment that is available only in an established hospital is required. Short of this point of specialization, the extra-mural hospital functions just like an established hospital, bringing together the medical, nursing, and ancillary services in the same way as in the hospital.

One may scoff at the extra-mural hospital concept and say that it appears to be just another type of home health care organization. To a limited extent that is true. However, the extra-mural hospital functions more like a hospital than a

*This section is based on "Putting It All Together—The New Brunswick Extra-Mural Hospital" by Gordon Ferguson. This paper was presented at the Ninth Annual Health Administration Forum, University of Ottawa, Canada, June 7, 1983.

home health care organization. Patients of the extra-mural hospital are admitted and discharged, just as in an established hospital. The only difference is that the patients remain in their homes and need some form of supervision and support by family members or friends.

In the New Brunswick example, the extra-mural hospital is intended to have an impact on both hospitals and nursing homes, providing a viable substitute for both hospital and nursing home care.

Objectives

The mission of the New Brunswick Extra-Mural Hospital is best described by its objectives:

- to provide an alternative to hospital admission
- to facilitate earlier discharge from the hospital
- to provide an alternative to, or postponement of, admission to nursing homes
- to provide continuous health care to those with long-term illness
- to provide continuous health care and rehabilitation to disabled persons of all ages
- to provide care at home for persons terminally ill
- to provide assessment and rehabilitation services to the elderly
- to facilitate the co-ordination and provision of support services, either directly or through other agencies.

The basic objective of the extra-mural hospital is thus to reach out into the community to carry a wide range of clinical and support services to the ill and disabled in their homes. In this way, it is possible for a physician to care for a wide range of patients suffering from a variety of problems in a home setting.

The extra-mural hospital clearly does not replace the established hospital or the physician's office. Rather it fills the gap between ambulatory and institutional care and precludes institutionalization for those patients who can be treated in a home setting.

In New Brunswick, the extra-mural hospital has the legal status of a hospital. As such, admitted patients have the same status as established-hospital patients and thus are covered by the same hospital insurance as established-hospital patients.

Service Delivery Units

Services of the extra-mural hospital are delivered through service delivery units. The service delivery unit forms the local base for the staff. Each service delivery unit has a unit coordinator who manages the day-to-day activities of the unit. Physicians wishing to admit patients do so through the unit coordinator. The unit coordinator is responsible for the allocation of staff, decisions to accept or reject patients in consultation with the referring physician, the quality of care, control of the unit budget, management of supplies, and so on. The unit coordinator must of course be a health professional and typically is a registered nurse.

Physicians who want to be affiliated with the extra-mural hospital must apply to the hospital board for admitting privileges. The affiliated physician admits patients and directs their management and discharge, thus playing the familiar role of attending physician.

When it was established in 1981, the New Brunswick Extra-Mural Hospital functioned initially with one service delivery unit in Frederickton. By 1985, seven service delivery units were in operation, and about 25 percent of the physicians in New Brunswick were affiliated with the extra-mural hospital.

The patient case load of the extra-mural hospital is heavily slanted toward providing services to the elderly. In 1985, 55 percent of the patients were 65 and over and 9 percent of patients were 85 years and over.

Patients are admitted to the extra-mural hospital with a wide range of disease conditions. The elderly tend to suffer from multiple chronic, often serious, health problems. Conditions identified at admission are similar to those in the established hospital, with patients differing mainly in the level of care required. The four major disease categories displayed by patients of the New Brunswick Extra-Mural Hospital in 1985 were respiratory problems (14.5 percent), cardiovascular problems (13.9 percent), all types of cancer (11.9 percent), and musculo-skeletal problems (10.7 percent).

Patients admitted directly from home account for 40 percent of admissions. The remainder are admitted from acute-care hospitals. On discharge, 63 percent of the patients remain at home, 34 percent are admitted to acute care hospitals and 3 percent die at home. Although the impact of the extra-mural hospital on the acute care hospital is difficult to measure, approximately 70 percent of its admitted patients have been identified as replacements for established-hospital patients for at least some portion of their stay.

By 1985, the New Brunswick Extra-Mural Hospital had treated 9,000 people since its inception in 1981. Its staff consisted of 100 nurses, 3 physical therapists, 2 respiratory therapists, and 2 occupational therapists, plus 267 affiliated physicians. The daily patient cost amounted to $21 compared with approximately $300 in an acute care hospital. The extra-mural hospital's budget for 1985 amounted to $6.6 million, out of New Brunswick's total health care budget of

$632.0 million. By keeping more patients at home, New Brunswick hopes to avoid the capital costs of building any new acute care hospitals before the turn of the century (Kelly 1985).

Some Observations

A common question raised about the Auckland, New Zealand, and the New Brunswick extra-mural hospitals concerns the extent to which they differ from home health care organizations.

Basically, the extra-mural hospital is organized and attempts to function like an acute care hospital. As such, it utilizes formal admission and discharge processes. It also uses affiliated physicians. Of course, the typical home health care organization can also claim that it also utilizes admission and discharge processes and has physicians at least loosely affiliated with it through referrals and ongoing physician supervision.

In light of this, why create extra-mural hospitals in communities already serviced by established home health care organizations? On the other hand, one could certainly argue that, in a community not now being served by a well-developed home health care organization, an extra-mural hospital would seem to be able to fill an important need.

In any event, to be successful, an extra-mural hospital clearly needs strong support from the local medical community. In deciding whether to provide such support, one would have to ask what benefits the extra-mural hospital would bring to physicians? Would it help them in the care of their patients? Or would it hinder them by imposing more time-consuming home visits?

The New Brunswick Extra-Mural Hospital was established with strong support from the provincial government, which regarded it as a means of avoiding new hospital construction in the province for at least the next several years. To what extent governments elsewhere would be willing to provide the health care financing mechanism needed to support the formation of extra-mural hospitals similar to those in New Brunswick and Auckland, New Zealand, remains an open question.

CONCLUSION

Institutionalization has been the traditional way to deal with the infirm and disabled elderly. Following the appearance of Medicare and Medicaid, however, it became apparent that institutionalization was not the most desirable way of dealing with the infirm or disabled elderly. Especially for those who could be cared for in a home environment, that appeared to be the ideal care setting. This realization led to demands for deinstitutionalization, or at least reduced institutionalization, and these demands are still very much in vogue today.

An interesting alternative to institutionalization may be the extra-mural hospital. As shown by the New Brunswick example, the extra-mural hospital can become a potent mechanism for keeping ill people in general and the ill and disabled elderly in particular out of institutions.

REFERENCE

Kelly, C. "New Brunswick Hospital Provides Low Cost Care." Toronto, Ontario: *Globe and Mail*, September 30, 1985.

Chapter 8

Rehabilitation of the Elderly*

INTRODUCTION

Rehabilitation is a fairly well accepted medical procedure for the younger handicapped or disabled individual. It is not, however, universally accepted as desirable or necessary for older people. This is unfortunate because older people can usually benefit immensely from even moderate rehabilitation programs.

Rehabilitation is often viewed as the third phase in medical care, the first two phases being prevention and specific medical/surgical care. But successful rehabilitation also involves preventing further disability or related deterioration and aiding ongoing medical or surgical treatment (Williams and Jones 1985).

The simple recognition that aging and disease are not synonymous will go a long way toward creating an environment in which rehabilitation becomes a routinely applied medical approach. The prejudices and myths about aging must be attacked and conquered on many fronts, including the field of rehabilitation. In particular, the all-too-common point of view that the normal aging process inevitably results in physical and mental deterioration, much of which is viewed as untreatable, is a notion that must be overcome.

Research has shown that many of the disabilities experienced by older patients are the result of identifiable and treatable pathological processes. Even in cases where the disease process can only be controlled, rather than cured, it is a legitimate goal of the clinician to treat disabled persons and to help them achieve whatever degree of productivity their functions will allow.

Population projections clearly demonstrate why rehabilitation medicine must occupy a more prominent place in the future practice of medicine. By the year 2000, the number of people 65 and older in this country is projected to reach

---

*This chapter is based on and has numerous excerpts from the four referenced articles which appeared in *Aging*, No. 350, Administration on Aging, U.S. Office of Human Development, U.S. Department of Health and Human Services, 1985.

35 million. Those 85 and older, the most vulnerable, will more than double in number, to 5.5 million.

An increased emphasis on rehabilitation therapy also has an economic basis. About half of all federal funding of health care is on behalf of older Americans. For many elderly, the alternative to costly rehabilitation therapy is even more costly institutional care. Studies of patients with selected impairments have shown that patients who received rehabilitation therapy are much more likely to return home and avoid institutionalization than are patients who do not receive such therapy. It is therefore economically justified to invest in rehabilitation measures that will somewhat shift the focus from acute and long-term institutional care to home and self-care.

The rehabilitation goals for the elderly patient must be set at a realistic level. For younger patients, a successful return to work is a normal measure of the success of treatment. For older patients, a simpler, but no less important goal, may be independence in such activities as household work, walking, grooming, or doing similar daily tasks. Realistic goal-setting also includes accepting small gains in function, many of which mean the difference between living at home and living in an institution.

The greater susceptibility of older patients to secondary disabilities makes it mandatory to begin rehabilitation immediately. By taking too long to investigate the geriatric patient or ignoring the need for rehabilitation therapy, care providers risk creating additional disabilities for the older patient.

THREE SUCCESSFUL GERIATRIC REHABILITATION INSTITUTIONS

To see what can be accomplished in the field of geriatric rehabilitation we examine in this chapter three rehabilitation institutions: the Piersol Rehabilitation Center of the Hospital of the University of Pennsylvania; The Burke Rehabilitation Center of White Plains, New York; and The Montefiore Hospital Home Health Agency.

The Piersol Rehabilitation Center

The Piersol Rehabilitation Center of the Hospital of the University of Pennsylvania in Philadelphia is the oldest rehabilitation center in the United States. The Piersol rehabilitation program, as presented in the following description drawn from Segal (1985), brings together resources in rehabilitation, mental health, and gerontology to meet the diverse needs of older people with disabilities.

Piersol's rehabilitation activities are not just restricted to geriatric rehabilitation; only 17–20 percent of the hospital's acute care patients are 65 years and older, but 50 percent of Piersol's cases are people over 65 years of age.

The center's primary objectives are to help patients live as independently as possible, to increase their functioning in activities of daily living, to help them achieve a satisfying life role, to reduce their social isolation, to increase their ability to maneuver in a home setting, and to develop their bowel and bladder control. To meet these objectives, the criteria for admission include consideration of the patients' medical stability as well as their potential for improvement. Attention is also given to what will happen to patients upon discharge. Attempts are made to steer them away from negative perceptions about themselves and instead to focus on their disabilities and how to adapt to them. The primary objective is to help patients retain their independence.

During a patient's first week at the rehabilitation center, members of the rehabilitation team evaluate the patient's potential for improvement. Following this evaluation, a team group meeting is held with the patient and members of the patient's family. At this meeting, a possible discharge date for the patient is projected so that the patient is aware that rehabilitation is a finite process.

The average length of stay in the rehabilitation center is from four to six weeks. A substantial portion of the patient's time is spent in physical therapy. The physical therapists in the center have the advantage of being able to refer to the patient's acute care therapy records and thereby add to their understanding of the patient's functioning.

Another important component of the patient's care is occupational therapy, which uses activities to achieve functional goals. The elderly are concerned with self-care, and the majority want to be independent. After standardized testing for coordination, strength and endurance, range of motion, sensation, cognition, perception, and balance, the occupational therapists work on the activities of daily living: eating, dressing, grooming, bathing, hygiene, and homemaking. Occupational therapy also includes gross motor exercises and functional activities that involve following directions, participation in competitive games, and doing memory tasks.

The patient is also subjected to music and speech therapy, which provides an outlet for verbalization. Especially with stroke patients, there is a loss of the power of expression or the ability to comprehend the written or spoken word. This condition is referred to as aphasia. A number of diagnostic and therapeutic techniques are used to stimulate the patient's communicative function.

In addition to the above therapies, the patient is treated by a recreation therapist. The recreation therapist takes patients to sporting and cultural events to help them overcome any embarassment at being seen in public with their disability. Family members are encouraged to go on these trips to help them feel more comfortable about being seen with the patient.

The Burke Rehabilitation Center

The Burke Rehabilitation Center, as described by Miner (1985), is a private nonprofit hospital in White Plains, New York, dedicated to helping disabled persons attain maximum independence. Its three main divisions are a 150-bed inpatient hospital, a research division, and an ambulatory division, which offers a wide range of services for outpatients with stroke, amputations, Parkinson's disease, orthopedic disabilities, arthritis, low back pain, various neurological disorders, cardiac and pulmonary disease, speech and hearing problems, and other disorders.

The mission of the outpatient department is to provide top quality rehabilitation to persons in the area with physical impairments. The services provided are physical therapy, including hydrotherapy; occupational therapy; speech, language and audiology; nursing; social services; orthotics, prosthetics, and bioengineering; laboratory and x-ray; urology; nutrition counseling; medical supervision; and subspecialty medical consultation. Basic outpatient services range from single therapy treatment sessions to multidisciplinary care involving several therapies. The core services are physical therapy; occupational therapy; speech/language therapy and audiology; and orthotics, prosthetics, and bioengineering.

Each patient receives a comprehensive evaluation from the appropriate therapy departments upon arriving at the Burke center for outpatient therapy. After evaluation, which identifies specific problem areas, goals are set, and a treatment plan is formulated to achieve the goals of the patient.

Physical therapy takes place in a gymnasium setting. Occupational therapy areas include a clinic room, a room for activities of daily living, a computer room for cognitive evaluation and retraining, a kitchen, and a bathroom. Speech/language therapy is conducted in individually designed treatment rooms.

The Burke center also has the following special programs for particular groups of the aging population:

- The Geriatric Evaluation Service, which identifies dementias and other related disorders and makes recommendations based on evaluation results
- The Dementia Day Care Program, which provides activities for persons with Alzheimer's disease and other dementias and gives respite to the families of the participants
- The Senior Day Program, which offers an interesting environment for elderly people who lack social and sensory stimulation
- The Community Care Program, which places elderly or disabled adults with foster families who can provide assistance with daily living routines

Most patients of the Burke center are from the community, although some travel a substantial distance for outpatient treatments. Outpatients who do not have access to a personal automobile use a minibus service provided by the county to reach the Burke center.

Exhibit 8-1 lists the physical, occupational, and speech/language therapy activities for the major groups of older outpatients treated at the Burke center. Some of the activities are applicable to more than one type of therapy.

The Montefiore Hospital Home Health Agency

The Montefiore Hospital Home Health Agency, started in 1947, is one of the first hospital-based home health agencies in the United States (Koren 1985). Since its inception, rehabilitation has been an important feature of the agency's functions. The 1965 Medicare Act made available to persons who were homebound such skilled services as physical therapy, occupational therapy, and speech therapy, in addition to nursing care. This enabled the Montefiore program to expand to 750 patients, 85 percent of whom are over 65 and 15 percent of whom are over 85 years of age.

Although services similar to Montefiore's home health program are available in clinic settings, the patients in those clinics must be transported to the clinics and this can create major problems and costs, especially for the homebound patients. By providing treatment at home, transportation costs are avoided—costs that are not reimbursable by Medicare, although they are reimbursed under Medicaid.

At Montefiore's home health agency, recent hospitalization is not a requirement for acceptance into the program, although hospital discharges account for the majority of patients. However, each patient must have a physician of record to be accepted into the program. If it is decided that a patient will benefit from the program, a therapist visits the patient's home to assess the home environment and the patient's current level of functioning. A rehabilitation program is then developed, equipment is ordered and installed in the patient's home, and treatment is tailored to the patient's home environment.

Rehabilitation therapy in the home is often questioned because of the greater range of equipment and services available in the institution. Montefiore has found that, with the exception of whirlpool units and diathermy machines, all of the necessary equipment and treatment modalities can be supplied. Parallel bars, mats, traction sets, TENS units, canes, hot packs, ultrasound units, and infrared lights—all can be ordered from a supplier of durable medical equipment, delivered to the patient's home, and set up. In addition, hydraulic lifters can assist caretakers in transferring heavy or inert patients from bed to chair, agitators can be put on bath tubs to give whirlpool-like effects, and rails and bars can provide safety for unsteady ambulators.

Exhibit 8-1 Burke Rehabilitation Center Therapies for Various Conditions

---

Stroke
Physical Therapy
Pre-gait activities, if the patient is not ambulatory
Gait training, if the patient is ambulatory
Ambulation on different types of surfaces, e.g., stairs, ramps
Education and provision of appropriate bracing
Range of motion, strengthening, and coordination exercises
Functional electrical stimulation, when appropriate
Family education in managing the individual at home
Occupational Therapy
Training in activities of daily living, including grooming, dressing, cooking, etc.
Transfer training, e.g., to toilet, bathtub, car
Activities and exercise to improve functional use of affected upper limb
Training to compensate for visual-perceptual problems, when indicated
Providing patients with adaptive devices, such as reachers and special utensils
Speech/Language Therapy
Language production work
Reading, writing, and math retraining
Functional skills practice, e.g., checkbook balancing, making change
Therapy for swallowing disorders
Oral musculature strengthening
Amputees
Physical Therapy
Fitting and providing of temporary and permanent prosthetic devices
Teaching donning and doffing of prostheses
Progressive ambulation
Training in proper stump care
Instruction in range of motion, strengthening, and endurance activities for both involved
    and uninvolved extremities
Occupational Therapy
Teaching donning and doffing of prostheses
Stump care training
Transfer training
Training in activities of daily living
Parkinson's disease
Physical Therapy
Gait training
Training in changing positions
General conditioning, strengthening, breathing, and range of motion exercises
Encouragement of motor activities outside Burke Center, e.g., swimming, bicycling,
    walking, as appropriate
Occupational Therapy
Improving fine gross motor coordination of the upper extremities
Providing patients with adaptive devices, e.g., reachers and special utensils
Basic self-care activity training, e.g., dressing and grooming
Transferring training from one surface to another
Speech/Language Therapy
Improving respiratory control
Improving coordination between respiration and speech
Improving control of rate of speech
Use of voice amplifiers and/or alternate communication devices

Exhibit 8-1   continued

Arthritis
  Physical Therapy
    Joint protection techniques
    Conditioning, strengthening, and range-of-motion exercises
    Gait training
    Hot packs, ice, hydrotherapy, ultrasound (deep heat) treatment
    Electrical stimulation
  Occupational Therapy
    Range-of-motion and strengthening exercises for the upper extremities
    Splinting to protect involved joints, decrease inflammation, and protect deformity
    Joint protection techniques
    Provision of adaptive devices to increase independence and avoid undue stress on in-
      volved joints
Low-back pain
  Physical Therapy
    Heat and cold treatment
    Ultrasound, electrical stimulation
    Strengthening and flexibility exercises
    Instruction in proper posture and body mechanics, e.g., proper lifting, sitting, and
      sleeping positions
  Occupational Therapy
    Advice and practice in labor-saving techniques
Cardiac disease
  Physical Therapy
    Patient education
    Conditioning and endurance programs, e.g., on a bicycle or treadmill
    Breathing exercises
    Strengthening and flexibility exercises
    Monitoring of patients' vital signs during exercise
  Occupational Therapy
    Labor-saving techniques
    Improving overall endurance to increase ability to participate in activities of daily living
    Monitoring of patient participating in activities of daily living
Pulmonary disease
  Physical Therapy
    Education about the disorder
    Breathing control exercises
    Conditioning exercises, e.g., using a treadmill, or general strengthening and flexibility
      exercises using a stationary bicycle
  Occupational Therapy
    Training in use of labor-saving techniques to increase independence in all areas of
      activities of daily living, including dressing and homemaking
    Monitoring of patient participating in activities of daily living
    Improving endurance of upper extremities

Source: Aging, No. 350, pp. 9–13, Administration on Aging, U.S. Office of Human Development, U.S. Department of Health and Human Services, 1985.

Another benefit of home rehabilitation is that the patients, after rehabilitation, must function on their own in the home environment. By rehabilitating the patient in the home, the environmental variable is removed and the patient is likely to perform closer to the optimum level. In short, treating the elderly in their own homes allows them to regain their functioning and to carry out their activities of daily living in the setting in which they must, in fact, manage if they are to maintain their independence.

CONCLUSION

Rehabilitation services for the elderly population is about to become one of the major growth areas in health care. Although initially this may result in increased health expenditures, there is evidence that rehabilitation of the elderly delays or avoids institutionalization, which involves a health care expenditure that far exceeds the cost of rehabilitation.

Yet, before rehabilitation of the elderly handicapped becomes more prevalent, there will have to be wider acceptance of the concept that rehabilitation is the third phase of medical care, the first two phases being prevention and specific medical/surgical care.

By the year 2000, the 65-and-older age group will number 35 million, and the 85-and-older age group will total 5.5 million. By the year 2030, the elderly population is expected to grow to 18 to 20 percent of the population. Fortunately, not all of these people will need rehabilitation care, but many will be able to benefit from it. Thus, it is imperative that efforts begin to develop the manpower and provide the financial sources needed to develop the capacity to provide appropriate rehabilitation care for the older American population. The alternative will be to see many of them reduced to a lower quality of life in an institutional setting.

REFERENCES

Koren, M.A., and Bills, D. "Home May Be the Best Place for Rehabilitation." *Aging*, no. 350 (1985):14–17.

Miner, S. "Outpatient Services for the Disabled." *Aging*, no. 350 (1985):9–13.

Segal, W.M. "A Hospital Rehabilitation Center—Preparation for Going Home." *Aging*, no. 350 (1985):4–8.

Williams, T.F., and Jones, P.W. "Rehabilitation in Our Aging Society." *Aging*, no. 350 (1985):2–3.

Chapter 9

Indicated Needs in Home Health Care

INTRODUCTION

The rapid growth of home care and home health care has made these areas the prime growth industry in the health care field. Will home health care continue to grow, or will it stabilize at its present size? The studies examined in this chapter do not provide a definitive answer to this question, but they certainly provide material to ponder in our attempts to find a response.

In the first study, based in Manitoba, where home health care is freely available at no cost to the patient, it was found that home health care has grown only to the point where 5 to 6 percent of the elderly population is admitted to home health care annually. However, a larger percentage, about 10 percent, receive some form of home care during the year.

In a survey in Lucas County, Ohio, there appeared to be little knowledge of home health care among the elderly, and little anticipation that they would ever need it. But then we are all optimists, even the elderly and the very old.

In another study, the experience of ventilator-dependent polio victims in the 1950s indicates the very real potential in substituting home care for institutionalization. The results of this study should be examined by everyone who feels institutionalization is inevitable for many people.

Finally, we cite the success of a home care study in Rochester, New York. Here, it was found that a targeted group of chronically ill patients could be served by a home care medical team at a cost below that of a traditional approach.

In the light of these studies, home health care is clearly not just a flash in the pan. It has been shown to be cost-effective. It has also proved capable of improving the quality of life for those who can benefit from it.

PATTERNS AND PREDICTORS

The question has often been posed, ''What would happen to home care if eligibility were determined solely on the basis of assessed need for help to return or remain at home, with no requirement that the individual needs a medical service, assuming the home care service were provided at no direct charge and as long as necessary?'' Shapiro (1986) attempted to answer this question in a study on the utilization of home care services by the elderly in the Canadian province of Manitoba.

In U.S. jurisdictions, there is usually some constraint on reimbursed home care services. The result is that home care services are frequently severely limited by government edict or because of substantial charges. In fact, utilization of home care services in the United States by Medicare enrollees ranges from 2 to 5 percent, depending on where they live. In New England, about 4 to 5 percent of the elderly are recipients, while in the South only about 2 percent of the elderly are recipients. Of all Medicare home care utilizers, about 90 percent are the elderly.

In Manitoba, home care became part of a province-wide health assurance system in 1974. The system has the responsibility for assessing persons for both home care and nursing home placement. Available services include therapy, nursing, homemaking, equipment and specific supplies, social services, adult day care, and respite care.

The Shapiro study revealed that about 5 to 6 percent of the elderly are admitted for home care service each year, and about 10 percent receive home care service at some time during the course of the year. Costs of this home care program are difficult to determine. Based on 1976 data, the annual cost per person served during the year was about $385. Based on monthly costs divided by the number served each month, the average monthly home care cost per person served was about $60. Thus, home care costs per person served in the province varied widely. Some people utilized the home care service only occasionally, while others used it on a long-term and regular basis.

The results of the study make a strong argument for multiple-entry admissions to home care programs. In the Manitoba group, only 6 percent of new home care admissions had recently been hospitalized.

The study also revealed that the function of home care changes with advancing age. Mortality rates of home care users under 85 years are higher than nonhome care users of the same age and sex. However, the opposite was found to be the case with home care users over 85 years of age. Apparently, the under-85 group used home care services as a hospital or nursing home replacement program. For the 85 and over, elderly home care was used primarily as a way to avoid institutionalization. Thus, in this case at least, it appears that home care played a large role in permitting the very old, those over 85, to continue living in the community for a relatively long period of time.

Supporting this conclusion, a 1983 Canadian federal-provincial home care study found that, during 1978, 35 percent of new home care admissions during a two-month period would otherwise have required nursing home placement.

The study revealed that average monthly cost savings of using home care instead of nursing home services ranged, in 1978 dollars, from $300 to $558, depending on the level of care required (Shapiro 1986).

The above study of the Manitoba environment shows that an essentially open admission approach to a home care program admits only a small minority of the elderly. The home care services appear to supplement family efforts that enable the elderly to remain at home for a relatively long period of time. It may now be worthwhile to investigate the effects that open admission to home care, under Medicare financing, would have on the very old, say 80 and over, in the American setting.

PERCEPTION OF HOME HEALTH CARE BY THE ELDERLY

The institution of the prospective payment system (PPS) for hospital care of America's elderly has made it more likely that those elderly who become hospitalized will also come in contact with home health care. Because the PPS system provides incentives for hospitals to discharge people earlier, many of the hospital-discharged elderly now require posthospitalization home health care.

Studies have found that the utilization of services by the elderly is partially determined by various sociodemographic factors. Complementing these, a study by Starrett (1986) explored how the elderly feel about home health care and how much they know about it prior to its utilization. The study pays particular attention to the role of needs, knowledge, and risk factors in the use of home health services. It was based on a stratified sample of 400 elderly individuals 65 and over in Lucas County, Ohio. The sample was stratified by age, sex, and zip code to ensure accurate representation of the elderly.

The main findings from the study indicated that the elderly had little knowledge of home health care and did not expect to need it. Specifically, about half of the elderly were not aware of home health care services and did not know where to go for home health care service information. A summary of the respondents' needs and knowledge is shown in Table 9-1.

The author suggests a need for home health care educational and marketing programs to inform the elderly about the appropriate use of home health care. In addition, home health care programs need to develop mechanisms to identify elderly people in need of such care before their conditions deteriorate to the point where they need hospitalization or nursing home institutionalization. Indeed, the purpose of home health care is to provide services to the elderly as a substitute for institutionalization in either hospitals or nursing homes.

THE VALUE OF HOME CARE: A CASE EXAMPLE

In the early 1950s, before the discovery of polio vaccine, a serious polio epidemic left hundreds of ventilator-dependent polio victims. The victims were

Table 9-1 Need for and Knowledge of Home Care

Factor	Variable	Value	Number	Percent
Need	Need home care in last five years	No	371	92.8
		Yes	29	7.3
	Current need of home care	No	387	96.7
		Yes	13	3.3
	Future need of hospital care	No	302	75.5
		Yes	98	24.5
Knowledge	Home health care	No	203	50.7
		Yes	197	49.3
	Know hospital to go for treatment	No	26	6.5
		Yes	374	93.5
	Aware of information services	No	191	47.7
		Yes	209	52.3
Health Status	Excellent		86	21.5
	Good		186	46.5
	Fair		103	25.8
	Poor		25	6.2
Age	65–69		128	32.0
	70–74		124	31.0
	75 and over		148	37.0

Source: Adapted from "Home Health Care: The Elderly's Perception" by R.A. Starrett in *Home Health Care Services Quarterly*, Vol. 7, No. 1, pp. 69–80, with permission of Haworth Press, Inc., 12 West 32nd St., New York 10001, © Spring 1986.

heavily equipment-dependent and ended up in hospitals where they faced life-long institutionalization. Responding to the situation, the National Center for Infantile Paralysis developed 16 regional respiratory polio centers to provide home care services to the ventilator-dependent polio victims. The objective was to enable them to return to their homes and live as normal lives as possible within the constraints imposed by their disability. The following report on this project was provided by Lauri (1984).

The sixteen regional centers were established at medical school/teaching hospitals to accept groups of the chronic ventilatory patients and to develop a positive approach to their care.

The first home care approach under the program was established in the Los Angeles Rancho Los Amigos Hospital, which had 158 ventilator-dependent polio patients. The cost of caring for these patients amounted to $37 per day per patient in 1953 dollars. The home care program that was developed to allow these patients to go home was provided at $10 per day per patient and included attendants, equipment, maintenance, and other supporting services. Of the 158 patients in the hospital, 152 were able to take advantage of the program and went home.

The transition from hospital to home was implemented carefully and gradually. Emphasis was placed on training family members and the patients in the use and maintenance of the ventilators and in assisting the patients to resume their roles in the family and the community.

The disabled individuals and their family members had to become expert in maintaining and operating the equipment and in training others. At first, the home care services provided attendants, but it was soon discovered that the family members were more dependable and more expert at attending the disabled individual than the attendants supplied by the home care service. The home care facility, however, continued to provide equipment maintenance services and social and advisory services to the disabled and their family members.

In 1959, the National Foundation for Infantile Paralysis reported that the home-based ventilator-dependent people were being cared for at one-tenth to one-quarter of the cost of hospital care. What was even more important was the achievement of a greater degree of self-sufficiency and independence for the ventilator-dependent people. Many of the ventilator-dependent individuals were able to complete their education and become professionals, such as attorneys, clergy, computer programmers, engineers, physicians, professors, teachers, and writers. Most of them reached a high degree of independence. Since the equipment made them dependent on assistance, they could never be completely independent. However, most of them were able to solve their problems as individuals.

This program shows how important the availability of home care can be when the alternative is institutionalization. Today, although the scourge of polio has been eliminated, many handicapped elderly find themselves in a similar situation. Unless home care is made available to them, the alternative of institutionalization hangs constantly over their heads.

THE COST-EFFECTIVENESS OF HOME CARE: A CASE EXAMPLE

Researchers at the University of Rochester have developed a new approach to home care for the elderly who are homebound and chronically ill (Groth-Junker 1984). In this program, a team consisting of a physician, a geriatric nurse practitioner, and a social worker provided round-the-clock, on-call medical care to elderly patients in their homes. A randomized, controlled trial showed that the approach provided effective, less costly care to the terminally ill.

The program used two groups of patients, each randomly selected. The study group was provided with round-the-clock, on-call medical care; the control group received traditional home care services, such as regular check-ups by a visiting nurse at home, but had to travel to a physician's office or clinic for additional treatment.

The experiment showed that aged patients who were treated by the home health care team but who died during the course of the study received more services at home and were hospitalized about half as much during their final two weeks than patients in the control group. The costs of home care provided by the home health care team were higher than costs of traditional home care because more services were provided. Yet, because of decreased hospitalization, overall costs for the patients of the health care team were about a third less than those for patients receiving traditional at-home care. An additional nonfinancial benefit achieved was the significantly greater satisfaction among the health care team patients, especially among their family members.

CONCLUSION

The studies reviewed in this chapter indicate that home health care is here to stay but that it is by no means a complete substitute for traditional care given in hospitals and nursing homes. Where home care is freely available, its utilization remains at modest levels. However, where it has been used, its effectiveness on the basis of lower cost and quality of life for the patients involved has become apparent.

With the prospective payment system (PPS), home health care will undoubtedly continue to become an extension of hospital care, especially for the elderly covered by Medicare. However, as we have seen, home care has its limitations. It nearly always assumes that the person receiving the home care has relatives or family members who can provide the physical and mental support system that is so necessary for the success of the program.

REFERENCES

Callahan, J.J., Jr. "Long Term Care and Home Health Services." *Bulletin of the New York Academy of Medicine* 59, no. 1 (1983):69–74.

Groth-Junker, A. *Home Health Care Team: Randomized Trial of a New Team Approach to Home Care*. Springfield, Va.: National Technical Information Service, 1984. (PB84–163955)

Lauri, G. "Polio Survivors Prove the Value of Home Care Services." *AAR Times* 8 (April 1984):47–48.

Shapiro, E. "Patterns and Predictors of Home Care Use by the Elderly When Need Is the Sole Basis for Admission." *Home Health Care Services Quarterly* 7 (Spring 1986):29–45.

Starrett, R.A. "Home Health Care: The Elderly's Perception." *Home Health Care Services Quarterly* 7 (Spring 1986):69–80.

Chapter 10

Critical Issues in Home Health Care

INTRODUCTION

A number of important issues relating to home health care should be addressed at this point. The first concerns the merging of community-based service programs and the kinds of comprehensive health care that health maintenance organizations can provide. Such facilities can provide a comprehensive array—in effect, a form of safety net—in the care of the elderly citizen. The major problem, of course, is cost. For such facilities to be successful, some form of cost sharing between Medicare, the community that provides the community-based services, and the client will be required.

The second issue concerns the importance of the network concept in caring for the elderly. A home support network is in fact critical for the successful implementation of a home health care project.

The third issue concerns the element of choice by the elderly person regarding various types of health care services. Ideally, of course, there should be complete freedom of choice. But in terms of cost-effectiveness, that ideal situation is usually not available, unless the individual is able and willing to pay for private care.

The fourth issue thus relates to the cost-effectiveness of home health care—a subject much debated in recent years. In some cases, home health care was found to be cost-effective; in other cases, it was found to fall short of acceptable cost-effective standards. The fifth issue concerns medical and legal aspects of home health care standards. In this connection, it has been suggested that, to avoid legal liability, home health care organizations must follow the hospital model of patient charting and adequate screening and training of their health care personnel.

The final issue we address concerns the advantages and disadvantages of a nonprofit versus a for-profit status for a home health care organization. Each type of organizational form has its advantages and disadvantages. Which form should be selected will depend on a variety of factors as they relate to the individual situation.

THE MULTIPURPOSE HEALTH CARE MODEL

The multipurpose senior services project (MSSP), originating in California, is a combination of community-based service programs and health maintenance organizations. Services provided through the MSSP include adult social day care, housing and home repair, in-home support, legal services, medical respite care, nonmedical transportation needs, nutrition, protective services, and preventive health care (Minkler and Blum 1982).

In April 1980, the Health Care Financing Administration (HCFA) initiated through the University Health Policy Consortium at Brandeis University a demonstration of the multipurpose concept (Jackson 1984). The demonstration project, called a Social/Health Maintenance Organization (S/HMO), was intended to create incentives to provide care in the most appropriate and cost-effective settings by allowing flexibility in service patterns. The project placed a cap on program expenditures, incorporated case management structures, and emphasized prevention and nonmedical supports.

Today, the financing of the S/HMO package is handled through Medicare for services rendered under parts A and B and for incidental services on the basis of a capitated rate per enrollee of 100 percent of the average adjusted per capita community rate. To provide the comprehensive package, private premiums are charged to make up the difference between revenues and cost. These premiums, however, cannot exceed the current Medicare supplemental premium. Medicaid subscribers are covered for all included benefits at a negotiated rate.

As Jackson (1984) reports, the S/HMO concept represents most clearly the trend away from the strictly medical model of health care for the elderly, as represented by Medicare regulations. The problem with the S/HMO model is that it is open-ended in the area of community support services, that is, it has a tendency to expand and become too expensive. Thus, the strictly health care delivery part of the S/HMO model, provided by the health maintenance organization, works well because the incentive of the HMO is to strive for cost-containment. Provided that the premiums provided to HMOs by Medicare are reasonable, the prospective payment system for health care also works quite well; indeed, it has already shown to be quite cost-effective for the younger working-age population. What is needed now to make the S/HMO system a success is a prospective payment system for the community, nonhealth-related services that need to be provided to elderly citizens.

THE NETWORK CONCEPT

The network concept of caring for the elderly is based on the recognition that society is becoming increasingly complex and interrelated and that there is a need for correspondingly complex concepts and descriptive analysis in caring for our older citizens. The resulting network of care should include friends, neighbors, and relatives—all functioning together to enable the elderly to maintain independent lives in the community (Cantor 1975).

Several studies, like the one reported by Johnson and Bursk (1977), have emphasized the critical significance of the affective relationship between elderly persons and their adult children. The General Accounting Office (GAO) reports that studies have shown that families and friends are indeed involved in providing the daily living requirements of older people (U.S. Congress, General Accounting Office 1977). The services provided include transportation, shopping, and financial assistance. However, the question remains: How long can the family be expected to carry the burden of long-term care? Often the family provides resources to the point of exhaustion, asking for help only when strained beyond endurance.

Eggert et al. (1977) confirm the family's willingness to assume the burden of care for seriously impaired individuals; but they also suggest that, without supportive services, the family's capacity to provide care is fragile. They found that 70 percent of patients who were institutionalized had been cared for at home after a previous hospitalization. However, after a second hospitalization, only 38 percent of the families were willing to continue providing care. This break-even point is at odds with the break-even point referred to in the above-cited GAO cost comparison. Indeed, the Eggert study suggests that the lack of available support services erodes a family's willingness and capacity to care for an elderly relative who is ill and is responsible for a rise in institutionalization.

Historical and social changes have created new constraints on families. Demographic changes have reduced the number of descendents to whom an older person may turn for assistance. Changes in the economy have decreased a parent's power to ensure support by grown offspring. Various forces acting on the family— social legislation giving individuals more independence, greater mobility, more emphasis within the family on raising children, more mothers working—have distorted the traditional interdependencies between the elderly and their children.

Probably most significant is the change in women's social roles. At present, approximately 60 percent of all women between 18 and 64 are working outside the home. This figure will no doubt increase steadily as the level of education increases. And as more and more women work, the opportunity to take care of elderly parents declines.

The research on intergenerational relations has obvious implications for policy and planning. The consensus of findings by Cantor (1975) and Shanas and

Sussman (1977) is that the capacities and capabilities of formal and informal systems differ significantly. For instance, with both husband and wife working, the capability of caring for a parent still exists, but the capacity is no longer available. There are indications that the best situation is one in which families can rely on the "bureaucracy" for assistance in economic and health care while continuing to draw on their own resources to meet the emotional and environmental needs of their older members. Studies suggest that policy makers and practitioners should pay greater attention to intervention strategies aimed at improving the correlation between poor health and poor intergeneration relationships.

Supportive services that would strengthen the network concept include improved transportation, home medical services, financial assistance (when needed), day care centers, and respite care services (the latter are temporary care services that give needed relief to families of the aged).

The economic approach to the study of home health services can provide administrators and policy makers with valuable information regarding the optimal level in the delivery and allocation of alternative services. However, the economic approach to planning can be greatly enhanced by the inclusion of sociological and psychological factors. The above-cited GAO report does not take such factors into account (U.S. Congress, General Accounting Office 1977). Thus, while many would concur with the GAO that family support is the key element, the GAO's recommendations (cited below) should not be accepted as is; improvement in the management of relevant services must be based on data that are more reliable and diverse.

THE ELEMENT OF CHOICE

At present, the elderly's choice of health care options is limited and influenced by reimbursement mechanisms. Although full freedom of choice is an ideal in our democratic society, in reality it is an option only for the affluent. Indeed, some say that, with regard to home health care, unlimited individual choice may in fact place unreasonable demands on other segments of the population and thus infringe on their own economic and social freedom. In any event, the issue of choice clearly has economic, philosophical, and political dimensions when applied to health care alternatives.

Home health advocates claim that, if home health services were available, they would be the choice of many elderly and that the resulting earlier discharges and decreases in admissions would lead to considerable savings. Realistically, however, choice in this case must be combined with an accurate assessment of the level of impairment. This has prompted efforts to find a better way to determine the appropriateness of services on an individual basis. In some states, the responsibility to do this has fallen to hospital utilization review committees. For example, New York State mandates an organized discharge planning program that must be submitted to the commissioner of health in writing to ensure that each patient has a planned program which meets the patient's postdischarge needs. There is some disagreement among health care providers as to the effectiveness of this approach, and administrative problems need to be ironed out. Discharge planners, on the other hand, criticize the lack of coordination in and the varying levels of quality of home health care systems that tend to inhibit their effectiveness.

Unfortunately, as noted previously, choice is limited for the dependent elderly in our society. For this reason, most of the studies that have compared home health care with nursing home care have addressed the cost issue in considerable detail but have given only token attention to the choice issue. Another drawback of these studies is that they rarely consider the abilities, attitudes, and needs of both the elderly and their families in regard to providing home health care as well as receiving it.

The previously cited 1977 GAO report makes the following recommendations:

> Until older people become greatly or extremely impaired, the cost of nursing home care exceeds the cost of home care including the value of the general support services provided by family and friends. However, for the greatly or extremely impaired, the value of services provided by family and friends becomes a dominant factor in their care and well being. Thus, those greatly or extremely impaired elderly who live alone are the most likely to become institutionalized. The Congress should consider focusing the jobs to be created to assist the sick and elderly under the President's welfare reform proposal to those elderly who live alone and are without family support.
>
> Because the states and HEW are experiencing considerable difficulty in coordinating the many federal programs which offer home health benefits, HEW should develop for the Congress' consideration a comprehensive national policy for the delivery of home health services. (U.S. Congress, General Accounting Office 1977)

This report is a prime example of how misleading and incomplete data can lead to the assumption that expansion of home health care is the universal solution to the problem. In a review of home health care effectiveness studies, Hammond (1979) points out that our available data are based on existing programs rather than on systematic research designs and that they rarely include consideration of direct, indirect, and tangible benefits and costs. Thus, although it has received a great deal of attention in the literature on gerontology, the concept of the informal support or natural helping network has not been integrated into home care cost-effectiveness studies.

THE COST-EFFECTIVENESS ISSUE

In a review of 70 studies on the cost-effectiveness of home health care, it was found that home health care was cost-effective for two major types of cases but was not cost-effective for a third major type (Wolkstein 1984). The three major types of home health care considered in the review were those that:

1. facilitated earlier institutional discharges
2. prevented institutional admissions
3. were provided to medically needy individuals who were likely to remain at home even without third party coverage

In the first two major types, the home health care was found to be cost-effective; in the third it was not. Given the description of the third type, it is not surprising that cost-effectiveness was not achieved in this case. If people are likely to remain at home in any event, because they have a strong home care network consisting of family members, friends, or relatives, the provision of home care will serve only as a substitute for the care now provided by the patient's home care network. The studies did indicate, however, that in the third type of care the provision of home health care would improve both the quality of care and the quality of life for the patient, as well as provide relief for the patient's home care network. In the first two types of home health care, cost-effectiveness was achieved because the cost of the care was offset by the substantial charges that would have been incurred if the patient had been institutionalized in a hospital or in a nursing home.

The review of the 70 studies identified several conditions as key to the development and delivery of cost-effective home health services. One such condition was patient assessment. Indeed, it was found that the functional assessment of a patient was more important than the patient's diagnostic category.

The review found that the methods for determining a patient's functional capabilities and level of impairment will have to undergo considerable refinement if they are to become generally accepted. Determining the functional status of an individual is a more subjective process than that involved in identifying the individual's diagnostic category. In this regard, there is a definite need for refinement and possible further research in determining the functional status of disabled and impaired individuals.

The review also suggested the imposition of a dynamic limit on the reimbursement levels for home health care to ensure that home health care costs for a given patient will not exceed the cost of institutionalization, if that option were selected. In fact, several states have set such limits, usually at 75 percent of the average skilled nursing facility rate. By tying the rate directly to the skilled nursing facility rate, one could be assured that the maximum daily home health care rate would increase as the skilled nursing facilities rate increased.

Another advantage of tying reimbursement rates to skilled nursing facility rates would be the assurance that patients who belong in skilled nursing facilities or hospitals would not continue to be treated in the home environment. Obviously, extensive and comprehensive health care can usually be more effectively provided in the specifically designed environment of the hospital or nursing home.

HOME HEALTH CARE STANDARDS: MEDICAL AND LEGAL ASPECTS

One of the less publicized problems of home health care is that of legal liability. This is somewhat surprising in light of the fact that the legal liability issues in health care in general have been so prominent in recent years. In fact, home health care services are particularly subject to legal liability problems because health care in a home care environment is frequently delivered in a less-than-ideal environment. Although in the home environment, the patient and family members are probably more relaxed and less likely to launch malpractice suits in borderline cases, with regard to outright malpractice cases there is little difference between the home setting and the institutionalized setting. In either setting, outright malpractice should of course be actively investigated to ensure that it does not occur again.

Shinnick (1984) suggests several ways by which home health care organizations can avoid or prevent malpractice cases:

- by careful screening of potential employee credentials
- by increased emphasis on continuing education of employees
- by keeping abreast of state-of-the-art technology

In particular, Shinnick argues that physicians and other health care professionals must remain current with the latest developments in medical technology. It is also important that they maintain prompt, complete, and accurate charting and provide adequate nurse supervision of each home care patient. In short, from a patient management point of view, the home care patient should be treated the same as the hospital patient.

Apart from the legal implications, the benefits from providing quality home health care are obvious. The creation of a loving and nonthreatening environment in the home can provide a strong psychological boost for the patient. In such a situation, the loving care of a member of the family or household can maximize the potential for rapid improvement in the patient. To be sure, not all health care can be provided in the home, but much of what is now provided in an institutional setting can now be provided in the home environment.

To avoid legal liability for malpractice, home health care organizations must follow the hospital model of timely and accurate patient charting, adequate screening and training of health care professionals, and continuing education of current employees. In this sense, home health care may be viewed as an extension of, and frequently a substitute for hospital care. As such the same discipline, control, and management standards should apply.

In some recent cases, hospital health care professionals have been found liable for the following:

- failure by a physical therapist to follow and adhere to a physician's order
- neglect in the administration of an enema and failure to report the incident in a timely fashion to the attending physician
- mislabeling and mishandling of a blood sample by a nurse
- improper injection of medication by a nurse
- insufficient number of nurses assisting a patient in walking to a restroom

Each of these incidents of negligence could also occur just as easily in a home care setting. Clearly, the home health care organization must be just as zealous in maintaining a high quality of care as a hospital or other health care delivery organization. They must be able to anticipate the risks associated with delivering home health care. It is, of course, impossible to avoid completely the risks of legal liability; that is why medical liability insurance is available. Still, home health care organizations can do much to protect themselves from exposure to health care liability by proper screening and training of their health care personnel and by insisting that their professionals follow accepted and proven methods and procedures.

NONPROFIT VERSUS FOR-PROFIT STATUS

Home health care agencies have traditionally been nonprofit organizations, especially in the northeastern United States. This is not surprising, since hospitals have been traditionally nonprofit, as a result of their initial charitable nature and, more recently, because of hospital building financing available through the Hill-Burton Act. In recent years, however, there has been a move away from nonprofit to for-profit health care organizations. Many hospitals, especially in the south-western and southern United States, are now for-profit. Health maintenance organizations, which began as nonprofit organizations because of federal grants for feasibility and planning, are also now moving to for-profit status.

To aid prospective home health care organizations in deciding whether to organize as for-profit or nonprofit organizations, Pyles (1984) suggests a number of factors to consider. First, although a nonprofit organization is relatively easy to establish, it usually is required by state nonprofit corporation statutes to be organized for a limited number of purposes, that is, charitable, scientific, benevolent, and so on. Second, though the availability of tax-exempt status is a well-known advantage of a nonprofit corporation, that status can be conferred only by the Internal Revenue Service (IRS), and it is not automatic. Also, control of the tax-exempt status by the IRS is fairly strict, and income and operations reporting is mandatory. In other words, a nonprofit status does not mean avoidance of close scrutiny by the IRS. If violations occur, removal of the tax-exempt status can be quick and final.

A third consideration is the exemption from federal Social Security taxes and federal unemployment taxes for nonprofit organizations approved by the IRS. These exemptions can result in considerable savings for home health care organizations, which tend to be highly labor-intensive operations. Also, tax-sheltered annuities are available for the employees of a nonprofit agency, though with the introduction of IRAs for the entire population, this benefit may no longer be quite as valuable as it used to be.

On the other side of the coin, there are a number of problems associated with nonprofit corporations, especially smaller nonprofit corporations with limited assets. First, it is very difficult for such organizations to borrow capital for expansion purposes. Since they usually have little or no collateral, banks and other lenders are very reluctant to provide funds. For-profit organizations, in contrast, have the potential to build equity and even to provide equity sharing for potential lenders. They therefore are in a much stronger position to acquire capital for expansion if necessary.

Second, a lack of motivation for growth can be a problem for nonprofit organizations. Such organizations, especially those with weak boards, are usually dominated by their management. In such cases, management usually has little to gain from growth, especially if it means an increase in risk, as growth usually does. Hence, nonprofit organizations tend to be rather stagnant as far as growth is concerned. For-profit corporations, in contrast, are usually able to provide their management with incentives tied to growth through equity participation, and thus are better able to expand and prosper.

One final consideration in deciding whether to organize as a nonprofit or a for-profit home health care organization concerns the attitude of the people in the community toward a nonprofit versus for-profit status. On this issue, the attitudes of the physicians who will refer patients to the home health care organization will be particularly important. In summary, before making the decision on what organizational form to select, the best interests of the organization must be kept constantly in mind.

CONCLUSION

Because home health care is a relatively new area in the general health care industry, it is still coping with a lot of uncertainty, with new types of organizations, and with numerous unresolved issues, problems, and difficulties. In this chapter, we do not claim to have addressed all of these issues adequately, but we hope the information presented will at least contribute constructively to the ongoing debate.

Home health care is now going through a natural process of evolution. New ideas are being tried, some are being tested, some are being accepted, others are being disregarded. New problems are coming to the fore—and also new opportunities that had not been anticipated.

Over the next ten years, home health care will mature into a more stable industry, and it will take its place among other health care institutions, such as the hospitals, the nursing homes, and health maintenance organizations. In the process, many of these organizations including home health care agencies, will become part of comprehensive health care systems to provide a wider and more comprehensive array of services to the community.

REFERENCES

Cantor, M.H. "Life Space and the Social Support System of the Inner City Elderly of New York." *Gerontologist* 15 (1975):23–27.

Eggert, G.M.; Granger, C.V.; Morris, R.; and Pendleton, S.F. "Caring for the Patient with Long-Term Disability." *Geriatrics* 32 (October 1977):102–115.

Hammond, J. "Home Health Care Cost Effectiveness—An Overview of the Literature." *Public Health Reports* 94 (July/August 1979):305–311.

Jackson, B.N. "Home Health Care and the Elderly in the 1980s." *American Journal of Occupational Therapy* 38 (November 1984):717–720.

Johnson, E.S., and Bursk, B.J. "Relationships Between the Elderly and Their Adult Children." *Gerontologist* 17 (1977):90–96.

Minkler, M., and Blum, S.R. *Community-Based Home Health and Social Services for California's Elderly: Present Constraints and Future Alternatives.* Berkeley, Calif.: Institute of Governmental Studies, University of California, 1982.

Pyles, J.C. "Operating as a Non-profit or For-Profit Home Health Agency." *Caring* (March 1984):17–19.

Shanas, E., and Sussman, M., eds. *Family Bureaucracy and the Elderly.* Durham, N.C.: Duke University Press, 1977.

Shinnick, L. "Home Health Standards Present Unique Medical and Legal Challenge." *AAR Times* 8 (April 1984):70–71.

U.S. Congress. General Accounting Office. *Report to the Congress: Home Health—The Need for National Policy To Better Provide for the Elderly.* Washington, D.C.: U.S. GPO, 1977.

Wolkstein, I. "Cost-Effective Home Care." *Caring* (May 1984):57.

Chapter 11

Home Health Care Programs

INTRODUCTION

In this chapter, home health care as an alternative to institutionalization in the nursing home or hospital is discussed. An inventory of home health services is presented indicating the wide variety of home health services and home care services that are available to the elderly population. Next a brief summary of what home health care intends to accomplish is presented. This is followed by a discussion of the ways home health care and home care services can be segmented. In this context, recommendations for implementation of a sound home health care system are presented.

Because the growth of home health care is heavily influenced by hospital participation, we next review the pros and cons of a hospital entering the home health care business. Finally, we address the issue of increasing physician involvement in expanding systems of home health care delivery. How do physicians feel about their growing role in this area? This subject is explored in some detail in the final section of the chapter.

USES, DEFINITIONS, AND OBJECTIVES

Home Health Care As an Alternative to Institutionalization

As an alternative to long-term institutional care, home health care has become a valuable resource in many communities. It provides needed services to many people, especially to those elderly ill who are functionally impaired. Although many of these persons receive needed emotional and physical support from relatives or friends, professional assistance in the form of health problem treatments and health care therapy is an important element, permitting early discharge from hospitalization and, in many cases, preventing institutionalization.

A chronic condition, such as arthritis or diabetes, can cause functional impairment, but it is usually not enough to indicate the need for long-term institutional care. The degree of functional impairment is determined by the elderly person's ability to handle daily activities and to move about without assistance. Elderly persons who are functionally disabled are often bedridden and need assistance with dressing and bathing, or they need help in moving around outside the home. Such people do not necessarily require institutionalization and thus are typical candidates for home health care. The availability of institutional facilities, the willingness of family or friends to care for the person, the costs of care, the person's reluctance to enter an institution, and the availability of home care—all of these are important variables to consider when deciding whether a person should enter an institutional facility. For those elderly for whom institutionalization is not the answer, home health care can provide a viable alternative.

The recent growth in home health care can be attributed largely to the substitution of home health care for hospitalization. The prospective payment system (PPS) for Medicare-reimbursed hospital patients has generated considerable demand for home health care among hospital patients who are being discharged earlier than in the past. Because of the success of the early-discharge approach for elderly patients, it is now also being used increasingly for younger patients whose hospital costs are reimbursed by third party organizations, such as health insurance companies and health maintenance organizations.

Home Health Care Definitions

To facilitate understanding of the remaining sections in the chapter, we present in Exhibit 11-1 a list of health-care-related terms, as defined by the Health Systems Agency of Western New York (Health Systems Agency 1982).

Types of Home Health Services

The Council of Home Health Agencies and Community Health Services has defined home health services as comprising the following (Council of Home Health Agencies 1974):

- An array of health care services provided to individuals and families in their places of residence or in ambulatory care settings for purposes of preventing disease and promoting, maintaining, or restoring health or of minimizing the effects of illness and disability.

Exhibit 11-1 Home Health Care Definitions

- *Home health services* are services provided to acutely or chronically ill or injured patients at their residence according to a plan of treatment prescribed by a physician. Home health services may include nursing care, medical social services, home health aide care, nutritional and dietary services, medical supplies and equipment, occupational therapy, speech therapy, physical therapy, and other specialized services.

- *Support services* are social and maintenance services that enable a disabled person to live at home. They include, but are not limited to, housekeeping/chore services, personal care, transportation, pastoral services, telephone reassurance, friendly visiting, shopping, and laundry services.

- A *certified home health agency* may be sponsored by a public or voluntary nonprofit home care agency, residential health care facility, or hospital. In order to be certified in New York, a home health agency must provide directly or through contract for nursing services, home health aide service and at least one of the following: physical therapy, occupational therapy, speech pathology, nutrition services, and medical social services.

- *Proprietary home health agencies* deliver a variety of health and support services. They are not licensed or regulated by the state of New York and cannot be certified to receive Medicare or Medicaid reimbursement.

- *The Long-Term Home Health Care Program*, or "Nursing Home Without Walls," is a coordinated and comprehensive package of home care services, available on a 24 hour basis, for persons who qualify for residential health care. Certified home health agencies, voluntary hospitals, or residential health care facilities may be authorized to provide long-term health care services. Total annual expenditures may not exceed 75 percent of the average reimbursement rate for comparable institutional care.

- *Channeling programs* provide various services, including screening of clients, assessment of service needs, prescription of services, acquisition and coordination of services, monitoring of services, and reassessment. Such programs can exist as independent channeling agencies or as separate functional units within existing agencies. Channeling programs emphasize provision of care at the least restrictive but appropriate level, stressing coordinated home care.

- A *community health nurse* is a nurse whose primary functions, under qualifying nursing supervision, are to provide, direct, and evaluate nursing care in a variety of settings and to offer instruction and guidance in health practice for individuals and families.

- *Medical social services* include such services as identification, assessment, and management of social problems related to illness and medical care, as provided by a qualified social worker.

- *Home health aide services* include assistance with simple health care tasks, personal hygiene, light housekeeping essential to a patient's health, and other related supportive tasks. A home health aide is required to complete a basic training program approved by the New York State health department and must be supervised by a nurse or other professional.

- *Homemaker services* include assistance and instruction in managing and maintaining a household and in dressing, feeding, and incidental household tasks. A homemaker must complete a training program approved by the New York State Department of Social Services.

- *Housekeeper/chore services* are light work or household tasks that do not require the services of a trained homemaker. Such services may be provided for persons at home because of illness, incapacity, or the absence of a caretaker relative.

Source: Annual Implementation Report, Health Systems Agency of Western New York, 1982.

- Services appropriate to the needs of the individual and family are planned, coordinated, and made available by an organized health agency through the use of agency employed staff, contractual arrangements, or a combination of administrative patterns. Medical services are primarily provided by the individual's private or clinic physician.

Numerous organizations in this country are currently providing home health services. Unfortunately, as with the nation's health care delivery system, there is a great disparity in home health services from one region to another in the amount and variety of services available. In thinly populated areas, home health services are often minimal or unavailable.

The essential home health services that are often eligible for insurance coverage are listed below in two categories: basic and other. Those services that would normally be arranged by a home health agency and facilitated by patient transportation services are marked with an asterisk.

1. Basic Essential Services
   - home health aide/homemaker
   - medical supplies and equipment
   - nursing
   - nutrition
   - occupational therapy
   - physical therapy
   - speech pathology services
   - social work
2. Other Essential Services
   - audiological services*
   - dental services*
   - home-delivered meals
   - housekeeping services
   - information and referral services
   - intravenous medication services
   - laboratory services*
   - ophthalmological services*
   - patient transportation and escort services
   - physicians' services*
   - podiatry services*
   - prescription drugs
   - prosthetic/orthotic services*

- respiratory therapy services
- x-ray services

In addition, there are certain desirable services that may be obtained through other community support programs designed to help those elderly who are well but still dependent. These include:

- barber/cosmetology services
- handyman services
- heavy cleaning services
- legal and protective services
- pastoral services
- personal contact services
- recreation services
- translation services

Home Health Care Objectives

The primary objectives of coordinated home care are summarized by Littauer (1963):

- to furnish comprehensive medical, nursing, social work, and related care to patients whose needs can be satisfactorily met in their homes
- for selected types of patients, to furnish "better" care in the home than would be possible in institutions
- by using the home for treatment, to furnish comprehensive care at lower cost than in the institutional setting
- to shorten the hospital stay or to prevent the hospitalization or rehospitalization of selected patients
- by releasing hospital beds for those who need them, to improve utilization of existing facilities and reduce demand for more beds
- to expedite recovery, prevent or postpone disability, and maintain personal dignity by restoring patients to normal family living and useful functional activity

Thus, clearly quality home care programs can provide an array of services that satisfy the needs of the homebound elderly. However, many problems will have to be solved before home care programs can reach their true potential value as part of a total health care delivery system.

Segmentation of Home Care Services

Home health care services can be segmented into nonhealth home services and health-oriented services to the patient at home (Kittelberger 1982). The nonhealth services include chore services, homemaker services, telephone reassurance, shopping services, and meal preparation services. The health-oriented services are those provided by trained health care professionals. They include, in addition to skilled services, such health-related services as health assessment, health care planning and intervention, taking of blood pressure, giving an injection, family education, counseling, nutrition training, occupational therapy, physical therapy, speech therapy, and intravenous medication therapy.

Another model of segmented home health services has been proposed by Hennessey and Gorenberg (1980). They divide home health care services into three segments: preventive care, supportive care, and therapeutic care. Types of care in each of the three segments are listed in Table 11-1.

Regardless of how types of home health care are categorized, an important element must be the availability of a social support system for the patient. Ideally, this means a family-linked support system. Unfortunately, this type of support is not always available. Hence, community support services need to be available to provide this important component in a home health care system.

Kittelberger (1982) makes several related points regarding the provision of home care services:

Table 11-1 Three-Way Segmentation of Home Care Services

Preventive	Supportive	Therapeutic
Dental care	Legal	Nursing
Health education	Financial	Physical therapy
Police assistance	Home help	Occupational therapy
Outpatient care	Nutrition	Inhalation therapy
Protective services	Social	Dental care
Home safety	Religious	Mental health therapy
Recreation	Recreation	Medical
Peer interaction	Transportation	Pharmacy services
Employment	Shopping	Laboratory services
Volunteer work	Grooming	Family respite services
	Visitors	Night sitters
	Handyman	Trustee services
	Laundry	
	Information and referral	

Source: Reprinted from Nursing Clinics of North America, Vol. 15, pp. 349–360, with permission of W.B. Saunders Company, © 1980.

- A standard means of classifying and assessing the services required by a family or individual must be developed. This would allow a choice of programs based on individual needs as well as cost factors.
- A comprehensive home health care program requires the coordination of a number of agencies, including hospitals, nursing homes and clinics, as well as existing community services, to provide a wide variety of multidisciplinary services.
- Successful comprehensive home health care programs will require the resolution of the debate between proponents and opponents of home health care so that reimbursement policies can be determined.
- Supportive services for the family or primary care giver are essential to the success of home care programs. In this way, the home care organization becomes an extension of the family and is subject to the family's control.
- Methods of providing services to rural areas need to be developed. In some areas, this may include start-up grants for the creation of new agencies.
- Reimbursement policies and procedures need to be less restrictive, especially in relation to the skilled care requirement. Direct third party reimbursement to nurses should be available.
- Health insurance companies and large corporations should consider home health care policies as providing both a new benefit and a new opportunity to reduce health care costs.

THE HOSPITAL'S MOVE INTO HOME HEALTH CARE

A hospital's move into home health care means, in effect, a move toward forward vertical integration. This means that the hospital extends forward its responsibility for its patients beyond the discharge point. Such a move is particularly applicable to those patients who are now discharged earlier because of the prospective payment system (PPS) for Medicare patients. Just from a responsibility point of view, hospitals would feel more comfortable with early patient discharge if they retained total control of the patient's postdischarge health care needs by effecting the early discharge through their own home health care service.

In fact, many hospitals have already moved into home health care. Kaye and Hitchcock (1984) report that the growth rate of hospital-based home health care agencies is outstripping that of independent home health care agencies. Indeed, it is reported that Medicare-certified, hospital-based home health care programs increased by 60 percent between February 1984 and February 1985, whereas the total increase in all Medicare-certified home health care programs in the same period was only 25 percent ("Home Care Agencies" 1985).

The logical type of home health care for a hospital to move into is that of personal care for its discharged patients. In fact, for a hospital, discharged patients form an ideal base on which to establish a home health care system. Without such a base, considerable marketing would be required to establish a home health care facility with the necessary clientele.

Besides the personal care area, three other areas may be suitable for a hospital-based home health care system:

1. high technology services, such as intravenous care and medication administration
2. respiratory therapy and the supply and maintenance of equipment for respiratory therapy
3. the supply of and education in self-care services, largely for diagnosis and illness prevention and early diagnostic purposes.

The advantage for the hospital in the high technology aspects of home health care stems from its already established expertise and experience in the area. Basically, the hospital would be administering the same service on a home-care basis as on an in-hospital basis. The same applies to respiration therapy, another area in which the hospital has considerable expertise. Why should it not apply this established expertise to the home health care system? In fact, the only areas in which the hospital does not have the requisite experience or expertise would appear to be the areas of self-diagnosis and self care. If the hospital decides to enter these markets, it may consider doing so on a joint-venture basis.

There are several factors a hospital must consider before deciding to move into the home health care field. First, on the positive side, if the hospital already has an excellent reputation as a health care provider, lending its name to home health care activities would bring considerable benefits in its marketing operations (this applies to all four of the home health care areas cited above). Second, the hospital would have to determine whether it wants to deliver health care on a home-centered basis or on an inpatient basis. Normally, a hospital has experience only in the latter area.

It has been suggested that if hospitals decide to enter more than one home health area, they should establish separate entities, preferably separate companies, to deliver the various services. In this way, the hospital can use its reputation to the maximum for marketing purposes, even though the home care operations are functioning independently.

Another question that hospitals must face before deciding to enter the home health care field is: should they do it on their own or should they do it through joint ventures or acquisitions? Many hospitals have the requisite reputation and technical experience but not the management experience. In such cases, a joint venture or acquisition would enable the hospital to acquire valuable experience in the management of home health care. Joint ventures and acquisitions are, of course, feasible only if there are corporate partners available or if there is an established home health care corporation that can be acquired.

A final factor that hospitals must consider is the probable evolution of the prospective payment system (PPS). Currently, it is restricted mainly to Medicare patients and HMO patients. If PPS proves to have substantial cost-reducing advantages, we can expect that it will expand quickly to other health care populations. In that case, the potential demand for home health care would expand still further, and a hospital that is not ready to take advantage of forward vertical integration would be at a severe disadvantage.

To take a conservative view, one could argue that a hospital should stick to what it knows how to do well, that is, hospital-based health care. Many still adhere to this view. There are, however, considerable risks in clinging to it. Given the major restructuring of the health care industry that is taking place, together with the potential expansion of PPS and the rapid growth of HMOs, hospitals might be well-advised to remain flexible so that they can take the right steps at the right time to ensure their future.

PHYSICIANS' VIEWS ON HOME HEALTH CARE

Because physicians are the gatekeepers to home care, their views on its future viability are critically important. In practice, the physician refers patients to home care and then serves as the coordinator of the health care professionals— the nurse, speech therapist, physical therapist, and occupational therapist—who are employed by the home care agency to provide the required services.

The current literature indicates that, for numerous reasons, physicians do not like the home care concept. The reasons that physicians prefer to avoid home care has to do with the malpractice issue, the loss of control over patients, the quality of care given, and the lack of reimbursement for the managerial responsibilities required by home health care.

Many physicians believe that the home care movement is, in effect, replacing the physician with other health care professionals. This claim cannot be substantiated. In fact, in many cases, home care has actually strengthened the control physicians have over their patients' welfare (Jenkins 1982).

The quality of the care provided by home health agencies is another controversial issue for physicians. Most physicians would like to retain more control over the care being delivered by such agencies. Clearly, in the traditional hospital setting, the physician plays a major role in the health care delivery process, whereas in the home health care field the physician is only indirectly involved in the delivery process.

Many physicians also feel that state licensing of home health care should be required. At present, not all states require the licensing of home care agencies. Beyond that, some physicians would like to see state commissions established to certify home health care agencies.

However, the major reason for many physicians' dislike of home care is probably the lack of reimbursement for the various management responsibilities required for home care (Alper 1985). These responsibilities include the review and signing of assessment and progress forms that permit the home care professionals to be paid. They also require numerous telephone calls. All of this takes up a good part of the physician's time. Yet, the physician is paid only for office and home visits, not for the time spent certifying and recertifying patients for Medicare home services, nor for telephone or direct consultations with members of the home service team.

Several suggestions have been made to help reduce the negative feelings about home care held by many physicians. Alper (1985) suggests the following four measures should be pushed by medical organizations:

1. Develop a system for certifying early hospital discharges. Existing utilization review committees could identify those patients who can leave the hospital, and above-average nursing and medical supervision could be provided at home.
2. Create incentives for patients to cooperate. Reducing or waiving the Medicare deductible might motivate patients to give up extra days of hospitalization. Patients who leave voluntarily would be easier and less risky to treat.
3. Work on the liability issue.
4. Eliminate payment anachronisms. Hassle-free payment for frequent home visits shortly after hospital discharge would help.

CONCLUSION

Though home health care is rapidly becoming an important component of the health care delivery chain, along with traditional hospitals and nursing homes and emerging health maintenance organizations, it is still very much in a formative stage. The rapid growth of the home health care field in recent years has led to a proliferation of various types of organizations. The stage is now being set for a consolidation of home health care organizations. Hospitals will become important participants in this consolidation process. What finally emerges is not clear, but it will certainly be different from the situation in 1987. For one thing, home health care will become both better organized and more specialized. There is also likely to be more cooperation among and integration of community support services for the elderly. Community support services are particularly adept at providing support services to the elderly; home health care services, on the other hand, are skilled in home health care delivery. Together, their close cooperation in providing complementary services can generate valuable benefits for both types of organizations.

REFERENCES

Alper, P.R. "Count Me Out of the Home Care Boom." *Medical Economics* (15 April 1985):90–92.

Council of Home Health Agencies and Community Health Services, National League for Nursing. *Proposed Model for the Delivery of Home Health Services.* Washington, D.C.: National League for Nursing, 1974.

Health Systems Agency of Western New York. "Home Health Services Definitions." In *Annual Implementation Report.* Buffalo: Health Systems Agency of Western New York, 1982.

Hennessey, M.J., and Gorenberg, B. "The Significance and Impact of the Home Care of an Older Adult." *Nursing Clinics of North America* 15 (1980):349–360.

"Home Care Agencies Up 25 Percent Since 1984." *Hospitals* 16 May 1985, 64.

Jenkins, C.R. "Home Care: The Doctor Comes Out Ahead, Too." *Medical Economics* (18 January 1982):108.

Kaye, H.M., and Hitchcock, K.A. "Home Healthcare: The Hospitals' Target." *Caring* 3 (July 1984):37–39.

Kittelberger, S.B. "Long Term Care Currents." *Ross Timesaver* 5 (July-September 1982):9–14.

Littauer, D. "The Principles and Practices of Home Care." In *Selected Papers from the Institute of Coordinated Home Care.* Pittsburgh, Pa.: Institute of Coordinated Home Care, 1963.

Chapter 12

Adult Day Care Programs

INTRODUCTION

Whereas nursing homes' rapid growth in the 1960s and 1970s was the result of Medicare, and especially Medicaid, financing, the growth of adult day care in recent years has occurred with no clear-cut support from governmental financing programs. It can even be said that adult day care has flourished largely because of a definite need, which was only subsequently followed by the emergence of funding sources.

In fact, adult day care in the United States has grown from only 15 programs in 1974 to about 800 programs in 1984 (Mankoff 1984). Since then, growth has continued unabated, and adult day care is now considered to be a full-fledged member of the health care system, especially for the elderly.

Adult day care is an innovative, effective, and efficient approach to solving the psychological, social, nutrition, rehabilitation, medical, and other health care problems of those elderly who need attention and care but who do not require institutionalization in a nursing home.

In this chapter, we address the various issues associated with adult day care and demonstrate that adult day care is just another component of the health care spectrum comprising acute hospital care, nursing home care, home health care, and ambulatory care.

ADULT DAY CARE DEFINED

There are a variety of adult day care programs currently in existence. They differ on goals and objectives, terminology, and in many other ways. Rita Munley Gallagher, legislative chairperson of the Michigan Association of Adult Day Care Centers, suggests the following common elements:

Day care for the older adult is a category of service that encompasses a variety of program types. In general, it may be identified as programs of social health and mental health services for the frail elderly who cannot completely care for themselves, are isolated, recovering from acute illness, or have chronic illness or disability. These programs vary in their goals, but all, in some way, work to maintain a person's ability to live independently in the community. (U.S. Congress 1984)

The classification of adult day care can be based on a program's primary service objective and target population. Using these criteria, two general types of programs can be identified: medical programs and social day programs.

Medical day programs are structured to have a close affiliation with a hospital or nursing home. Medical day programs are aimed at providing intensive rehabilitative and support services, generally to recently hospitalized clients. The primary service objective of the medical day program is to restore physical and mental functional ability to the maximum extent possible.

Social day programs are structured to meet the needs of clients who are suffering the disabling effects of degenerative diseases and chronic conditions. Social day programs provide socialization opportunities, recreational activities, monitoring, and other social services. The primary service objective of the social day care program is to maintain social and physical functioning to the maximum extent possible and to prevent or postpone institutionalization.

THE BENEFITS OF ADULT DAY CARE

Adult day care is viewed by many health care experts as a feasible solution to the problem of caring for the frail elderly. The frail elderly can be defined as those aged individuals who are in need of supervision, personal assistance, grooming, meals, social and recreational opportunities, and other services on a daily basis. The adult day care center can provide these individuals with the care, attention, and service they require.

Adult day care centers are beneficial not only to dependent adults but also to families, the government, hospitals, and nursing homes. It is for this very reason that adult day care is appealing to those who are even casually familiar with the problems of the frail elderly.

Adult day care programs enable the frail elderly to avoid a nursing home admission and to remain in their comfortable surroundings at home. The elderly can thus enjoy a more complete lifestyle, interacting with family and friends, which would be impossible to provide in a nursing home setting.

Adult day care programs also serve a definite need for the family members who care for the frail elderly. Since many of the frail elderly require personal assistance, supervision, and other types of specialized care, a special burden is placed on family members to provide such services. In such situations, family members find themselves in a precarious situation: they do not want to institutionalize their mother or father, but they would have difficulty in providing the required care themselves. They would have to deal not only with the normal problems of raising the children, paying the bills, and doing their work, but would also be obliged to see that adequate care is provided to their dependent relative. In today's modern society, characterized by the two-income household, adult day care provides the elderly with the required care in such situations, giving the family of the elderly "peace of mind" and eliminating the potential guilt often associated with placing a relative in a nursing home.

Adult day care can also be viewed as a solution that can help the government contain and even reduce overall health care expenditures. In a prepared statement before the congressional Subcommittee on Health and Long-term Care of the Select Committee on Aging, Congressman William R. Ratchford reported on a model day care program in southeastern Connecticut (U.S. Congress 1980). In the report, he compared the full public cost of adult day care with the total public cost of chronic and convalescent nursing homes (the cost estimates for adult day care reflected actual program expenses, net daily living expenses of the client, based on Bureau of Labor statistics figures, plus the cost of other services provided to the participant). The total public cost of the Connecticut adult day care program was calculated at $113.87 per client in weekly expenses, with a per diem of $16.27. In contrast, skilled nursing facility costs amounted to a weekly expense of $228 per client and a per diem of $32.57. The report also indicated that adult day care in the Connecticut program actually decreased family stress and tension. It concluded that adult day care thus appears to have a most favorable impact on the quality of the older person's life.

Hospitals and nursing homes can also benefit from offering adult day care programs. As reimbursement for services provided by hospitals and nursing homes is gradually being squeezed under the DRG system, hospitals and nursing homes are seeking new ways of generating income. In this situation, adult day care programs are attractive to both hospitals and nursing homes, in that they require relatively modest outlays of capital investment and have the effect of significantly increasing cash flow. Nursing homes are perhaps the most logical setting for the provision of adult day care, as well as for home health care and hospice services, because they have the knowledgeable staff and other resources necessary to provide such services economically.

COMPARISON OF COST AMONG DAY CARE MODELS

In a study by Hannan and O'Donnell (1984), adult day care models were compared on the basis of services offered and costs incurred. Three adult day care program models were identified: support programs, mixed programs, and ancillary programs. The support program provides a minimal amount of therapy and is largely oriented toward recreational, social, personal care and nutrition services. However, it meets the normal expectations for a nursing adult day care center. At the other extreme is the ancillary health therapy support center, which offers a full array of medical and therapeutical services and where recreational activities appear to be nonexistent. Mixed adult day care programs offer a full array of services; they differ from support programs in their provision of social services and therapeutic services, but they place less emphasis on medical care and therapy than the ancillary programs.

There is definitely a need for all three types of adult day care programs, based on clients' needs. However, one could argue that the support and mixed programs could serve the vast majority of day care clients. Clients not in need of medical care or therapy would clearly benefit more from the support program. Clients requiring rehabilitation services, on the other hand, would benefit more from the services provided by a mixed or ancillary services program.

An accompanied cost study of the three types of adult day care programs revealed that the cost per hour increases with the degree of intensity of medical and health therapy services. In 1980, the total direct cost of operating a support program amounted to $2.74 per hour per client; for a mixed program, the comparable cost was $5.21; for the ancillary services program, it was $9.19. The ancillary service direct costs were particularly affected by a high transportation cost, which probably resulted from the necessary use of wheelchair vans, a service not extensively used in the other two types of programs. Both medical and therapy service costs were considerably higher for the ancillary services program than for the other two programs.

The comparative figures in the study were based on data from six support programs, five mixed programs, and two ancillary programs. Total pooled hours of care provided during 1980, on which the cost data are based, amounted to over 100,000 hours for both the support and mixed programs and about 75,000 hours for the ancillary services programs.

These statistics strongly suggest the need, from both a care and cost point of view, to place clients in the appropriate adult day care program, based on their condition as determined by a professional assessment.

TYPES OF ADULT DAY CARE SERVICES AND FACILITIES

Since there are a variety of adult day care programs, offering a range of services designed to meet specific goals, the service needs of an adult day care program will be unique to its particular situation. However, the following services seem to be basic (Wilensky 1983):

- patient assessment and case management, including conferences with the attending physician to establish a plan of care
- one to three meals per day, plus snacks (with attention to special diets)
- personal care, including bathing and grooming
- ancillary services (as needed), such as physical and occupational therapy, nursing treatments, and the monitoring of blood pressure, weight, and other indicators
- therapeutic recreation, for example, in activities of daily living
- socialization, for example, parties, games, music, discussion groups, and pet therapy
- educational opportunities related to mental and physical well-being
- group activities for physical fitness (exercise and diet) and other needs

In addition, the delivery of adult care services will require a physical plant with at least the following facilities (Wilensky 1983):

- male and female toilets, with sufficient room to accommodate wheelchairs
- showers and/or tubs for bathing
- separate space for beds/recliners for those who require a rest period
- dining and recreation area of 35 to 50 square feet per person, depending on the state requirements
- an outdoor recreational area
- safe storage for each person's possessions
- provision for temporary care in case of illness

FUNDING OF ADULT DAY CARE

The lack of a national policy has forced states providing adult day care to use various funding mechanisms. Various states have applied Title 3, Title 19, or Title 20 funds or have used community-developed or revenue-sharing monies with fees-for-service to finance their adult day care programs (U.S. Congress 1984).

New York State has the distinction of authorizing, in 1970, the first adult day care program to be covered by Medicaid funding. In the mid-1970s, California, Massachusetts, and Georgia expanded their Medicaid coverage to include adult day care. By September 1984, over 125 adult day care programs were paying for medical day care through Medicaid. Still, due to the variety of payment sources, adult day care funding continues to be fragmented and is not yet available to all those in need.

Yet, despite the lack of a national policy for funding adult day care, adult day care programs continue to grow in number. In fact, in a seemingly uninviting financial environment, the growth of these programs has been phenomenal. The only logical explanation for such growth is widespread recognition of a definite need.

CASE EXAMPLES

As we have seen, adult day care centers differ widely in the range and scope of the services they provide; no two adult day care programs are identical. In this section, we describe briefly two established adult day care programs: The Support Center in Wheaton, Maryland, and the Heathwood Health Care Center in Amherst, a suburb of Buffalo, New York.

The Support Center, Wheaton, Maryland

The Support Center in Wheaton, Maryland, is described by the center's activity coordinator, Francis Goldstein, and the center's director, Stephanie Egly, as "a place where impaired or frail adults can receive care and emotional support during the day and go home to their own beds, families and residences at night" (Goldstein and Egly 1985). Here, frail adults are defined as those who are 18 or older, although the majority of the center's clients are elderly.

The center is designed to accommodate 24 people, but it can handle an additional 20 clients at another nearby location. The center's clients come from all races and are afflicted with a variety of illnesses, including Parkinson's, arthritis, Alzheimer's, the aftereffects of stroke, and even mild retardation. Goldstein and Egly note that, "without the Support Center, many [of these people] would be forced to leave families and familiar surroundings and enter a long-term care institution" (Goldstein and Egly 1985).

The Support Center is decorated to promote a feeling of hominess in colorful and pleasant surroundings. In its rooms, one can see bright, comfortable furniture, green plants, large windows to allow the sun to shine in, a fish tank, arts and crafts in various stages of completion, and even a live rabbit. The rabbit serves an important function in the center; it plays a part in the center's pet therapy and is an object for affection for the center's clients.

Supportive services include a noon meal, which is provided by the Montgomery County Senior Nutrition Program. Occupational, physical, and speech therapies are offered when prescribed by a client's physician. The center also provides transportation to the clients for dental and medical appointments.

The center employs a professional staff that uses a multidisciplinary approach to develop individual care plans for each client. The plans document and highlight problems, cite strengths and weaknesses, establish goals, and describe the best approach for meeting each individual's special needs.

The center also sponsors a number of activities for its clients. Films, slide shows, and field trips take place on a regular basis.

The Support Center is funded from a combination of sources. Care of lower- and moderate-income clients is subsidized by a grant from the Maryland Department of Health and Mental Hygiene. The center is Medicaid-certified and receives reimbursement for Medicaid-eligible clients. Many clients and/or their families pay for their care privately, based on their ability to pay on a sliding-fee scale. Private fees range from $20 to $33 a day. The center also receives support through donations from community groups.

Heathwood Health Care Center, Amherst, New York

In 1986, in the Buffalo, New York, area, there were three adult day care programs in operation. The Heathwood Health Care Center, located in the suburb of Amherst, and the Episcopal Church Home, located in downtown Buffalo, are classified as Subchapter C or medical day care models. The Lord of Life Adult Day Health Center, located in the suburb of Cheektowaga, can be classified as a social day care model, meeting the needs of those suffering from degenerative diseases and chronic conditions.

The Subchapter C classification of the Heathwood Health Care Center refers to a New York State code to which health care providers wishing to establish a medical type day care program must adhere. The application process for the classification is similar to that for a certificate of need.

The Heathwood program provides skilled physical, occupational, and speech therapies as well as nursing services (Oldenburg 1985). The program employs a social worker and offers a variety of activities, including films, group singing, arts, and crafts—all of which are designed to ensure the maximum functional abilities of clients.

Under its Subchapter C classification, the Heathwood program is allowed to accommodate up to 15 people per day. Clients are never admitted or rejected by diagnosis. Individuals are excluded only if the facility cannot provide the care, service, or monitoring they require. The decision to exclude individuals is thus based on staffing, environmental, and physical concerns.

The majority of clients at Heathwood are stroke victims, although several have spinal cord injuries, visual handicaps, end-stage renal disease problems, or arthritis. The program operates daily from 11:45 A.M. to 2:45 P.M., during which time it is structured to provide a meal and up to three 45-minute skilled sessions of speech, physical, and/or occupational therapy, as needed.

The cost of the three-hour day care program is based on the services a client needs. The base rate of $21.50 a day includes fees for skilled occupational therapy, dietary, nursing, and social work, but does not include costs for skilled physical and speech therapy.

Funding for the Heathwood program comes from three main sources: private pay, Medicare and Medicaid, and various types of insurance. The percentages from the three funding sources fluctuate with the case mix of the clients but tend to be roughly 40 percent from private pay, 30 percent from Medicare and Medicaid, and 30 percent from various types of insurance coverages.

CONCLUSION

Adult day care in the United States has evolved in 15 years from virtually no facilities to about 1,000 adult day care centers. This phenomenal growth has occurred despite the lack of fixed financing mechanisms. In fact, adult day care has advanced to the point where it is now considered to be an important link in the portfolio of services that should be available to the elderly to provide them with the proper array of health, social, nutrition, rehabilitative, and medical services.

Generally, three types of adult day care programs can be identified: support programs, mixed programs, and ancillary services programs. Each of these programs serves a particular segment of the population in need of adult day care. Also, within these broad categories, no two adult day care centers are alike; each must be designed appropriately to serve the needs of the elderly citizen in its particular community.

REFERENCES

Goldstein, F.M., and Egly, S.R. "Adult Day Care—An Extension of the Family." *Aging*, no. 348 (1985):19–21.

Hannan, E.L., and O'Donnell, J.R. "Adult Day Care Services in New York State: A Comparison With Other Long-Term Care Providers." *Inquiry* 21 (Spring 1984):75–83.

Mankoff, L.S. "Adult Day Care—A Promoter of Independent Living." *American Health Care Association Journal* (January 1984):19–21.

Oldenburg, M. "Adult Day Care." Paper prepared as an MBA student project, School of Management, State University of New York/Buffalo, 1985.

U.S. Congress. House. Select Committee on Aging. *Hearings on Trends in Long-Term Care: Adult Day Care and Other Options in Michigan.* 98th Cong., 2d sess., 1984.

U.S. Congress. House. Subcommittee on Health and Long-Term Care, Select Committee on Aging. *Hearings on Adult Day Care Programs.* 96th Cong., 2d sess., 1980.

Wilensky, M. "Adult Day Care." *Nursing Homes* (September/October 1983):27–28.

Chapter 13

Health Care Assessment, Coordination, and Placement of the Impaired Elderly

INTRODUCTION

Determining who is to receive what service or mixture of services is critical to the allocation of health care resources. This country is beginning to realize that its wealth is not boundless. If increasing numbers of older Americans are going to have an opportunity to receive the best care that can be offered, their needs must be assessed and matched with the available services that can best satisfy those needs. The concept of utilization review is implicit in this process. Skilled nursing home care may be required during one period of a patient's treatment but would, hopefully, give way to a less intense type of care that could be provided through other services, such as home care or day care. For this reason, the screening process must be continuous, including periodic review to ensure that the patient is receiving the care prescribed in the most suitable service setting.

If the prime goal of assessment—health care coordination and placement—is to fulfill the needs of the patient, those affiliated with providing these services might well be biased in their judgments. To ensure proper patient assessment, health care coordination, and placement, it is important that the process be controlled by an unbiased organization.

ASSESSMENT AND PLACEMENT

Patient assessment has generally been limited to the activities of hospital discharge units that determine the need for continued institutionalization or discharge to a home environment where home or day care can be provided. In the hospital discharge unit, patient assessment is based on medical, functional, and social factors. The patient's physician usually performs the medical evaluation, a registered nurse performs the functional evaluation, and the social services unit handles the social and environmental evaluation. The latter evaluation considers the patient's home environment and ability to return to it. If they no longer need acute care hospital services, some patients may still require care in a skilled nursing facility (SNF). However, SNF admittance may result in permanent institutional residence.

Of course, the primary orientation of the hospital discharge unit is toward the discharging of patients. Because of this natural bias, the discharge unit may make a proper recommendation for discharge at a particular time; yet, from a longer perspective, it might in some cases be better for the patient to remain in the hospital a while longer and then be discharged to the patient's home or to an alternative home care environment. Similarly, if the person responsible for assessment and placement is affiliated with a long-term facility, that affiliation may influence the decision in the direction of institutionalization. Despite the enormous increase in the number of nursing home beds, utilization of beds is still a direct function of bed availability. This underscores the need for an equitable method that allocates nursing home beds to those patients who need them most urgently.

When patients are institutionalized, the medical directors of the social services or health departments also monitor and review placement. However, these reviews are usually made after the patient has been transferred from the hospital to the nursing home. At that point, it is difficult to cancel the placement. Moving patients from a SNF or health-related facility (HRF) is extremely difficult in that numerous social and political pressures can affect the process. For these reasons, the placement or nonplacement decision should be made before the institutionalization takes place.

The variability of quality assessment among hospitals is yet another problem associated with the assessment activities of a hospital discharge unit. To minimize such variability and guarantee that patient placement recommendations are made on an equitable basis, some sort of centralized patient assessment procedure, such as that depicted in Figure 13-1, might be used.

TWO MODELS OF PLACEMENT COORDINATION SERVICES

In this section we review experiences in two different urban areas in dealing with the problems of assessment and placement: Hamilton, in Ontario, Canada, and Erie County in New York State. In considering the models of placement coordination services in these two areas, it should be remembered that, although assessment and placement activities are heavily oriented toward the nursing home patient, noninstitutionalization of a patient usually implies the need to supply that patient with home health care or day health care, or both.

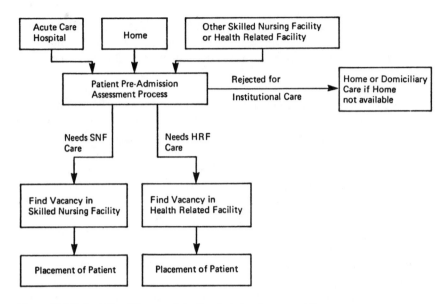

Figure 13-1 Patient Flow Diagram of the Preadmission Assessment Process

The two organizations we review below initially started as assessment and placement organizations but have since evolved into assessment, health care coordination, and placement service agencies. In each case, given the multitude of health care and social services normally available in a community, these organizations fulfill an important function in coordinating the care needs of patients. In that respect, they serve as useful models for similar coordinating organizations in other communities.

The Hamilton Program

The assessment and placement service (APS) in Hamilton, Ontario, Canada, was established in 1971 on the advice of the then newly-formed Extended Care Committee of the Hamilton District Health Council. The project was funded in April 1971 by the Ontario Ministry of Health and commenced operation in September 1971 (Placement Coordination Service 1983, 1984).

One of the concerns of the Health Council had been the promotion of optimal utilization of services for the disabled and chronically ill. The Extended Care Committee was formed to study the needs of this group and the relevant services that were available. Based on the study, a coordinating body was formed to obtain the medical, social, and nursing evaluations of the disabled and chronically ill and make recommendations for appropriate programs or levels of care to develop their assets and potential.

Following the Hamilton initiative, other regions in Ontario began to form assessment and placement services. By 1982, ten placement coordination services had been developed, all based to some extent on the Hamilton model but designed to meet unique local requirements.

The initial assessment and placement services in Hamilton have now been replaced by the Placement Coordination Service (PCS), which in turn has been incorporated by a long-established home health care services organization called the Victorian Order of Nurses (VON). This organization administers a large coordinated home care program and provides many community services, including nursing, rehabilitation therapy, palliative care, meals-on-wheels, and volunteer friendly visiting. It was felt that, with the addition of PCS, the VON would be in an excellent position to develop a proper balance in the use of community services with temporary or permanent institutional care.

Though the PCS and the traditional home health care unit of the VON have retained their separate administrations and budgets, the cooperative relationship between their services permits an individual to gain access to either or both, according to identified need. For example, someone in need of long-term care might remain at home for as long as possible with community support services and an occasional admission to an institution for care. In these circumstances, the individual's family would probably be willing to provide a great deal of care over a lengthy period of time, knowing that if arrangements break down or a crisis arises, further support, including institutional care, could be arranged.

The combined PCS/VON organization can also call upon other service organizations to provide detailed functional assessments by experienced nurses, physical therapists, occupational therapists, social workers, speech therapists, and so on.

The Hamilton experience shows that the demand for health care and support services for the elderly continues to grow. In this context, of particular concern is the care and management of persons with impaired mental function, many of whom have senile brain disease of the Alzheimer type. For such persons, it is essential to establish the correct diagnosis and to find treatable conditions that may mimic senile brain disease. Once the diagnosis is clear, the burden of care falls upon the family and the long-term care support network. In such situations, the amount and kind of care is very variable. Some persons, particularly in the early phases, may require minimal supervision in a stable environment. Help can be given to the family to understand the condition, prognosis, and management. Other persons may require protection and close supervision, help with personal care, or very patient and skilled management of aggressive behavior. The optimal location for the person will depend on the willingness and ability of the family and the staff of various institutions and on geographic factors.

Depending on the unique factors in each case, institutions will vary in their ability to provide care and protection to such persons.

The Hamilton program has found that, for persons with impaired mental function, placement was possible in various types of settings. In other words, rather than locate all such persons in the same place, it has seemed better to locate them according to their personal and individual characteristics. The ability to do this, however, requires a flexible array of services and a wide range of resources, as well as a solid coordinating system.

The Hamilton PCS uses an assessment tool to provide the information necessary to make appropriate recommendations. This information falls into the three categories: demographics, medical condition, and functional capacity. The demographics encompass age, sex, marital status, next-of-kin, education, employment history, cultural background, present location, and income level. The medical category includes diagnosis, prognosis, treatment, level-of-cognitive function, and emotional status. The functional capacity category includes degree of ability to walk, talk, see, hear, comprehend, dress, bathe, undertake personal care, and do household chores. The demographic and functional capacity data are provided by a social worker-nurse team; the medical information is provided by the client's personal physician. An information flow diagram of this assessment process is presented in Figure 13-2.

Based on the information derived from the assessment and on an intimate knowledge of available facilities and programs, the placement recommendations are made. The recommendations include appropriate level of care and/or programs of rehabilitation or recreation and programs whereby the client may be assisted toward fulfilling a meaningful role in the community.

Referrals to the Hamilton PCS program are made by health professionals in the community or health care institutions or by members of the community. The referral may be as simple as a telephone call asking for the process to be set in motion.

The Erie County Program

The Erie County Coordinated Care Management Corporation in New York State is a nonprofit corporation committed to helping elderly and chronically impaired persons obtain appropriate health and social services in a timely, cost-efficient fashion. Using a community-oriented approach, it involves government officials, private sector providers, and consumers in a search for solutions to complex problems in long-term care (Coordinated Care Management Corporation 1986).

Coordinated Care is not a direct service; rather it obtains for the client the highest quality, most appropriate, least costly service package. This is accom-

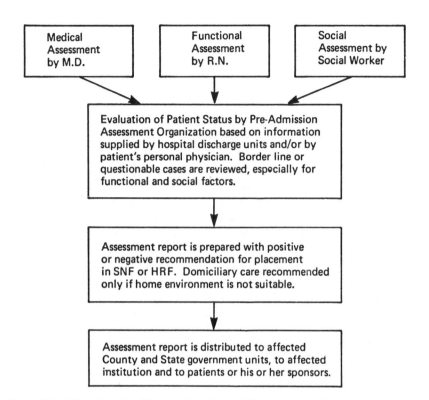

Figure 13-2 Information Flow Diagram of the Preadmission Assessment Process

plished by providing assessment; care plan development; case management; financial and family counseling services for clients; community education and care giver training for family members, friends, and volunteers who provide care for elderly and impaired persons; client-tracking and program planning services for community agencies; and data collection and research for policy makers.

Since its establishment in 1980, Coordinated Care has helped over 10,000 chronically ill people receive the services they need to become as independent as possible. Major funding for its operations is provided by the Commonwealth Foundation, the Robert Wood Johnson Foundation, the United Way of Buffalo and Erie County, the Erie County Department of Senior Services, the Erie Department of Social Services, and the New York State Office for the Aging.

Coordinated Care activities comprise four major components: the Health Evaluation and Asset Review Team (HEART), the Community Alternative Systems Agency (CASA), the Management Information System (MIS), and the Central Client File (CCF).

HEART, which was initiated in 1986, provides comprehensive patient assessment, care planning, and financial counseling to non-Medicaid-eligible Erie County residents. The HEART care plan recommends the most appropriate and least costly services that will meet a client's needs. A total of 27 community agencies work with Coordinated Care to help impaired persons remain independent in their own homes whenever possible. The HEART project is funded with grants from the Commonwealth Foundation and the United Way.

The CASA is a joint venture operated by Coordinated Care and the Erie County Department of Social Services. It provides assessment case management and linkage to appropriate home care services for Medicaid clients of all ages. During 1985, CASA services resulted in savings of approximately $6 million in Medicaid funds by directing people to home care services instead of long-term institutional services. In 1986, CASA served about 4,500 clients. In comparison, the HEART program served only 180 clients during the first seven months of its operation in 1986.

Coordinated Care's MIS collects, tabulates, and analyzes data from completed multidisciplinary adult assessment forms that are used by the CASA program, local hospitals, and a variety of community-based organizations to evaluate client needs. The MIS database includes valuable data on clients' functional abilities and the services provided. This information is available to health and social service agencies, program planners, and policy makers concerned with the long-term care system.

Coordinated Care's CCF allows maximization of interagency service coordination and client information sharing. The CCF is a database containing client demographic, assessment, and service information. This central database allows hospitalized clients to be linked with the agencies that have previously served them and facilitates communication between multiple agencies serving the same client. The CCF ensures that no client known to the system receives an unnecessary assessment or duplicated services.

In its implementation of these various services, Coordinated Care has, since its inception, made significant progress in improving Erie County's long-term care delivery system. By building alliances between county human service departments, hospitals, nursing homes, home health care service organizations, community-based service organizations, and community-based social service financing organizations (such as the United Way), the Coordinated Care Management Corporation has played a major role in the creation of an integrated network of long-term care services for Erie County residents.

Some Observations on the Two Models

The Hamilton and Erie County placement coordination programs serve two different communities in different countries and under different health financing and coordinating systems. However, the problems faced by the two services are similar. Basically, they boil down to the question of how to provide the most appropriate type of health care service for a client, based on the client's needs and the availability of services. Yet, because health care services vary greatly in the levels of care provided in different settings, different environments, and different geographic locations, it is extremely difficult for any one individual or family, or even for any one health care provider, such as a physician, to recommend the most appropriate care. In this situation, the experience, knowledge and database access available to a health care coordination service become valuable resources in providing appropriate information to health care institutions, individual health care providers, and their clients. Based on such resources, health care services can be optimally allocated, and clients can be placed with service institutions or organizations that can provide the best care available for their particular needs.

TRANSFER TRAUMA

Basic Issues

Transfer trauma in an elderly person is a trauma that results from a change in environment. This type of trauma can produce high death and morbidity rates among patients who are transferred to new environments. Thus, it becomes an important factor to consider when outlining the role that independent agencies should play in assessing the elderly who are presently in or about to enter long-term care facilities. Several questions about transfer trauma have been raised in the literature: First, what are the possible ill effects of transferring patients to another, more appropriate, level of care? Second, do transfers to different levels of care within the same facility differ in terms of benefits to patients from transfers to other facilities or transfers between a home environment and a long-term care facility? Third, are there informal or documented procedures by which long-term care facilities presently manipulate patients' movements through the health care system for their own purposes? And finally, what are the costs involved in the various types of patient transfers?

A Case Study

In the late 1970s, a study was undertaken among nursing homes in the Buffalo, New York, area to identify patterns of patient flow between levels of care in the health care system (Gworek 1979). First, an exploratory design obtained data on unusual or significant patterns of patient flow and the reasons for such movement. An absorbing Markov model, a statistical model, was then used to explore transfer traumas among elderly nursing home residents. Causes and implications of patient transfers were investigated in light of relevant assessment and placement activities. In the following discussion, the methodology and technical aspects of the Buffalo study have been omitted for the sake of simplicity.

Background

A number of investigators have documented the apparent increase in morbidity and mortality rates following a change of residence by elderly people. Though some studies have found the evidence for such transfer trauma results inconclusive, other research has pointed up certain differences in morbidity and death after involuntary versus voluntary change of residence.

One might speculate that people's decisions about changes in life status are generally made commensurate with their resources. Such decisions are facilitated by the freedom associated with economic independence and the existence of alternatives. When this freedom of choice is reduced and a person is forced to move out of sheer economic necessity or because of the influence of others in more dominant positions, strain and trauma can result. Simple economics explains why Medicaid and public assistance recipients are more prone to involuntary change than is the average person.

Transfers can be described in terms of two kinds of movement: positive and negative. Negative movement is movement from a less intensive level of care to a more intensive level (for example, from a nursing home to a hospital). Positive movement is movement from the same level of care or to a less intensive level. Some skeptics of transfer trauma findings suggest the relevant data include only those who were being transferred because of a decline in health status. They contend that this would automatically bias the conclusions, that is, the patients, when observed after the transfer, would appear to be in worse condition, and this would be associated with transfer trauma. These skeptics maintain that, in order to be accurate, conclusions about transfer trauma must be drawn from data that includes positive movement as well as negative movement.

Results

The Buffalo study found that trauma also occurred after interfacility patient transfers when the movement was in a positive direction, that is, to the same or less intensive level of care. The important factor was found to be involuntary change, for example, in the case of a Medicaid patient who had no assets or someone in the community to provide care and who had no alternative to the transfer.

Apart from the question of transfer trauma, patient admission data from the sampled nursing homes showed significant differences in method of payment for care, depending on where a patient was admitted from. Of those who paid for their own care, 45 percent were admitted from the community. This compares with only 12 percent of Medicaid recipients who were admitted from the community. In both groups, the majority of admissions to nursing homes represented elderly who were living alone. Admissions from a hospital or mental institution were relatively the same for both payment groups. However, a significantly greater percentage of Medicaid patients (37.0 percent versus 7.5 percent) had been transferred from other nursing homes. Most of these inter-nursing home transfers resulted in a positive change in the level of care, from a skilled nursing facility (SNF) to a lower and less expensive health-related level of care (HRF). In only 15 percent of all inter-facility transfers was the flow negative, from HRF to SNF.

In the study, the patients transferred from other nursing homes were compared over a five-month period with patients who were not transferred. It was found that those who transferred:

- experienced a high death rate

- were more likely to become seriously ill and require a stay in the hospital

- were less likely to be discharged home (in general, it was noted that, once an elderly person was placed in a nursing home, the likelihood of a discharge was slim)

Nursing homes that featured both levels of care, HRF and SNF, experienced minimal patient movement between levels. No significant trauma appeared to exist after a transfer from one level of care to another within the same facility. Essentially, the social and physical environment remained unchanged in this type of transfer, hence, there was no traumatic effect.

It is important to note that a majority of the transfers between nursing homes were originally private payers who had initially been admitted to proprietary nursing homes. They were transferred from those homes after their money ran out and they were forced to seek state aid. As noted earlier, for-profit nursing homes can make more money from private-pay residents. Since these nursing homes turn over patients faster than do nonprofit homes, a hospital wishing to discharge a senior citizen to a less expensive, lower level of care and treatment will find an open bed more quickly in a for-profit nursing home. And since a number of such proprietary nursing homes provide only one level of care—that is, skilled nursing care—a patient may be placed in this level of care even though the patient's condition actually warrants less expensive HRF care. A hospital discharge unit whose function is to discharge patients as quickly as possible is not necessarily concerned with appropriate placement. If the patient is private-paying, the for-profit nursing home is more than willing to accept to its skilled nursing facility an elderly resident who is actually healthy enough to be in a HRF.

After the resident runs out of funds and must go on Medicaid, the nursing home wishes to discharge its obligation. The procedure that follows is simple. The nursing home suggests that the resident has progressed and should be in a lower level of care, that is, an HRF. Since the for-profit home may have only skilled nursing care, the resident will have to be transferred to another facility, in many cases, to a nonprofit institution.

Transfers to lower levels of care are considered to be good indicators of positive movement through the health care delivery system. Yet, the profit motive is always present, though hidden. In this way, for-profit homes can take credit for efficient, effective management of elderly health care.

The Buffalo study suggests an increased likelihood of the type of involuntary transfer we have described. And this is likely to result in increased trauma among patients. In such cases, the individual suffers, and the general public bears the burden of transfer trauma. The related increase in morbidity means a greater likelihood of yet another transfer—this one to the hospital for a lengthy stay. And the costs of the hospital care, which are approximately five times that of nursing home care, will be reimbursed by Medicaid and ultimately passed on to the public in the form of taxes.

CONCLUSION

Patient assessment and health care coordination and placement organizations are excellent means of allocating long-term health care resources. Because of the many conflicting pressures faced by hospitals, nursing homes, home care agencies, and physicians in dealing with their own special interests, and because society ultimately bears the high costs of institutional care, it is of paramount importance that public policy encourage the development of organizations that can carry out the functions of patient assessment, coordination, and placement.

Health care coordination is especially important because it provides the best type of care for the client while simultaneously considering the availability of health care resources. Finding the optimal health care modality for the client also generates considerable savings for those financing health care, as demonstrated by the Erie County program.

In this context, transfer trauma becomes an increasingly significant risk, in that more frequent client assessment may cause agencies to consider transfer of a client from one type of service to another more frequently.

REFERENCES

Coordinated Care Management Corporation. *Annual Report 1986*. Buffalo, N.Y.: Coordinated Care Management Corp., 1987.

Gworek, P. "Transfer Trauma for Nursing Home Patients." Unpublished report, School of Management, State University of New York, 1979.

Placement Coordination Service. *Annual Report 1982–83*. Hamilton-Wentworth, Ontario: Placement Coordination Service, 1983.

———. *Annual Report 1983–84*. Hamilton-Wentworth, Ontario: Placement Coordination Service, 1984.

Chapter 14

Hospital Utilization and Quality of Care

INTRODUCTION

The issue of health care utilization, especially hospital utilization, by the elderly is a popular topic, both in the media and among health care researchers, because of government funding of much of the hospitalization of the elderly through Medicare. Similarly, the issue of quality of care for the elderly, especially the hospitalized elderly, has become a topic of concern since the introduction of the prospective payment system (PPS) for Medicare beneficiaries who are hospitalized. Under the PPS, hospitals are reimbursed on the basis of the patient's diagnosis, based on the diagnostic related grouping (DRG) system.

The issue of hospital utilization by the elderly is of particular concern to health care planners because of the tremendous demands placed on Social Security payments to fund the Medicare system. Health care costs have been rising steadily over the past 20 years and now amount to about 11 percent of the gross national product (GNP). As noted earlier, the elderly, although constituting only about 11.5 percent of the population, incur over 30 percent of all health care costs. It is thus not surprising that growing concern is being expressed about rising health care expenditures, especially for Medicare beneficiaries.

To be sure, health care for the younger employed is also expensive. But the employed can fund their health care costs directly out of earnings. The elderly, who are generally retired, must pay out of savings for that portion of their health care costs that is not paid by Medicare. Moreover, Medicare is funded largely from premiums paid by the currently employed population and only to a small extent by the premiums paid by those people who are now retired and benefiting from Medicare health care coverage.

Although health planners are searching for ways to reduce Medicare expenditures, they are not likely to be successful. The PPS has been able to achieve a small reduction in Medicare reimbursements for hospital costs. But this small reduction is only a one-time savings that is not likely to be repeated. The only possible sources of future reductions in the cost of Medicare-reimbursed illnesses are in technological breakthroughs in therapeutic drug development.

With regard to the quality of care provided to the elderly, the Health Care Financing Administration (HCFA) will have to ensure, through provider review organizations (PROs), that the quality of care is maintained, even though earlier hospital discharges occur. The elderly, especially the very old, are in a precarious situation when they need hospitalization. They are in a weak position to judge the quality of care they receive, and they are in a disadvantageous position if they complain that they are being discharged too early. In such situations, a watchdog agency, such as the PRO, is an absolute necessity. However, the PRO only does retrospective reviews. There may also be a need for reviews at the time of discharge, especially in those cases where early hospital discharges appear to be the pattern. How this can be accomplished is not clear. In any event, as problems proliferate, there is certain to be an increasing demand for reviews at the time of discharge.

HOSPITAL UTILIZATION BY THE ELDERLY

The elderly utilize hospitals much more extensively than the rest of the population. This is not surprising, since health care utilization generally increases as the age of an individual increases. The young, once they are past the critical first few years, generally require little health care; if required, it is usually for injuries incurred. Also, as women enter their childbearing period, their utilization of health care increases, and health care utilization for both men and women generally continues to increase with age. People in their 60s use more health care than people in their 50s, who in turn use more health care than people in their 40s. The highest utilizers of health care, generally institutional care, are the very old, that is, people over 80, and especially over 85 years of age.

Garnick and Short (1984) report that Medicare claims for people 85 years and older reveal about 50 percent more hospitalization than for all those 65 years and older. Institutionalization in facilities other than acute care hospitals is also very high for those 85 years and older. Since the 85-years-and-older group is expected to increase rapidly, we can expect a commensurate increase in acute care hospitalization in the coming years.

The 65-years-and-older group constitutes about 11.5 percent of the population but utilizes about 30 percent of acute care hospital space. Since this group is projected to increase to about 18 to 20 percent of the population in about 40 years, we can also expect a considerable increase in acute care hospital care demand in this age group.

Introduction of the Medicare prospective payment system (PPS) for hospital care has already begun to reduce hospital utilization, at least in terms of length of stay for Medicare patients. However, the reduction in utilization is only moderate, and it is not likely to continue. In fact, because of the many problems associated with providing posthospital specialized home care, the current lower rate of hospitalization for the elderly may actually creep up again.

The Hospital Cost and Utilization Project (HCUP) of the National Center for Health Services Research and Health Technology Assessment has summarized data on hospital utilization by three different age groups, from 40 years of age and up, as shown in Table 14-1. These data are a bit old, but, although average length of stay has since declined, the relative hospitalization rates are still valid. Using the 40–64 age group as a base, the 65–79 age group and the 80-and-older age group had longer average lengths of stay and a larger average number of diagnoses. However, the average number of surgical procedures and the percentage operated were lower for the older age groups.

Garnick and Short (1984) report that elderly patients admitted to rural hospitals have fewer procedures, shorter stays, and less surgery than those admitted to urban hospitals. Also elderly patients are discharged to other health facilities from rural hospitals more often than from urban hospitals. These results are not surprising, since urban hospitals usually have more facilities and more specialists on their staff to treat patients with complications. One wonders whether some patients in rural hospitals are not treated because of the lack of available technology, facilities, and specialized staff.

QUALITY OF HEALTH CARE UNDER PPS

HCFA Monitoring

With the implementation of the prospective payment system (PPS) for Medicare patients, the question arose: What effect would it have on the quality of care? The primary concern was with the built-in incentives for hospitals to discharge patients earlier. The Health Care Financing Administration (HCFA) has the means to monitor both quality and utilization through contracts with Utilization and Quality Control Peer Review Organizations (PROs). Thus, although PROs had previously been concerned primarily with excessive utilization, with the introduction of PPS the HCFA became increasingly concerned to use PROs to monitor the quality of medical care provided to in-hospital Medicare beneficiaries.

During the period 1984–1986, HCFA emphasized PRO monitoring of the medical necessity of admissions. This emphasis was the result of expectations that the maximum reimbursements on diagnostic related groups (DRGs) would encourage hospitals to increase admissions in order to increase hospital revenues. In the 1986–1988 period the requirements for PROs emphasized the monitoring

Table 14-1 Characteristics of Patients in Short-Term, General, Nonfederal Hospitals, by Age Group

	40–64 Years		65–79 Years		80 Years and Over	
	Actual Number	Base Percent	Actual Number	Percent of 40–64 Group	Actual Number	Percent of 40–64 Group
Average length of stay (days)	8.4	100	10.8	129	12.0	143
Average number of diagnoses	2.5	100	3.1	124	3.5	140
Average number of surgical procedures	1.3	100	1.2	92	1.0	77
Percent operated	52.2	100	41.5	80	30.2	58
Percent discharged to other health facility	1.9	NA	6.3	NA	17.4	NA
Percent Medicare	8.1	NA	93.3	NA	95.7	NA
Percent female	54.2	NA	53.4	NA	62.3	NA
Sample size	104,584		64,603		23,773	

Note: Hospital Cost and Utilization Project (HCUP) patient sample is for 1977. Hospitalizations for conditions that would not occur in the elderly—for example, the entire range of conditions associated with childbirth, complications of pregnancy, and abortions—are excluded. All differences between age groups are significant at the 0.05 level, using a standard two-tailed t-test.

Source: Hospital Studies Program: Hospital Cost Utilization 6, National Center for Health Services Research and Health Care Technology Assessment, Department of Health and Human Services, 1984.

of the quality of care provided. The GAO report on these efforts was based on results in three states: California, Florida, and Georgia (Zimmerman 1986). It identified a technique that the HCFA should require PROs to utilize to monitor quality issues. The technique is based on the profiling of data on hospital and physician quality-of-care problems.

Profile Data

PROs were created under the Tax Equity and Fiscal Responsibility Act of 1982 (Public Law 97-248) to serve as the primary organizations for monitoring Medicare hospital utilization and quality of care. The PROs, usually private statewide organizations, are under contract with HCFA to monitor hospital performance, and if necessary, initiate corrective action. The first contracts became operational in 1984.

To participate in Medicare reimbursements, hospitals must agree to allow the appropriate PRO to conduct utilization and quality of care reviews. To correct hospital and physician abuse of Medicare or provision of substandard care services, PROs use two primary tools:

1. They can deny Medicare payment to hospitals for medically unnecessary admissions or substandard care.
2. They can recommend suspension, removal, or monetary penalties against hospitals and physicians participating in Medicare who are repeatedly associated with cases found to have quality-of-care problems.

During the 1984–1986 contract period, as noted, PROs concentrated on utilization review and did only limited profiling of hospitals and physicians. However, even that limited profiling showed potential quality problems requiring PRO attention and action.

In Georgia and Florida, profiled data on quality problems during the 1984–1986 contract period revealed patterns of substandard care for certain hospitals and physicians. PROs were able to identify providers with a relatively high number of cases involving substandard care. In Georgia, the results of PRO review of hospital and physician quality of care for cases admitted during the 16-month period from August 1984 to November 1985 showed 7 hospitals provided substandard treatment for 30 or more Medicare beneficiaries and 44 physicians provided substandard treatment to 5 or more beneficiaries. Table 14-2 presents a summary and analysis of the Georgia data.

The data show that there were 1,245 hospital quality problems and 1,314 physician quality problems. Of course, a quality problem does not necessarily mean that there was abuse or neglect in actual care. In the context of PRO

Table 14-2 Profiled Hospital and Physician Quality Problems Identified by
Georgia PRO, 1984–1985

Hospitals			Physicians		
Number of Problems	*Number in Category*	*Mean Total Number of Problems*	*Number of Problems*	*Number in Category*	*Mean Total Number of Problems*
Over 39	4	160	Over 20	2	40
30–39	3	103	15–19	2	34
20–29	7	171	10–14	12	144
10–19	27	391	5–9	28	196
5–9	34	238	2–4	161	483
1–4	73	182	1	417	417
0	48	0	0	8810	0
Total	196	1245		9432	1314

Note: To determine the mean total number of problems, the middle number in each number category
was used.

Source: *Medicare—Reviews of Quality of Care at Participating Hospitals,* by M. Zimmerman, Report
to the Administration, Health Care Financing Administration, U.S. General Accounting Office, September
1986.

activities, a quality problem case is any hospitalization in which a PRO's physician determines that some aspect of the medical care provided was substandard. This may range from poor documentation of treatment to physician practices that cause injury to the patient.

A more detailed analysis of the Georgia results is provided in Table 14-3. These data identify hospitals and physicians with the most Medicare cases receiving substandard care. For Provider A, a hospital, the PRO identified 82 cases with quality problems; one physician was responsible for more than half of these cases. Again, because of the uncertain definition of quality, the degree of seriousness of the substandard care provided could not be determined.

In any event, as the GAO report points out, the profiling of PRO data can provide a valuable tool to identify repeat offenders. Necessary actions can then be taken against the offenders to ensure the maintenance of quality of care for Medicare beneficiaries.

CONCLUSION

The issue of hospital utilization has become a matter of concern because of the anticipated rapid growth in the elderly population over the next 40 years.

Table 14-3 Hospital and Physician Quality Problems, by Targeted
Providers, Identified by Georgia PRO, 1984–1985

Hospital			Physician			
Provider	Bed Size	Quality Problems	Provider	Quality Problems	Number of Months	Percent of Total
A	123	82	A1	43	15	52
			A2	15	10	18
B	73	50	B1	25	9	50
			B2	13	10	26
C	257	47	C1	17	13	36
			C2	9	12	19
D	87	39	D1	11	8	28
			D2	10	12	36
E	40	34	E1	13	12	38
			E2	7	11	21
F	75	34	F1	12	14	35
			F2	7	5	21

Source: Medicare—Reviews of Quality of Care at Participating Hospitals by M. Zimmerman, Report to the Administration, Health Care Financing Administration, U.S. General Accounting Office, September 1986.

The elderly now utilize over 30 percent of all health care in the country; during the next 40 years, their numbers will increase to the point that, by 2030, they will constitute between 18 and 20 percent of the population.

Concern about quality of care has also increased, largely because of the advent of Medicare's PPS, which provides incentives to hospitals to discharge patients as early as possible. Since it is not always possible to agree upon the correct discharge point, the concern about early discharges from hospitals for Medicare beneficiaries is very real. Though an HCFA-supervised system of PROs is supposed to identify quality of care violators, the problem is that, because such a system works in a retrospective mode, quality-of-care offenders may not be identified until after the offense has been committed.

REFERENCES

Garnick, D.W., and Short, T. "Utilization of Hospital Inpatient Services by Elderly Americans." In *Hospital Studies Program: Hospital Cost Utilization Project 6.* Washington, D.C.: U.S. Department of Health and Human Services, 1984.

Zimmerman, M. *Medicare—Reviews of Quality of Care at Participating Hospitals.* Report to the Administration, Health Care Financing Administration. GAO/HRD–86–139. Washington, D.C.: General Accounting Office, September 1986.

Chapter 15

The Nursing Home and Its Problems

INTRODUCTION

There are two major reasons why people are in institutions. First, they are likely to be suffering from one or more disabling chronic conditions. Second, they are likely to lack the psychological, social, and/or economic means for dealing with their condition outside an institution. Naturally, more than any other group, it is the elderly that fulfill these requirements.

This chapter examines the legal, economic, and organizational structure of the nursing home industry. With the passage of the Medicaid and Medicare laws in the 1960s, the nursing home industry has mushroomed almost overnight. In particular, the rapid growth of the private sector nursing home has resulted in a shortage of trained administrators, which has led to a variety of problems for the industry.

In this context, we examine the issue of nursing home funding. Although many individuals enter a nursing home as patients who are able and willing to pay, the accumulating expenses quickly exhaust their life savings, and most of them end up as publicly funded patients.

Who is the typical present nursing home resident? About 5 percent of those over 65 are institutionalized and, as a result, have little contact with the rest of society (U.S. Congress, Senate, Comm. on Aging 1982). Yet, although the percentage of persons over 65 keeps rising, and indeed is expected to continue to climb over the next 50 years, it is unlikely that the absolute number of people in institutions will continue to rise at the same rate. The reason is that there is now increasing pressure to provide alternative forms of care in noninstitutionalized settings.

There will of course continue to be a need for the nursing home to provide care for the chronically ill who need constant supervision, that is, for the type of nursing home usually known as a skilled nursing facility (SNF). But what of the many patients in health related facilities (HRFs) and in intermediate care facilities (ICFs)? In such facilities, many of those who can ambulate and are afflicted with relatively minor problems will, in the future, most likely be cared for in alternative settings.

STRUCTURE OF THE NURSING HOME INDUSTRY

Legal and Economic

In order to understand the economic structure of the nursing home industry, one must consider the legal basis of the institution. Government regulation and legislation affect not only the services provided for clients, they also have broad implications for the nursing home industry as a whole. For example, the nursing home industry experienced its greatest growth after the enactment of Medicare and Medicaid, as shown in Table 15-1. Today, public funds account for a little more than 50 percent of the total nursing home bill (U.S. Congress, Senate, Comm. on Aging 1982). Indeed, it often seems that, through the enactment of Medicare and Medicaid, the government has created an industry that is almost totally dependent upon it. Yet, 80.9 percent of the nursing homes in the United States are still operated for profit, and 67 percent of all nursing home beds are controlled by these institutions. Of all U.S. nursing homes, 15 percent are philanthropic, accounting for 25 percent of the beds; only 4.1 percent of the

Table 15–1 Nursing Home Statistics

Category	Year			
	1971	1976	1978	1980
Nursing Homes (Total)	22074	20468	18722	23065
• Government Control	1368	1402	1214	936
• Profit Control	17049	15343	14023	18669
• Nonprofit Control	3587	3723	3485	3460
Capacity 6–24 Beds	8266	5675	5414	8498
25–75 Beds	8259	7531	6306	6362
75+ Beds	5479	7262	7002	8205
Residents (1,000)	1076	1293	1240	1396
Full-Time Employees (1,000)	568	653	664	798

Source: Health Resources Statistics, National Center for Health Statistics, U.S. Government Printing Office, 1981.

homes and 8 percent of the beds are government controlled (National Center 1981).

Organizational

Basically, two levels of care are provided by nursing homes—skilled and intermediate. Skilled care is that level of care most like hospital care. Intermediate care, as the term suggests, is intended to help those who do not need round-the-clock nursing care or other mandatory services provided by a skilled nursing facility. In some states, the term *health-related* is used instead of intermediate care.

Originally, federal funding under Medicare was available only for skilled nursing care, but in 1967 an amendment to the Social Security Act made possible direct payments as well to recipients in intermediate care facilities. Eventually, the funding program was moved from its cash grant status under Title 16 of the Social Security Act into Title 19 (Medicaid), thus providing a base for adequate federal regulation.

A study conducted in 1982 revealed that there were 25,849 nursing homes in the United States, caring for 1,493,406 residents. Approximately 850,000 people were employed full-time in these facilities, resulting in 57 employees for every 100 residents (National Center 1983).

NURSING HOME FUNDING

As noted earlier, the nursing home industry is funded mostly by public monies. In fact, publicly funded long-term care administered through nursing homes is increasing its share of the nation's health dollar; in 1960, it accounted for a little more than one percent; this grew to four percent in 1970 and to over nine percent in 1982 (Bureau of Data Management 1984). In 1982, 40.9 percent of Medicaid payments went to nursing homes (Bureau of Data Management 1984). Today, nursing homes receive assistance from various government agencies through more than 50 programs.

Because the nursing home industry is so dependent on the government, it is quite understandable its interests are a significant factor in the making of government policy. In particular, laws and regulations that control the quality of care and the proficiency of staff members in nursing homes are directly influenced by various local and state entities that constantly evaluate the system and provide feedback to the policy makers. This dynamic system of evaluation and feedback provides a continuous check on the effects of any proposed policy on the nursing home industry and the nursing home resident.

CHARACTERISTICS OF NURSING HOME RESIDENTS

General

Of all U.S. citizens 65 and over, 5.6 percent are in institutions. The number of persons 65 and over in the United States has increased 600 percent since the turn of the century. One-third of these people are over 75. Surveys show that though only 1 in 18 elderly people is in a nursing home or related facility on any given day, that 1 out of 5 of them will eventually spend some time in a nursing home (Bureau of the Census 1978).

In 1976, approximately 75 percent of the 1,027,850 persons over 65 living in institutions were in nursing homes, 11 percent were in mental hospitals, and 14 percent were in all other types of institutions (National Center 1978). Eighty-nine percent of nursing home patients, 28 percent of mental hospital patients, and nearly all residents of geriatric hospitals are over 65. Nursing homes supply the bulk of long-term care, and the elderly constitute the greatest proportion of the nursing home population. Nursing home patients are generally old, female, widowed, white, and alone; most are brought into the institution directly from their private homes. The percentage of the U.S. population residing in nursing homes from 1950 to 1980 is shown in Table 15-2.

Disabilities

One of the most common disabilities among nursing home patients is heart disease, constituting 27.6 percent of all patient disabilities. Chronic brain syndrome and mental illness account for another 16.1 percent. About one-quarter of nursing home patients suffer from some degree of physical handicap due to arthritis, hip fracture, or stroke. Nearly 40 percent suffer from four or more

---

Table 15-2 Number of Persons and Percentage of U.S. Population Residing in Nursing Homes

Category	Year			
	1950	1960	1970	1980
All Ages: Persons	296,783	469,717	927,514	1,426,371
% of Population	0.20	0.26	0.46	0.63
65 and Over: Persons	217,536	387,953	795,807	N/A
% of Population	1.77	2.32	3.96	N/A

Source: Bureau of the Census, U.S. Government Printing Office, 1982.

chronic disabilities. Usually, nursing home patients do not have isolated disabilities; they have multiple disabilities (Freeland and Schendler 1984).

The typical nursing home resident needs many kinds of assistance. Less than half the patients can walk. About 55 percent require assistance in bathing, 47 percent need help in dressing, 11 percent need help in eating, and 33 percent are incontinent. The extent of the care needed is indicated by a 1974 survey (U.S. Congress, Senate, Special Comm. on Aging 1975). The survey found that of the 3,437 patients surveyed, one-third were totally dependent on nursing staff for their bath, 17.5 percent required spoon feeding, 31 percent did not use the toilet room, and 13.3 percent could not put on day clothes. While this survey emphasized the elderly's need for help, it also pointed out that they can also do some things for themselves. A summary of survey's findings is presented in Table 15-3.

Demographics

Not only are institutionalized persons likely to be old, female, and white, they are also likely to be poor. Several factors are involved here. First, the elderly generally live on fixed incomes. Over time, this income and whatever savings they may have acquired over a lifetime are likely to be diminished in value by inflation. When illness occurs, high medical costs can rapidly erode their financial resources. Ultimately, when placement in a nursing home is required, the cost of long-term care is apt to be prohibitive. In 1977, average nursing home charges in the United States were about $670 a month (although many SNFs were in excess of $1,000 per month). By 1987, annual average nursing home costs had

---

Table 15-3 Patients in Nursing Homes with Physical and Mental Disorders

Diagnosis	Percent
Heart Disease	27.6
Hypertension	3.0
Stroke	10.5
Chronic Brain Syndrome	6.4
Other Mental Illness	9.7
Arthritis	3.6
Cancer	5.2
Diabetes	5.0
Hip Fracture	4.8
Other	23.7

Source: Health Care Financing Review, Vol. 5, No. 3, p. 42, Health Care Financing Administration, Department of Health and Human Services, Spring 1984.

increased to $22,000 per year; in New York City, the costs were $30,000 per year. Thus, it is not surprising to find that, as shown in Table 15-4, at least half of all residents in nursing homes are supported by Medicaid or some form of public assistance (Bureau of the Census 1978).

Transfers

Finally, it should be noted that an increasing number of the institutionalized elderly are discharged mental patients. Thousands of elderly patients have been transferred from state mental institutions to nursing homes. Between 1969 and 1973, the number of the elderly in state mental hospitals decreased 40 percent, from 133,264 to 81,912 (U.S. Congress, Senate, Special Comm. on Aging 1974). This trend is the result of public pressure to reduce patient populations in large and impersonal mental institutions. Another, perhaps more important, reason may have been cost—the desire to substitute federal dollars for state dollars. Unfortunately, the end result was merely the replacement of one inappropriate setting by another.

CONCLUSION

The passage of the Medicaid and Medicare laws in the 1960s initiated a period of tremendous expansion for the nursing home industry. However, as in other industries, the rapid growth led to problems. The result has been extensive government regulation and control to ensure quality care by trained staff members.

Table 15-4 Primary Source of Payment for Nursing Home Charges

	Percentages by Year	
Category	1973–1974	1977
All Residents	100.0	100.0
Own Income	36.7	38.4
Medicare	1.1	2.0
Medicaid	47.9	47.8
Public Assistance/Welfare	11.4	6.4
All Other Sources	3.0	5.3

Source: U.S. National Nursing Home Survey, National Center for Health Statistics, U.S. Government Printing Office, 1975; The National Nursing Home Survey, 1977 Summary for the United States, U.S. Government Printing Office, 1978.

Because of the movement to deinstitutionalize the elderly with only minor problems, those who remain in nursing homes are mostly the chronically ill with severe problems. The mental and physical conditions of these residents require constant care and supervision. Whereas age 65 commonly signals passage into senior citizenship, age 75 or older often signals the transition into an acute care nursing home.

Thus, although home and day care are desirable alternatives for those elderly afflicted with minor ailments, there will always remain a significant number of elderly who must be cared for in an institution, usually at public expense.

REFERENCES

Bureau of the Census. *Statistical Abstract of the United States*, 1977. Washington, D.C.: U.S. GPO, 1978.

Bureau of Data Management and Strategy, Health Care Financing Administration. *Nursing Home Survey*. Washington, D.C.: U.S. GPO, 1984.

Freeland, M.S., and Schendler, C.E., "Health Spending in the 1980s: Integration of Clinical Practice Patterns with Management." *Health Care Financing Review* 5 (Spring 1984):42.

National Center for Health Statistics. Health Resources Statistics. Washington, D.C.: U.S. GPO, 1978.

———. *Health Resources Statistics*. Washington, D.C.: U.S. GPO, 1981.

———. *1982, National Facility Inventory Survey, Vital Health Statistics*, Series 14, no. 32. Washington, D.C.: U.S. GPO, 1983.

U.S. Congress. Senate. Committee on Aging. *Development in Aging*, 98th Cong., 1st sess, 1982.

U.S. Congress. Senate. Special Committee on Aging. *Mental Health Care and the Elderly: Shortcomings in Public Policy*. 93rd Cong., 1st sess., 1974.

———. *Nursing Home Care in the United States*. 94th Cong., 1st sess., 1975.

Chapter 16

Housing and Living
Facilities for the Elderly

INTRODUCTION

Although many elderly stay in the houses or apartments they occupied prior to retirement, many of them, for one reason or another, leave their homes and search for other housing. As long as the elderly are relatively alert, healthy, and ambulatory, particularly if they are part of a family unit, appropriate housing is normally not a major problem. However, when the person is impaired in some way and is living alone, the security of sheltered community housing may be the only option. However, low-cost, high quality housing is usually already occupied, and waiting lists of up to ten years are not unusual. And for someone who is 70, a ten-year wait, even a five-year wait, is unrealistic. Hence, compromises have to be made. For the reasonably well-off, there are private sector developments that provide excellent services and facilities at rather high rental rates and fees. The person on Social Security with minimal savings, however, has a real problem. Public sector housing is not always available, nor is it always of high quality.

TYPES OF FACILITIES

Assisted Independent-Living Programs

Assisted independent-living (AIL) is a general term to describe a certain type of housing facility for the elderly. These facilities have different names in different countries. In the United States, they are called life care communities or elderly housing campuses. In England, they are called sheltered housing, while in West Germany they are referred to as Altenwohnheime.

In England, assisted independent-living programs have been around for 30 years; in fact, England is the world leader in this type of housing (Boldy and

Heumann, 1986). Sheltered housing units in England have as residents more than four times the number of elderly than any other Western nation.

The typical British AIL facility consists of independent apartment units that are designed to be barrier-free. Each apartment is connected by an intercom or alarm system for contacting nearby help in case of emergencies. If residents become partially disabled or frail, support services are available. Communal lounges and laundry facilities encourage socializing. The facilities do not accommodate the mentally confused, the seriously disabled, and the bedridden. These types of patients must be cared for in an institutional setting, such as a nursing home.

The need for sheltered housing in the United States is generally based on two broad criteria: functional impairment and social deprivation. It has been estimated that about 5 percent of the elderly are in need of sheltered housing because of functional impairment. This group, of course, does not include those elderly who are seriously impaired and need institutionalized care. When the socially deprived elderly, those who are isolated and lonely, are added to the functionally impaired, the number rises to 10–15 percent of the elderly population.

If we use the lower figure of ten percent, we can estimate that there is a need for sheltered housing in the United States with accommodations for about 3 million people. That is, ten percent of the approximate 30 million U.S. residents who are 65 and older. Although a variety of housing communities for the elderly exist in this country, there are clearly not enough to accommodate 3 million people.

The question then becomes, How do all those elderly people who are still in need of sheltered housing cope? Many of them clearly manage to live and survive on their own in less than ideal circumstances. Yet, the level of social deprivation for many of these people is severe. Those who are functionally impaired survive with the assistance of relatives, neighbors, or friends. If appropriate levels of sheltered housing were available, the burden on numerous other social programs, such as Meals-on-Wheels and community centers for the elderly could be lightened.

The type of sheltered housing appropriate for the older population varies widely. The typical city dweller, who is used to multifloor buildings, is likely to be quite happy with sheltered housing in such buildings. Elderly rural or suburban residents, on the other hand, would probably find such settings oppressive and confining; they would probably prefer sheltered housing consisting of single-floor housing units with communal facilities for recreation.

Another important factor in AIL programs is the level of support and supervision provided. Many retirement communities in Florida and Arizona can be considered semisheltered housing, since they are usually restricted to retired people and have community facilities for recreation, communication, and entertainment. They normally would not have intercoms or alarms in case of emergency. However, such communities usually maintain a high degree of communication among neighbors or fellow residents. In addition, telephone service is nearly always available.

A more complex AIL arrangement is represented by the typical older citizen's housing development found in cities, suburbs, and rural towns. Again, the nature of the sheltered living varies, but the residents usually have a high degree of communication and thus are able to enjoy most of the benefits of sheltered housing. Many of these communities, however, lack community service and recreational facilities and activities and thus do not provide appropriate protection from social deprivation.

In England, the sheltered housing communities employ "wardens" who are responsible for the welfare of the residents. What is meant by welfare is, of course, an open question; some wardens are very active in providing relief from social deprivation, while others view themselves simply as physical protectors of the residents. In the United States, one solution may well be to train the elderly to provide self-help and do volunteer work for the other residents of the community.

Life Care Communities and Elderly Housing Campuses

The major trend today in housing and health-related facilities for the elderly is the life care community or the retirement campus. Indeed, such communities are becoming increasingly popular (Thomas and Bobrow 1984).

The classic example of a life care community is the Motion Picture and Television Fund County in Woodland Hills, California, located on 41 acres of rolling landscape. The layout and design provide four levels of care: independent living in country-style cottages, congregate care in a lodge setting, skilled nursing and intermediate care in an appropriate facility and acute care in a community hospital.

Another example is the Kendall Retirement Community, located 30 minutes southwest of Philadelphia. The Kendall community is financed by the resident retirees themselves. It combines apartments, a health center, and skilled and intermediate care facilities on a wooded 85-acre site. A central dining and activity facility is included on the site. This community has become so popular that it has a seven-year waiting list.

Even for-profit corporations are moving into this market. National Medical Enterprises operates a life care community in Delray Beach, Florida, that includes acute care and skilled nursing facilities as well as apartments for elderly residents. This community is oriented toward the health-related facilities, whereas the emphasis in the other life care communities we have described is on independent housing facilities.

An example of a somewhat different and larger life care community is The Protectory, located in Lawrence, Massachusetts (Jsomides 1984). This community provides health care and housing for 350 frail, dependent, low-income elderly residents in three connected buildings. It is sponsored by the Grey Nuns, Sisters of Charity, of the Mary Immaculate Nursing Home. The nursing home and an in-house geriatric health center provide a variety of care services to the residents.

The Protectory offers a choice of one-, two- or four-bedroom apartments. Each apartment has a kitchen with built-in appliances. Bathrooms are longer than usual, with wider doors, and the bedrooms are wider than normal—all for easier access. Emergency bells are located in every bedroom and bathroom. The entire complex is completely accessible by wheelchairs. Thus, The Protectory, designed especially with the older resident in mind, illustrates what can be achieved by sensitive planning of human-scale residential spaces.

Thomas and Bobrow (1984) suggest three important guidelines for designing interior spaces for the elderly. They maintain that such space should be organized for (1) orientation, (2) sensory stimulation, and (3) control of the environment. Carefully chosen wall colors, lighting, and floor textures and varied interior landscapes can add measurably to the environment in which the residents spend so much of their time.

Thus, considerable planning—based on architectural, environmental, social, psychological, and communication factors—must go into the design of a life care community. A well-designed community, providing a pleasant environment for its residents, clearly will have a better potential for success.

DESIGN CONSIDERATIONS

Because elderly residents have certain limitations and will spend more time in their housing environment than the younger person, it is important to consider carefully their special needs when designing housing facilities for them. Based on a report by J.G. Sprague, Director of Design and Construction of the American Hospital Association, Thomas and Bobrow (1984) specify ten factors that should be considered in designing an elderly housing environment:

1. *Movement.* Because the elderly are less likely to be voluntarily mobile, the environment should introduce visual stimulation and incentives to physical movement.
2. *Orientation.* Traffic patterns and furnishings should be carefully considered to minimize the tendency for the elderly to wander.
3. *Physical impairment.* Because the elderly often suffer poor vision, hearing, and sense of touch, handles, handrails, knobs, and grab bars should be carefully designed and placed.

4. *Lighting*. Indirect and incandescent lights should be used to avoid glare and flicker. Indirect lighting of walls, especially near the floor, is especially effective in preventing tripping. All areas should be well-lit to avoid tripping.
5. *Acoustics*. Carpeting and other acoustic materials should be used to cut down on potential noise generation, which is disturbing to the elderly.
6. *Color*. To enliven the environment and to aid in orientation, bright colors and contrasts should be used.
7. *Texture*. Because sense of touch is often poor with the elderly, textures should be widely varied.
8. *Odor*. Because sense of smell usually remains acute in the elderly, disagreeable odors should be controlled; cleanliness should be emphasized to avoid odors.
9. *Privacy*. Opportunities for privacy should be available to all residents; this applies both to personal privacy and privacy with visitors.
10. *Safety*. Because of the risk of fire or for other reasons, emergency evacuation provisions should be available, and residents should be aware of what to do in case of an emergency.

In view of these guidelines, apartment complexes or other types of independent living units for the elderly should clearly be designed by expert architects who are familiar with the known needs of the elderly residents. Much remains to be learned about the ideal living environment—one that simultaneously provides physical security, health care, and independent living—for the older American. However, as more housing for the elderly is built in the years to come, new insights will undoubtedly lead to more satisfactory designs for life care communities.

FINANCING HOUSING FOR THE ELDERLY

The cost of housing for the elderly—whether it be AIL facilities, life care communities, or continuing care homes—is an issue of growing concern. There are a variety of ways to finance such housing. Many housing complexes are built by local jurisdictions, usually with federal funding. Such housing is usually heavily subsidized to make it affordable by people on Social Security and with modest savings. Rents in the subsidized housing units are usually keyed to the available resources of the residents.

Other housing communities for the elderly are operated and financed by agencies affiliated with churches or other religious organizations. Here, too, part of the building costs may be financed with the help of federal subsidies. In such cases, the rental rates are usually based on income from Social Security, pensions, and savings. Usually, the quality of the housing in church-affiliated communities is higher than in publicly subsidized communities. However, the rental costs in church-affiliated units are also usually higher than in publicly subsidized units.

The most expensive and also the most rapidly growing type of housing for the elderly is being built by the private sector. When incomes of the elderly are augmented by accumulated savings and generous pension plans, the market for higher-cost and higher-quality sheltered housing facilities increases.

Private sector housing for the elderly takes many shapes and forms ranging from moderate-cost facilities to high-cost luxurious facilities. Payment is usually based on services provided, and the leases are usually long-term. Many such units require substantial up-front deposits, which lower monthly charges for rent and other services but may also severely deplete an individual's life savings. Up-front fees of up to $100,000 are not unusual ("Life-Care Retirement Homes" 1982). In addition, the resident pays monthly fees to cover utilities and maintenance may also be charged for optional meals. Minimal health care costs are sometimes built into the fee, but major health care costs are usually covered by normal fee-for-service charges. Medicare, of course, covers part of hospitalization, and other supplementary insurance is also available.

The private sector communities for the elderly are usually of fairly high quality and offer more variety. They are also usually more accessible, without the lengthy waiting periods common with the better public sector and church-affiliated organizations.

Whatever housing choice is made by the elderly, it is important to check it out well before making the move. In fact, the decision-making process should develop gradually over a long period of time.

CONCLUSION

Although there may be about 3 million impaired or socially deprived elderly in the United States, it is not at all clear how many of them have the opportunity to live in a relatively sheltered or protected environment with opportunities for social interaction.

Clearly, in the years to come the need for sheltered housing for the elderly will grow rapidly. Especially, if incomes of the elderly increase over the next 10 to 20 years, as some anticipate, the elderly will be able to spend more to obtain better housing.

In designing these new housing communities, it is extremely important that the developers be aware of the special needs of the elderly. Private sector developers must be guided by these needs in making their planned communities more attractive.

The basic message for many elderly citizens is that available housing options are limited. Therefore, they must begin to plan early if they hope to move into sheltered community housing during their retirement years.

REFERENCES

Boldy, D., and Heumann, L. "Housing Options and Choices for the Elderly." *Home Health Care Services Quarterly* 7 (Spring 1986):59–69.

Jsomides, C.L. "Nursing Home Campus Features Housing for Frail Elderly." *Hospitals*, 16 February 1984, 114.

"Life-Care Retirement Homes—What They're Like, What They Cost." *Changing Times*, October 1982, 28–32.

Thomas, J., and Bobrow, M.L. "Targeting the Elderly in Facility Design." *Hospitals*, 16 February 1984, 83–88.

Chapter 17

National Health Policy for the Elderly

INTRODUCTION

Development of health care policies for providing and financing care for the elderly must be pursued vigorously. As noted previously, the number of Americans 85 and older will double in the next 18 years ("AHCA Policy Perspective" 1984); and it is particularly for those in this group—many of whom are highly dependent, lack family members who can care for them, and are likely to be institutionalized—that an adequate health policy must be developed. To a lesser extent, those in the 65-to-84 age group, which will also significantly increase as a percentage of the population, need to be assured of the availability of affordable health care.

Much of the literature on financing health care for the elderly focuses on government subsidies. This approach is clearly necessary for the two-thirds of the elderly who live on Social Security with little or no extra income. The one third of the elderly who are not poor usually are able to finance much or all of their own health care. Yet, even for this nonpoor group, creative, government-sponsored health insurance programs are needed to ensure the availability of various types of health services, from ambulatory care to long-term institutionalization. In return for this assurance, the vast majority of the nonpoor would probably be willing to pay their share in financing the health insurance mechanism. For the two thirds who cannot contribute toward their own health care, more generous financing programs need to be developed. Are we as a society willing to take on the responsibility of developing these types of programs?

MAJOR ISSUES

As the elderly population increases and the oldest of the old become more numerous, the need for services and care for the most vulnerable elderly increases. It is estimated that, by the end of the century, about 20 percent of the population will be over 60, and one-third of this group will be 75 or older. This growth in the elderly population has implications for all levels of society—from the family to the federal government, and from the private physician to the large health care institutions—and it will impose severe strains on the American economic system. These strains will be manageable, provided proper planning is done and proper health care policies are formulated.

The major issues facing the elderly have been summarized by New York State's Plan on Aging for 1984–1987 (Office for the Aging 1983). The issues—income, health care, and housing—apply particularly to New York State's elderly population, but they also reflect general trends and problems in the United States.

Income

Economic security is a major problem for the elderly. According to preliminary analyses of 1980 census data for New York State, the rate of poverty among persons 65 or older has increased by 23 percent since 1975. Nationally, the number of persons 65 or older with incomes near or below the poverty level increased by nearly 6 percent from 1978 to 1979, and by an additional 4 percent from 1979 to 1980.

Social Security is the principal source of income for two-thirds of the population over 65—with an average annualized benefit at the beginning of 1982 of just over $4,000. Roughly one-quarter of Social Security beneficiaries in New York State, some 700,000 people, have no income other than their Social Security checks. The most recent average annual income figure for persons 65 and older living alone in New York State is $5,222, well below the median level of $10,183 for individuals under 65 living alone. Families headed by a person 65 or older had a comparatively low median income of $11,941, versus $21,129 for families headed by someone under 65.

Health Care

Health care costs continue to soar. At the national level, health care expenditures increased from $26.9 billion in 1960 to $465 billion in 1986—a phenomenal increase. These rising health care costs have forced a dramatic increase in the elderly's out-of-pocket expenditures. In 1977, the average out-of-pocket expense for an elderly person for health care was $698; by 1983, it was approaching $1,600; in 1988, it could climb to $2,750. In 1977, the average out-of-pocket cost of $698 represented 11.9 percent of an elderly person's income;

in 1983, the $1,600 in expenses represented 15.5 percent; in 1988, the $2,750 in expenses represented 18 percent.

Housing

The 1980 census revealed that earlier projections of the housing status of older New Yorkers had understated some dramatic changes in housing and living patterns in the older population. The number of older New Yorkers living alone showed an unexpected increase of 25 percent. Affordable and secure housing and living arrangements supportive of independent living had become serious problems facing older New Yorkers.

Statewide, 50 percent of the elderly own their homes, and 50 percent are renters. In New York City, however, only 27 percent of the elderly are homeowners, while 73 percent of them are renters. Among those 65 and over, the rate of home ownership has increased by 21 percent in the last ten years; in the same period, the number of older renters has increased 5 percent.

Inflationary housing and utility costs consume an ever-increasing slice of income for both homeowners and renters. Older New Yorkers typically pay a larger percentage of their income for housing costs than the nonelderly. Many are forced to pay for adequate housing at the sacrifice of food, medical care, or other necessities.

As noted earlier, the growth in the number of elderly households is expected to continue to outpace that for the rest of the population. The number of elderly living alone will also increase. Similarly, female-headed households will increase in numbers. These trends, coupled with the very rapid growth of the 75-plus population, which has the greatest concentration of frail elderly, indicate that the housing needs of older persons will become more demanding and complicated during the coming decade.

Homemaker, residential repair, chore, and health care services, as well as housing assistance, are needed by the frail elderly. The Community Services for the Elderly Program, funded by New York State, provides needed support services to the elderly in their own homes and communities, thereby improving their ability to live independently. A special focus has been on the provision of services for the frail elderly. New York Area Agencies on Aging identify the at-risk elderly and coordinate the delivery of services.

Housing for the elderly is more than just "bricks and mortar." Suitable housing for the elderly must include supportive services that help overcome isolation, loneliness, and poor nutrition patterns that characterize many of the elderly. When we consider the prohibitive costs of institutional settings, it is surely more cost-effective and humane to provide preventive supportive services from the beginning, right where the elderly reside.

There is no one solution to all the housing needs of older New Yorkers. Severe cutbacks in federal housing and the high cost of construction have forced local housing providers to rely more on existing resources. Creative partnerships among local agencies present one of the best opportunities for meeting the need. The participation of private financial institutions would further strengthen efforts along this line.

THE NEW YORK STATE MODEL

New York State, in contrast with many other states, has a strong county government system. Many services affecting older persons in New York State are administered through county-level governments and the New York City government. For example, New York State's public social service system is state-supervised but county-administered. Therefore, adult services under Title 20 of the Social Security Act, the Food Stamp Program, and Medicaid are administered at the county level. Mental health services, both institutional and county-based, are administered in accordance with a plan for each county. Also, many health services, recreational services, and transportation services are administered at the county level.

In 1973, for the purpose of administering funds for Title 3 of the Older Americans Act, the New York State Office for the Aging divided the state into planning and service areas to conform with county boundaries and the boundaries of New York City. All 62 counties in the state, as well as the state's St. Regis Mohawk and Seneca Nation of Indians Reservations, now have an Area Agency on Aging. To promote better cooperation among governmental programs serving the elderly, the great majority of these Area Agencies on Aging are part of county governments and the New York City government, forming collectively the New York State Aging Services Network. Experience since 1973 has shown that, the closer the area agency is to local governmental and political structures, the more successful it is in obtaining local support for services for the elderly. Since 1980, all Older Americans Act programs in New York State have been administered through Area Agencies on Aging. In addition, the New York State Community Services for the Elderly Program, designed to strengthen the aging services network, is administered through Area Agencies on Aging.

There have been definite advantages in having the Area Agencies on Aging serve as the prime vehicles for planning and implementing services for the elderly in New York State. The area agency can improve coordination among the many providers of services for the needy elderly. It can also help to eliminate the confusion and frustration often experienced by older persons and their families when seeking programs and services to meet essential, and often chronic, care needs.

In New York State, the Area Agencies and their network of local subcontractors are currently providing a wide range of community-based services for the elderly. These services are designed primarily to assist older persons in maintaining their independence at home. The services include home health care, homemakers, chore services, home-delivered meals, protective services, crime prevention, congregate meals, senior center services, transportation, legal services, information and referral, health screening, housing assistance, and counseling on financial, health, and personal matters. Outreach activities are implemented to aid isolated, low-income, minority, and other "high risk" persons served by the network. Over $100 million a year in federal, state and local funds is spent by the Aging Services Network in providing these services. In addition, over 30,000 volunteers, mostly older persons, work in the network, helping to deliver various services to older people who need them.

New York State's Aging Services Network has made significant progress in providing services to the elderly throughout the state. It is the only federally supported system that is attempting to provide a counterbalance to the heavy emphasis on institutional care in such major programs as Medicaid, Medicare, and mental health. Through its system development activities, it has been particularly effective in increasing the resources allocated to older people under the broad auspices of other programs and services. For these reasons, the Aging Services Network might well become a model for other states to emulate.

THE BASIS FOR A VIABLE HEALTH CARE POLICY FOR THE ELDERLY

Access to Care

The foundation of today's national health care policy can be found in the 1965 amendments to the Social Security Act, which produced Medicare and Medicaid (Haffner 1985). Medicare was intended for the elderly, and Medicaid for the poor. Since many of the elderly are also poor, especially those institutionalized in nursing homes, Medicaid has also become an important medium to finance health care for many of the elderly.

Access to health care has always been an implicit right in the United States. Implementation of that right has, however, been handled mainly on a local basis, through care provided by local county or city-run hospitals or through free care (sometimes unintended) provided by physicians and community hospitals who are unable to collect on their service bills.

In recent years, however, cost of health care has risen more rapidly than other costs. As a percentage of GNP, we are spending twice as much on health care as we were 25 or 30 years ago. As a result, the community's obligation and society's motivation to provide health care to all has been seriously eroded. Though in many communities health care is still available to all, regardless of ability to pay, in numerous other communities it is unavailable to those who are unable to pay for it and who do not qualify for Medicaid. For such people, the health care access situation has become quite precarious. Especially in those areas in which the traditional county or city hospital has been converted to another, sometimes for-profit, type of organization, access to health care for those unable to pay with no Medicaid coverage may not be available at all.

Catastrophic Care Coverage

Medicare is of course available to virtually all those 65 and over. But Medicare covers only a modest portion of the elderly's health care costs. Usually, a considerable copayment is expected if they are being treated under Medicare. What happens if the elderly cannot afford to pay their portion of the medical bills?

Several forms of catastrophic health care coverage have been proposed to provide financing for that portion of the elderly population's health care cost not covered by Medicare. If an elderly person has a serious illness, such as a stroke or other chronic condition, requiring an extended period of care and therapy, the private payment is usually enormous in terms of available resources. If such persons are unable to pay, they are forced to apply for Medicaid, which may mean having to give up the savings or assets they have accumulated to carry them through their retirement years.

Recently, several proposals have been made in Congress to provide some form of government-sponsored, but participant-financed, catastrophic health insurance. Those elderly participating in it would, by paying a monthly premium, protect themselves from serious erosion or total depletion of their assets in case of a major illness. Thus far, these proposals have not made much headway, due to a reluctance to authorize new government expenditures that would add to the already huge federal budget deficit.

A weakness in most of the proposals for catastrophic health insurance has been the failure to include payment for long-term institutionalization costs for nursing home care. Today, only the wealthy can afford to pay for nursing home institutionalization over a protracted period of time. The policy maker's fear that complete financing of nursing home cost would result in another explosion in nursing home utilization, with a concomitant explosion of cost to be borne by federal subsidization, is understandable. Nevertheless, it must be admitted that the lack of availability of nursing home insurance, even if it provides only partial coverage, is a serious deficiency in our health care financing system.

The Prospective Pricing System

The prospective pricing system (PPS), introduced in the early 1980s, has resulted in lower hospital utilization, earlier hospital discharges, and the growth of posthospitalization home health care services. It thus appears that, at least in the case of hospitalization, prospective pricing and reimbursement will become universally accepted.

PPS was the result of Medicare's efforts at cost containment. Reductions in hospitalization have in fact been greater than anticipated. Yet, though many claim that the trend toward shorter hospital stays is a direct result of the introduction of PPS, the exact nature of the cause-and-effect relationship is not clear.

In general, prospective pricing mechanisms may be said to have beneficial effects on health care for the elderly by reducing institutionalization and using home health care and day care more effectively. Prospective pricing may also help to reduce health care cost, which will be an especially important factor if a catastrophic health insurance plan for the elderly becomes operational.

Evaluation of Treatment Alternatives

A deficiency in basic knowledge is yet another obstacle to the formation of a national health policy for the aged. We do not have enough information about the treatments that are available for particular conditions and about the value of any given treatment. Program evaluation procedures are, for the most part, nonexistent. The evaluation that does occur is usually only a count of the numbers served. What is required is unbiased appraisal of treatment alternatives in terms of their total value. Only this kind of evaluation can help answer that all-important question, Is it worth it? (Administration on Aging 1977).

The development of this type of evaluation program requires in-depth analysis of the elderly population. More needs to be known about those who require long-term care and those who have disabling conditions but are not actively seeking access to long-term care institutions. Similarly, more has to be known about the institutions themselves—their relationship to other long-term service systems, their operational incentives, and their manpower requirements. The establishment of databases on these issues can help overcome the barriers that stand in the way of developing a national health policy.

Tied to the evaluation issue is the important question of control. Who will determine the priorities? Who will implement them? What methods will be used? A holistic approach calls for priorities to be set nationally, with implementation performed jointly by federal, state, and local agencies. In particular, a study at the University of Pennsylvania has pinpointed the need for answers to the following questions:

What implications do alternative control structures have on the nature of political and professional accountability regarding programs for the elderly? To what extent does an increased role for citizens' advisory boards translate into client representation and improved services as opposed to a provider or administrator-dominated "rubber stamp"? To what degree might control structures be adjusted from one local area to another to reflect the needs and demonstrated service capabilities in different local settings? What effect do control structures have on the capabilities of agency directors to carry out the goal of effectively coordinating a variety of other programs and services?. . . Clearly the issue of local control and the role of local government in health and health related services for the elderly needs much greater attention across the nation as the multiple objectives of accessibility are pursued. (Gamm and Eisele 1977, 181)

CONCLUSION

The development of a national health policy for the elderly may be somewhat of a misnomer, since there always is an implicit health policy in effect. Thus, the development of a health policy really means to focus on those areas where no clear policies exist or where current policy needs to be modified.

There are of course other issues facing the elderly besides health care and its costs. However, many of those other issues are also health-related. For instance, adequate housing and adequate income are closely related to adequate health care, nutrition, socialization, and security. Thus, when we explore health policy for the aged, especially health care financing for the elderly, it is sometimes difficult to separate out the particular issues that should have priority. Among these related issues are access to care, catastrophic health care insurance, and the prospective payment system—all of recent vintage. Individually and in combination, these issues are having a considerable impact on the elderly and their future.

Today, there is a growing need for society and its representatives, our legislators, to face the issue of health care access and coverage for all of the elderly. Society, including the elderly, will have to pay the cost. In the past, we accepted the responsibility of caring for our elderly. Our affluent society of today can do no less.

REFERENCES

Administration on Aging. *Evaluation Research on Social Programs for the Elderly.* Washington, D.C.: Administration on Aging, U.S. Department of Health, Education, and Welfare, 1977.

"AHCA Policy Perspective." *American Healthcare Association Journal*, March 1984, 47–54.

Gamm, L., and Eisele, F., ''The Aged and Chronically Ill.'' In *Health Services*, edited by Arthur Levin. New York: Political Science Academy, 1977.

Haffner, A.N. ''The Nation's New Health Care Agenda.'' Paper presented at the Eighth Annual Meeting of the New York Chapter of the Association of Mental Health Administrators, Albany, N.Y., 5 June 1985.

Office for the Aging. *New York State Plan on Aging 1984–1987*. New York: Office for the Aging, New York State, 1983.

Chapter 18

National Network on Aging

INTRODUCTION

During the past two decades, the population of the United States, and also that of other industrialized countries, has been shifting from a youth-centered to an elderly-centered orientation. In this process, the term *older* has acquired a variety of meanings. In some statistics, the older population is presumed to consist of those 60 and older. A more common notion is that the older population consists of those 65 and older. And, in some quarters, there is even talk of considering the older population to be those 70 and over. Whatever the exact definition, however, there is little disagreement that the older population, by whatever measure, is growing rapidly and will continue to do so for at least the next 40 years.

Concern for caring for the elderly as a collective group became a formal movement when the Social Security Act was passed in the 1930s to provide at least a minimal measure of financial security to the elderly during their older years. Social Security continues to be a popular means of providing some financial security to the elderly, and any politician who has threatened or even considered cutbacks in Social Security has later regretted it. Social Security is as hallowed as the American flag and motherhood; it is something one takes for granted in the American system.

In the 1960s, Medicare, financed mainly by Social Security premiums or taxes, depending on what you prefer to call the FICA withholdings from paychecks, has also become a popular program and, indeed, is now considered as necessary as Social Security. The problem with Medicare is that its coverage is rather complex and it does not cover all health care costs for the elderly. Because of its complexity, many elderly are not fully aware of what it provides and what it does not provide. When illness strikes and hospitalization is required, however, the limitations of Medicare are revealed. Because of these limitations, Medicare reform is necessary and will undoubtedly be of major interest and concern during the next several years.

A somewhat less well known program of the 1960s is the Older Americans Act (OAA). This act laid the foundation for what was to become the National Network on Aging (NNOA). This network currently provides a host of services to the elderly through a national system of service centers, service activities, information and referral centers, and other means. Since the enactment of the OAA in 1965, amendments to the act have put more teeth in the legislation and further solidified the foundation of the NNOA.

THE OLDER AMERICANS ACT*

The OAA of 1965 consisted of three titles: Title I established a set of objectives that our society should achieve for older persons. Title 2 established the Administration on Aging (AoA), currently located in the Department of Health and Human Services (DHHS). The AoA's focus was intended to be on the development and coordination of programs at the federal level that directly benefit the elderly. Title 3 provided for the formation of focal points for programs for the elderly at the state level. Federal funds were made available to each state on the condition that the state governor designate a state unit on aging (SUA), an identifiable office within state government with its own commissioner, superintendent, or other state-appointed head. Each SUA was to develop its own state plan on aging, which then was to be submitted to the federal AoA for approval. Federal funding of state-level activities was dependent on federal approval of the state's plan on aging.

In 1973, a major amendment to the OAA provided support for the National Network on Aging, which was designed to avoid the proliferation and frequent overlap of federally funded activities for the elderly. Original federal expenditures for the OAA (in 1966) were only $6.5 million; by 1973, these had grown to $195.6 million. As OAA outlays expanded, they generated concern over how well the expenditures were being utilized.

The 1973 amendment specified that each SUA had to subdivide the state into planning and service areas, and that each of these areas had to have its own area agency on aging (AAoA). Each AAoA then would form the focal point for all aging-related activities in that area, and all federal funding for programs in that area would be screened by the AAoA.

Also, each AAoA was to develop an areawide plan on aging, which was then to be submitted to the SUA for approval. In other words, each AAoA in the

---

*The material in this section is based on R.C. Matalish, ''Reaching the Nation's Elderly through the Network on Aging,'' *Human Development News*, August 1985, 4–5.

state had a reporting and supervisory relationship with the SUA. In addition, each AAoA had to form an advisory council, 50 percent of whose members had to be elderly persons. The advisory council was to ensure that AAoA programs focused effectively on the needs of the elderly in the state area served.

By 1985, there were 673 area agencies on aging in the country. The designations for these agencies are not uniform. Some are called county offices on aging, others are called area councils on aging, and so on. However, each agency has the same mandated responsibilities as established under the OAA amendment of 1973.

Two more important amendments were made to the OAA in 1972 and 1978. The 1972 amendment created the National Nutrition Program for the Elderly (NNPE). The NNPE, implemented in 1973, provides for the funding of congregate nutrition sites in housing projects, senior centers, churches, and restaurants across the nation. The amendment also covered funding for the now popular Meals-on-Wheels program, which provides warm meals to the elderly who are unable to leave their homes. As of 1985, over 12,000 congregate nutrition sites were operational.

The 1978 amendment to the OAA required area agencies on aging to designate community focal points for service delivery to the elderly. These focal points generally are multipurpose senior centers, where various types of nutrition services, counseling, information and referral, health screening, and recreation activities are available. In addition, they provide such services as transportation, homemaker, visiting nurses, home-delivered meals, counseling, information and referral, outreach, legal, housing, and case management.

The OAA and its amendments have also led to the creation of other activities and advisory bodies regarding the elderly. For example, Title 3, operating at the federal level, is the basis for advising the Congress, the president and the AoA regarding aging issues. It provides for a Federal Council on Aging, which is composed of 15 persons nominated by the president and confirmed by the Senate. Its purpose is to represent, at the federal level, older Americans, health care professionals, the service provider community, and the research and academic communities.

Title 4 of the OAA provides funds for gerontology training programs, research projects, and demonstration projects. Title 5 provides funds for the Community Service Employment for Older Americans (CSEOA), which supports over 60,000 part-time employment slots for elderly persons. These employment slots provide for a broad range of jobs in aging organizations, service provider agencies, and the business community. The program is administered through eight national contractors and the designated state offices.

Since its formation in 1965, the National Network on Aging has thus evolved into a nationally coordinated and funded, but locally administered, organization. Its services are available to all of the nation's elderly. Indeed, it is difficult to imagine how any elderly person in the nation could not be touched or involved in some way with the national network. The input into the network's services provided by local organizations is evaluated by some 15,000 individuals who serve voluntarily on area agency advisory councils. These councils also provide direction in implementing the activities of the various components of the network at the local levels.

BASIC ELEMENTS OF THE NETWORK

Organizational Framework

Over the years the organizational framework of the Network on Aging through which services are provided has expanded extensively. Figure 18-1 gives an

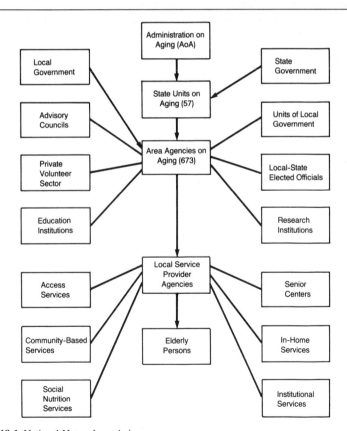

Figure 18-1 National Network on Aging

overview of this framework and shows how the service delivery process functions at each level. One of the major successes of the Older Americans Act is that it was able to establish this system in the states in conjunction with federal funding provisions. That is, federal funding could occur only if the proper local and state administrative and organizational units were in place.

At the top of the pyramid is the Administration on Aging (AoA) in the Department of Health and Human Services. Below it are the 57 state units on aging, covering the 50 states, plus the District of Columbia, Puerto Rico, the Virgin Islands, and other U.S. affiliated areas. The state units on aging are under the jurisdiction of the respective state governments and are usually a department or commission in the state government. Below the state units on aging are the area agencies on aging. As of 1985, there were 673 AAoAs. This number varies over time, because some area agencies may split while others may consolidate for a variety of administrative and other reasons. Reporting to and under control of the area agencies on aging are the local service providers. These service providers can be senior centers, transportation agencies, Meals-on-Wheels providers, and other service organizations.

Services

Thousands of inquiries regarding the elderly are received each year by the White House, state governors' offices, the Administration on Aging, members of Congress, Senators, congressional staffers, the Association of State Units on Aging, the Association of Area Agencies on Aging, and by other governmental agencies and office holders at all levels. Frequently, the inquirers want to know how they can link up with services or how a family member can have someone check on an elderly relative in a distant city. In the majority of these cases the inquiry is turned over to the local area agency on aging. As a rule, such inquiries are followed up within hours or days.

Thus, the Network on Aging is truly a working system for the entire country. It is there to serve those elderly who need the variety of services available in the community. Of course, not all elderly people are in immediate need of the services provided by the network. However, over the years, most elderly persons will utilize one or more of its many services, either directly through the network's affiliated agencies or through other agencies to whom they are referred by the network.

As the elderly population continues to increase during the next 40 years, it is comforting to know that the Network on Aging will continue to be there to serve it.

Information Management

An important function of the state units on aging is the handling of information to ensure that there is accountability for the various programs. To ensure continued and expanded funding of the various activities a solid database has to be maintained. For example, a clear and detailed knowledge of how and where funds are being spent is critical for acquiring new and continued funding. A well-developed and well-maintained SUA information system is able to provide that.

In early years of the SUA programs, extensive use was made of mainframe and minicomputers that also served other functions in state government. In recent years, however, the emergence of the microcomputer, especially personal computers such as the IBM PC, has rapidly expanded use of the computer as a monitoring tool in the state units on aging. In 1984, a survey revealed that about 90 percent of the SUAs have computer-assisted data storage and analysis at their disposal. About 30 percent of SUAs reported they were using a combination of mainframe and microcomputer computers for handling data storage ("Computers Aid State Units" 1985).

Specifically, computers in state units on aging are most often used to tabulate, analyze, and keep track of contracts, budgets, and agency expenditures. Spreadsheets are widely used. Other applications include word processing, graphic production, and telecommunications. A software package common to many SUAs is the dBase II/III database. In addition, the National Association of SUA has supported the development of special software packages to aid in the management of state units on aging.

CONCLUSION

Emerging from the Older Americans Act of 1965 and subsequent amendments, the National Network on Aging has over the years proved to be a model program in establishing and maintaining a nationwide system of services for the elderly. The means used to establish the network illustrate how objectives can be achieved by utilizing the power and influence of federal funding. Not to be ignored are the political benefits from serving a large segment of the voting population, those over 65 years of age. Politicians at any level can proudly point to the National Network on Aging and document what it is doing for the elderly at relatively modest cost.

Although the National Network on Aging is not directly health-care-oriented, it provides a considerable range of services that are health-maintenance-oriented. Such services as nutrition services, Meals-on-Wheels, congregate meals, and social programs at senior centers have a powerful influence in maintaining the health status of the American senior citizen. Thus, the network can be viewed both as a senior citizen service program and as a senior citizen health maintenance program.

REFERENCES

"Computers Aid State Units on Aging." *Human Development News*, August 1985, 6–8.

Chapter 19

Medicare: Its History and Its Future*

INTRODUCTION

The rapid growth of the Medicare program is threatening the financial solvency of its Hospital Insurance Trust Fund. Since 1970, Medicare outlays have been increasing at an average annual rate of approximately 17 percent; in fiscal year 1986, they totaled $76 billion (U.S. Congress, House, Comm. on Ways and Means 1985). Current projections indicate that the Hospital Insurance Trust Fund may be depleted by 1992 if policy changes are not made to restore its solvency. Since over 30 million people in this nation are dependent on Medicare to provide medical insurance protection, it is imperative that something be done immediately to restore its credibility and reduce the apprehensions of those who are dependent upon it.

In this chapter, we review Medicare's history and describe its eligibility and benefit provisions. The severity of its financial problems and their causes are discussed, and the 27 options examined by the Social Security Advisory Council to deal with these problems are briefly summarized and their pros and cons explored. The revenue/expenditure implications and the council's specific recommendation for each option are presented.

Finally, by use of a simple evaluation model, we draw some conclusions as to which of the council's options offers the greatest potential in resolving Medicare's financial problems. Each option is evaluated on the basis of four criteria: (1) cost competition, (2) distributive equity, (3) administrative ease/minimal compliance costs, (4) revenue/expenditure certainty and stability. Each of these criteria is considered to be a vital factor in determining the political and economic viability of the council's proposals.

BACKGROUND

A Brief History of Medicare

Medicare was enacted in 1965 after several years of debate dating back to the years of John F. Kennedy's presidency. As Title 18 of the Social Security Act,

---

*Much of this chapter is based on a paper entitled "Medicare: Options and Recommendations for Dealing with Its Present Fiscal Crisis" by Jeffery Morgia, School of Management, SUNY/Buffalo, December 1985.

it was established during the closing days of an era when federal policy was aimed at making the benefits of health care more widely available. The nation's economy was strong, and continued high GNP growth rates were anticipated in future years. Thus, Medicare supporters argued that this country could afford to protect the aged from the insecurity arising from the cost of health care and/or health insurance.

In the first six years of the program's operation, Medicare's administrative policies were designed to create a peaceful, cooperative atmosphere with the hospitals and other service providers receiving payments. Its policies included payments of two percent above costs, payments covering accelerated depreciation, and prompt payment for services provided. Furthermore, under the program, physicians' charges to Medicare were considered reasonable at virtually any level (U.S. Congress, House 1984). Also, hospitals benefited, since Medicare insurance shielded them from the bad debts they often incurred in servicing elderly patients.

However, the government quickly became aware of how costly such generous policies could be; and, in 1967 and 1971, increases in the health insurance tax rate and earnings base had to be imposed. Soon after the 1971 increase, Congress began to consider what should be done to end Medicare's run-away costs. Finally, in 1972, it agreed on legislation designed to harness Medicare's costs. Among other things, the legislation established reasonable limits on costs, indexed limits on physician and medical service increases, allowed a health maintenance organization (HMO) enrollment option, and established a system of professional review organizations (PROs) to limit institutional payments. Although this legislation did provide some control over Medicare's finances, it was not able effectively to stop its sharply rising costs.

Medicare's expenditures continued to rise during the Carter years. Although President Carter attempted to control them by proposing hospital cost control legislation, he was not able to convince Congress of the merits of his proposal. In 1982 and 1983, President Reagan succeeded in getting legislation passed establishing the prospective payment system (PPS) for payment of Medicare's hospital services. The resulting changes in reimbursement produced some cost savings, but not enough to keep the trust fund solvent in future years. Thus, in 1983, Social Security amendments were passed raising additional revenues for the trust fund via increases in tax rates. Yet, these measures were still not enough. If further measures are not taken to restore Medicare's financial health by increasing revenues and/or decreasing outlays, its future will continue to look financially bleak.

Medicare Eligibility

Medicare is a federal health insurance program for people 65 or older, for people of any age with permanent kidney failures, and for certain disabled individuals. It serves as the principal insurer of acute health care expenditures for 29 million elderly and disabled persons (U.S. Congress, Cong. Budget Office 1983).

Medicare has two components: (1) hospital insurance (HI) or Part A and (2) supplementary medical insurance (SMI) or Part B. The HI component is supported almost entirely by the Social Security payroll tax. The SMI component is an optional insurance plan requiring a monthly premium, which covers approximately 25 percent of the costs; the other 75 percent is covered through general revenue financing.

Persons become eligible for Medicare's hospital insurance if they are 65 or older and have worked long enough to be insured under Social Security or railroad retirement benefits. They can also become eligible if they are younger than 65 and have been entitled to Social Security disability benefits for 24 months. Finally, they are eligible regardless of age if they need maintenance kidney dialysis or a kidney transplant and are insured under Social Security or the railroad retirement system. If persons are not eligible for Medicare's hospital insurance program at age 65, they may purchase it for a basic monthly premium ($226 in 1987), which represents the average individual cost of the insurance.

Under the SMI program, persons do not need Social Security or federal work credits. If they want this type of insurance, they must pay a monthly premium ($17.90 in 1987). If they receive Social Security or retirement benefits, they are automatically enrolled in the plan unless they state they do not want it. They are eligible to receive both Part A and Part B coverage, regardless whether they choose to retire or continue working after age 65. Thus, employment is not a requirement for receiving Medicare coverage after age 65.

Medicare Benefits

Medicare's Part A or HI plan can help pay for inpatient hospital care, inpatient care in a skilled nursing facility, home health care, and hospice care. If a person requires inpatient treatment, Part A will help pay for up to 90 days in any Medicare-participating hospital in each benefit period. In 1987, the hospital insurance paid for all covered services for the first 60 days, except for the first $520. For the 61st through the 90th day, it paid for all covered services except for $130 a day (U.S. Department of Health and Human Services 1987). If persons require more than 90 days of inpatient treatment, they can use some or all of their 60 nonrenewable reserve days. The use of reserve days covers all hospital expenses except for $260 a day.

Under Part A or HI, covered services include semiprivate rooms, all meals, regular nursing services, drugs, lab tests, x-rays, medical supplies, rehabilitation services, anesthesia services, intensive care, operating and recovery room costs, and coronary care. Part A also provides help in paying for needed skilled nursing facility care, for up to 100 days in each benefit period. In 1987, hospital insurance paid for all covered services for the first 20 days and all but $65 a day for up to 80 additional days (U.S. Department of Health and Human Services 1987). There are no limits on home health care services; Part A pays for all home visits at the approved full rate. Services covered under this category include skilled nursing care, physical therapy, and speech therapy. Finally, Part A can help pay for hospice care for the terminally ill; it pays for a maximum of two 90-day periods and one 30-day period. Covered services include doctor and nursing services, therapies, drugs, and medical social services. Medicare pays the full cost of covered hospice services.

Medicare's Part B or SMI helps pay for physician services and for a variety of other medical services not covered under Part A. This insurance covers 80 percent of approved charges after an annual $75 deductible has been paid by the individual. Covered services include physician charges, x-rays, outpatient hospital services (such as emergency department use), outpatient clinic treatment, home health care visits, and medical supplies and drugs administered in the physician's office. Medicare Part B does not cover custodial care, routine dental care, eyeglasses, hearing aids, prescription drugs, and routine medical check-ups and related tests.

An Example of Medicare Coverage

Table 19-1 illustrates how Medicare would help pay an individual's medical expenses, assuming the person was in need of both inpatient and outpatient medical care in the same benefit period and was covered under the program.

Medicare Financing Methods

Part A, hospital insurance (HI), and Part B, supplementary medical insurance (SMI), have different methods of financing. HI has its own separate trust fund provided under the Social Security Act and designed to operate on a self-sustaining basis. It is financed primarily from amounts appropriated to the Hospital Insurance Trust Fund under a permanent system of taxes paid by employees and their employers, and by the self-employed, in work covered by the hospital insurance payroll tax (U.S. Congress, Comm. on Finance 1984a). An individual's HI trust fund contribution is computed on annual wages and/or self-employment income up to a specified maximum amount. In 1987, the HI tax rate was 1.45 percent, and the maximum taxable earnings were $37,800, providing

Table 19-1 Examples of Medicare Coverage

Service	Cost	Medicare's Approved Charge	Medicare Share	Patient Share
Part A–Inpatient Services				
80 days inpatient care in semiprivate room at $500 per day	$40,000	a. 60 days—all but $520	$29,480	$ 520
		b. 61–80 days—all but $130 per day	7,400	2,600
40 days skilled nursing facility care at $100 per day	4,000	a. 20 days—100%	2,000	
		b. 21–40 days—all but $65 per day	700	1,300
Hospital phone	400	a. Not eligible	—	400
Physician's service while inpatient, including surgery	3,000	a. 80% of approved charge ($2,500)	2,000	1,000
Anesthesiologist services	800	a. 80% of approved charge ($600)	480	320
Total Part A	48,200		42,060	6,140
Part B—Outpatient Services				
Physician service for ulcer treatment	400	a. $75 deductible	180	220
		b. 80% approved charge ($300)		
Eyeglass exam and glasses	120	a. not eligible	—	120
Routine medical check-up	80	a. not eligible	—	80
Diagnostic tests	300	a. 80% approved charge ($250)	200	100
X-rays	400	a. 80% approved charge ($300)	240	160
Dental exam	50	a. not eligible	—	50
Total Part B	1,350		620	730
Total Parts A and B	$49,550		$42,680	$6,870

a maximum tax of $548.10. This amount was paid by both the employee and the employer; a self-employed person had to pay twice that amount.

The board of trustees of the HI fund have adopted a policy that annual inflows should equal annual outlays, plus an amount sufficient to maintain a permanent trust fund reserve equal to one-half year's expenditures. This reserve is intended to provide additional investment income earnings for the trust fund. The only exceptions to the above financing procedures for HI are for (1) people who are not eligible for Medicare and who voluntarily enroll by paying a monthly premium and (2) a small group of people who were grandfathered into the program and whose premiums are financed out of general revenues.

SMI, unlike HI, is not financed out of proceeds from Social Security taxes. The SMI program is financed by monthly enrollee premiums ($17.90 per month in 1987) and appropriations from general treasury revenues. SMI premiums are now allowed to increase to a level sufficient to produce premium income equal to 25 percent of projected SMI costs for aged enrollees. This is far less than that intended by the original Medicare legislation, which stipulated that premiums pay 50 percent of the program's expenditures.

MEDICARE'S FINANCIAL PROBLEMS

According to Congressional Budget Office (CBO) and HI trustees estimates, the HI trust fund will be depleted at the end of 1992. Year-end HI trust fund balances were scheduled to begin to decline in 1987; by 1995, the negative balance is projected to be more than $90 billion. These projections are based on the expected cost savings and revenue increases of existing legislation; the revenue increases are projected from increased payroll tax rates (1.45 percent in 1986 and thereafter), and the cost savings are projected from the implementation of PPS payment rates for hospitals as of 1985. Projections of trust fund outlays, income, and balances for the years 1986 through 1995 are shown in Table 19-2.

Over the 1985–1995 period, HI outlays are projected to grow at a 12.4 percent annual rate, while revenues from taxes are projected to increase at only a 7.9 percent rate (U.S. Congress, House 1984). The 12.4 percent annual growth in

Table 19-2 Projections of Hospital Insurance Trust Fund Outlays, Income, and Balances

Year	Outlays	Income	Annual Surplus	Year-End Balance
1986	$ 57.3	$66.4	$ 9.1	$ 22.4
1987	62.1	66.9	4.8	27.2
1988	68.3	67.1	− 1.2	26.0
1989	75.1	71.5	− 3.6	22.4
1990	82.6	75.9	− 6.8	15.7
1991	90.9	80.1	− 10.7	4.9
1992	99.9	84.6	− 15.2	− 10.4
1993	109.8	89.1	− 19.4	− 31.2
1994	120.8	93.6	− 24.1	− 58.4
1995	133.0	98.0	− 29.5	− 93.4

Note: Numbers are in billions, projected on assumption of more stringent DRG rates after 1985.

Source: *Background Material Related to Medicare Financing Issues*, Senate Committee on Finance, 98th Congress, 2nd Session, April 1984.

outlays takes into account general inflation, eligible population growth and its aging, and changes in the cost of hospital care resulting from more resources being applied per hospital stay. The 7.9 percent revenue increase assumes moderate economic growth in the national economy. If the economy's performance is less than moderate, fewer revenues will be realized, creating larger HI trust deficits.

There are several reasons for the HI trust fund's financial difficulties. First, it should be noted that hospital services account for 95 percent of HI trust expenditures; therefore the financial solvency of the fund is highly dependent upon what occurs in the hospital sector. Since hospital costs have risen much more sharply and faster than increases in other areas of the economy, these costs have had the most significant negative impact on the trust's financial status. Second, the eligible population and its average age have both been rising gradually each year, which places additional burdens on the fund. HI enrollment continues to rise an average of 0.5 million individuals per year; and, since the average age of enrollees is increasing due to longer life expectancies, there is a corresponding increase in their hospital service need. Finally, the value of the services provided to each Medicare hospital user is increasing; enrollees are receiving more tests, treatments, and other services per visit than they did in previous years. In combination, these factors have contributed directly to HI trust fund outlay increases, and to the growing HI fund deficits projected for the 1990s.

Problems anticipated from the rapid growth expected in SMI are closely related to the size of the federal budget deficit. Since, by law, appropriation from general revenues to SMI must be sufficient to guarantee solvency of the trust fund, SMI does not face a financing crisis per se (U.S. Congress, Senate 1983). However, financing is still a concern because SMI's projected growth is much higher than the growth of general revenues. SMI's outlays are projected to increase 16 percent per year; to keep pace, general revenues will have to increase 17 percent per year. Consequently the share of general revenues required to fund the SMI trust fund will rise from 3.7 percent to 5.7 percent between 1982 and 1988 (U.S. Congress, House 1984). Given the currently high federal budget deficit and related problems, continued general revenue absorptions of SMI cost increases are simply not realistic. SMI outlays and/or enrollee premiums will have to be adjusted sufficiently to lighten the burden on other budget sources.

There are two basic reasons for SMI's financial problems: (1) SMI enrollees have increased each year and (2) medical service prices and enrollee use have risen substantially over the years. About one-tenth of this growth (SMI outlays) is attributable to expansion in the enrolled population; the remainder is due to a combination of increases in prices and in the use of services; enrollees have increased an average of 0.5 million each year, and benefits have grown an average of 21 percent per year (U.S. Congress, House 1984).

POLICY OPTIONS

The 27 options developed by the Advisory Council on Social Security to deal with Medicare's projected deficits can be grouped in five categories (U.S. Congress, House, Select Comm. on Aging 1985):

1. options that affect program outlays
2. options that affect program revenues
3. options that affect revenues and/or outlays through benefit restructuring
4. options that affect program outlays via changes in provider reimbursement
5. miscellaneous options

A summary of the issues involved in the implementation of each option and a description of its projected cost/savings as calculated by the Advisory Council on Social Security, is presented below.

Options that Affect Program Outlays

1. *Index annual deductible.* Under this option, the annual supplementary medical insurance deductible would be indexed to the Consumer Price Index rather than remaining at the $75 annual level prevailing for the past five years (U.S. Congress, Special Comm. on Aging 1984; U.S. Congress, House, Comm. on Ways and Means 1985b).
   - Pros:
     a. The elderly's average income has risen each year so that they can afford the corresponding rise in Medicare's Part B deductible. Mean beneficiary income, which was under $2,000 for noninstitutionalized elderly in 1966, had more than doubled, to $4,212, in 1973, when the deductible was raised by 20 percent. When the deductible was raised to $75 in 1982, the noninstitutionalized elderly's mean income had risen to $9,704, nearly four times the average in 1966 (when deductibles were $50 annually) (U.S. Congress, Senate, Comm. on Finance 1984a).
     b. A larger deductible serves as a deterrent to unnecessary utilization of services.
   - Cons:
     a. The elderly's out-of-pocket liability has kept track with inflation, due to the widening gap in Medicare's "reasonable charge" and the physician's "actual charge."

b. A higher SMI deductible may encourage greater use of inpatient services, where the deductible may be lower. Thus higher HI outlays may result.

- Social Security Advisory Council recommendation: Approval.
- Projected cost savings: If this option had been implemented in calendar year 1985, SMI outlays would have been reduced by $680 million for the period 1985–1989. (U.S. Congress, Senate, Comm. on Finance 1984a).

2. *Increase age of eligibility.* Under this option, the age of Medicare eligibility would be gradually increased from 65 to 67 years old over the period 1985 to 1990, when it will become fully effective.

- Pro: Life expectancy has gradually increased over the years since Medicare was first established, increasing more than three years since 1966. Therefore, it is logical to assume that the need for Medicare at age 65 has decreased from what it once was, since people are remaining healthier longer.
- Con: People who are not covered by alternate forms of medical insurance after age 65 will suffer undue financial hardship if they become seriously ill before age 67.
- Social Security Advisory Council recommendation: Approval.
- Projected cost savings: $74.6 billion in savings for HI trust fund through 1995, and $4.89 billion in savings for the SMI trust fund, through 1989 (U.S. Congress, Senate, Comm. on Finance 1984a).

3. *Apply means test.* Under this option, enrollees' eligibility for benefits or level of premium payments would be tied to their financial need (in terms of income, savings, and so on).

- Pro: People who are in the greatest need for financial support with their medical bills would receive it, while those who are better able to absorb such medical expenses would be indexed according to their ability to self-pay. This could save billions of dollars while avoiding the placing of undue financial hardships on the elderly.
- Con: Medicare was designed as an entitlement program, not as a welfare program, therefore applying the means test is against the basic design of the program.
- Social Security Advisory Council recommendation: Rejected.
- Projected cost savings: No projections were given, since a specific implementation plan was not developed by the advisory council. However, Karen Davis and Diane Rowland of Johns Hopkins University propose that a premium equal to two percent of the income of Medicare beneficiaries be required. This could be done on a sliding scale, with

those making less than $5,000 per year exempt. By 1995, a premium set at an average of two percent of the income of Medicare beneficiaries would yield $10 billion (U.S. Congress, House 1984). Over the period 1985–1995, a $116 billion reduction in expenditures has been estimated under this plan.

4. *Extended coverage for specific diseases and treatments.* Several legislative attempts have been made to extend coverage to certain individuals having specific diseases. This option is based upon the success of such an extension to those suffering from end-stage renal disease. It has been argued that individuals with AIDS is another such group that should be covered by Medicare.

   • Pro: Such a protection extension would be humane and would distribute the costs equally throughout the nation for specific, high-cost diseases. This would take a burden off state and local funding sources via eliminating Medicaid's coverage responsibility, and it would be justified on the basis of the treatment provided to end-stage renal disease victims.

   • Con: This option would be costly to Medicare's already ailing trust funds, and, unless arbitrary guidelines were established, it would be difficult to determine which diseases should and which should not be covered.

   • Social Security Advisory Council recommendation: Rejection of further protection extensions of Medicare. Recommendation that specific funds be earmarked for special diseases from the general tax fund, as appropriate.

   • Projected cost savings: None at present, but billions could be saved in the future if this policy is not adopted.

Options that Affect Program Revenues

5. *Increase reliance on general revenues.* With this option, both the HI and SMI trust funds would receive either new (in the case of HI trust) or increased (in the case of SMI trust) revenues from the general revenue tax fund.

   • Pro: Receiving new/increased financial subsidies from general revenues would provide a simple means of resolving Medicare's financial concerns. Since general revenues (income taxes) are more progressive than Social Security taxes, lower- and middle-income workers would share less of the financial burden than upper-income individuals. There is precedent for the use of general tax revenues in financing health insurance programs, since SMI already receives over 75 percent of its funds from this source.

- Cons:
    a. There appears to be little financial logic in this approach, since the present federal deficit is enormous and cannot be increased further.
    b. Many people who contribute to general revenues do not receive Medicare insurance, such as state and local workers. Therefore, to use general revenues for a purpose that does not benefit them per se could become a major political battle.
- Social Security Advisory Council recommendation: Rejected.
- Projected revenue increase: Variable, depending on the general revenue contribution.

6. *Increase scheduled payroll taxes.* Under this option, HI payroll taxes would be increased even further than is currently legislated (presently 1.45 percent). This could be accomplished by increasing the tax rate percentage and/or increasing the maximum taxable ceiling (currently $37,800).
- Pro: This approach can be easily justified, in that the HI trust fund is supposed to be self-sustaining from payroll taxes collected.
- Cons:
    a. There is a concern that further HI payroll tax increases will affect employment levels and business activity adversely.
    b. The HI payroll tax is less progressive than general revenue taxes; and current workers who would be paying for the increases are, on average, less wealthy than those benefiting (the elderly).
- Social Security Advisory Council recommendation: Rejection.
- Projected revenue increase: Variable, depending on the HI tax rate and/ or maximum taxed income increases.

7. *Interfund borrowing.* Under this option, the HI and SMI trust funds would each be allowed to make short-term loans (under a repayment plan, including interest) from either of Social Security's other two trust funds (OASI and DI) at times when such loans would not jeopardize the finances of either of the latter funds.
- Pros:
    a. There is a precedent for this option: OASI borrowed $12.4 billion from the HI trust fund in 1982, an amount that will be repaid by 1990.
    b. This would help alleviate short-term financial cash flow problems of the HI trust fund.

- Con: This option will not resolve the long-term financial problems of the HI trust, and it may be a tool for procrastination in taking long-term remedies.
- Social Security Advisory Council recommendation: Approval.
- Projected revenue increase: None.

8. *Reallocate OASI tax rates to HI.* Under this option, the projected surpluses in the OASI trust fund in the next several years would be reallocated to the HI trust fund, which is running a deficit. The total tax rate of Social Security's three trust funds would remain the same; however, HI would receive a larger portion of the revenues than it currently does, while OASI and DI would receive smaller portions, since their trusts are relatively sound financially.

- Pro: This option would not impose additional Social Security tax increases on the working population; rather, it would distribute the taxes in terms of each fund's long- and short-term needs.
- Con: This option could jeopardize the financial solvency of the other trust funds if projections of revenues and outlays were inaccurate. And such projections are difficult to make with a substantial degree of accuracy, as history has shown.
- Social Security Advisory Council recommendation: Approval.
- Projected revenue increase: Variable, depending upon the degree of reallocation.

9. *Tax on health insurance fringe benefits.* Under current law, an employer's contribution to an employee's health plan is a tax-free fringe benefit. An estimated $20+ billion in additional federal income taxes would have been collected in 1983 if employer health plan contributions had been treated as taxable income (U.S. Congress, Senate, Comm. on Finance 1984a). Some of these taxes would then have been allocated to Medicare.

- Pros:
  a. This type of tax increase is progressive.
  b. This option may make health care consumers more cost-conscious, since employers would seek to lower the costs of health care insurance which would decrease the level of benefits to those covered. As a result of the increased health care cost consciousness, overutilization would be reduced, and competitive cost comparisons would be promoted, which would help lower the costs for all consumers, including the elderly.
- Cons:
  a. This progressive tax may increase the burden on the older worker and workers in hazardous occupations, thus becoming nonprogressive to some.

  b. The expected behavioral change (cost consciousness) may not occur.
  c. Employers may shift fringes to other areas, thus negating the tax advantage.

- Social Security Advisory Council recommendation: Approval.
- Projected revenue increase: Variable, depending on the tax rate and the amount allocated to Medicare.

10. *Excise taxes on alcohol and tobacco.* Under this option, federal excise taxes on alcohol and cigarettes would be increased with the revenues going directly to the HI trust fund.

  - Pros:
    a. Medical evidence suggests a strong correlation between use of alcohol and cigarettes and increased health care cost.
    b. This tax appears to be fair and equitable. Most important, it is the least objectionable of all tax increases considered.

  - Cons:
    a. Other products that have been shown to affect health adversely escape taxation.
    b. The producing industries may be detrimentally affected.
    c. Increased federal taxes may decrease demand for the affected products but not result in substantial revenue increases.

  - Social Security Advisory Council recommendation: Approval.
  - Projected revenue increase: Variable, depending on the tax increase, product demand, and the amount allocated to the Medicare trust fund.

11. *Expand number of covered employees.* Under this option, employees in nonprofit, state, local, and federal organizations would be mandated by law to join the Social Security (including Medicare) program. This would increase the base of contributors to the HI and SMI trust funds.

  - Pros:
    a. If more individuals were contributing to the Medicare program, it is presumed that more revenues would be collected, thus helping to support the trust funds.
    b. Uniform national coverage would end the confusion and reduce the medical cost risks of some individuals who are not presently covered by an alternative old-age medical insurance plan.

  - Cons:
    a. Attempts to extend Social Security coverage would be met with fierce opposition by certain elements.

b. Extended coverage will increase outlays, which may be greater than the revenue gains, thus putting the Medicare trust funds in an even more precarious position.

• Social Security Council recommendation: Approval.

• Projected revenue increase: Unknown.

Options Affecting Revenues or Outlays through Benefit Restructuring

12. *Restructuring HI benefits*. Under this proposal, HI benefits would be restructured to eliminate confusing definitions and clauses and improve administration of the program. Three proposed basic changes would (1) provide protection against catastrophic illness; (2) eliminate the present complicated definition of benefit period and provide for coverage of all hospitalizations, no matter how many, in any given period of time, and (3) eliminate confusing cost-sharing formulas and replace them with a single daily coinsurance rate of three percent.

• Pros:

a. Administration of the program would be easier, and costly and time-consuming records and calculating methods would be eliminated.

b. Better protection would result, and the beneficiary would be better able to understand the program's purposes and procedures.

c. The cost-sharing formula would encourage competition while discouraging overutilization of services.

• Cons:

a. Assuming that the plan would leave revenue and outlay totals unchanged, those suffering catastrophic illnesses would gain while the majority who experience few health problems would lose, due to higher deductibles and cost-sharing burdens.

b. Since there has been no experience in operating this plan, revenue and expense projections may be inaccurate. And if expenses were underestimated, it would add to the financial difficulties of the HI trust fund.

• Social Security Advisory Council recommendation: Approval.

• Dollar impact on the HI trust fund: The recommended restructuring plan would result in $12.83 billion savings in the Part A program and $24.98 billion in additional revenues during the period 1985–1995 (U.S. Congress, Senate, Comm. on Finance 1984a).

13. *Offer an optional Part A benefit improvement package.* Under this proposal, the restructured benefit package in option 12 above would be changed

to eliminate the three percent coinsurance rate by paying a premium equal to the improvements' average cost.

- Pro: This option would reduce the financial risks for the individual in need of medical care.
- Con: This option would result in higher administrative costs.
- Social Security Council recommendation: Approval.
- Dollar impact on the HI trust fund: None, assuming the premium covers costs.

14. *Offer an optional Part B benefit improvement package.* Under this proposal, the beneficiary would be allowed to choose an improved SMI protection plan at a premium cost increase that would cover all additional expenses incurred. Assuming implementation had occurred in 1985, a $227 annual cap would have applied to out-of-pocket expenditures (U.S. Congress, Senate, Comm. on Finance 1984a). After an individual meets this cap, SMI would cover 100 percent (rather than 80 percent) of all approved charges.

- Pro: This option would reduce the financial risks for the individual in need of medical care.
- Cons:
    a. This option would directly compete with private "Medigap" insurance plans, thus decreasing private sector employment while increasing governmental employment.
    b. This option would result in higher administrative costs.
- Social Security Advisory Council recommendation: Approval.
- Dollar impact on SMI trust fund: None, assuming the premium covers costs.

15. *Target long-term care benefits.* Under this proposal, long-term care needs would be studied further before a comprehensive long-term program is considered. As the nation's elderly population grows, so does its need for long-term custodial care, for example, nursing home care and home health care. Medicare presently does not cover the cost of this type of care beyond the first 100 days. This has created financial hardships for many beneficiaries who do not have supplemental insurance coverage for this purpose. It has been strongly urged that Medicare expand benefits in this area; however, such expansion would be expensive if appropriate financing methods are not devised.

- Pros:
    a. Medicare would not take on this new costly benefit extension before extensive studies are completed on various issues of this proposal.

b. Since many of the presently available long-term care services are extremely expensive, further study appears warranted, seeking less costly approaches to providing such service prior to offering insurance protection under Medicare.

- Cons:
    a. Many individuals would experience financial hardships because of their lack of insurance to cover their long-term care needs in the interim.
    b. It is argued that this insurance protection need should be left to private providers who can provide it more cost-efficiently than the government.
- Social Security Advisory Council recommendation: Approval.
- Dollar impact on Medicare: None, other than the insignificant costs associated with the study.

16. *Preventive services coverage.* Under this proposal, Medicare would begin to fund primary-protection medical services, such as breast examinations, physical exams, and various immunizations. While the literature and research concerning the cost-effectiveness of offering such services are inconclusive, it is possible that the offering of such services would improve the health and mobility of the elderly population, resulting in long-term care cost savings (U.S. Congress, Senate, Comm. on Finance 1984a).

- Pros:
    a. More expensive treatment needs could be avoided through such preventive service.
    b. This benefit extension could relieve unnecessary pain and suffering in the elderly population.
- Con: Many physicians currently provide preventive services during routine office visits, with no separate charge. Medicare funding of this proposal may serve as an incentive for physicians to begin separate billings, thus creating some unnecessary costs for Medicare.
- Social Security Advisory Council recommendation: Further study is warranted.
- Dollar impact on Medicare: Presently, only minimal costs associated with further study. Future cost/savings are unknown.

17. *Voluntary vouchers.* Under this proposal, the beneficiary would be provided with a credit to purchase health care services from a federally qualified health care delivery system. The voucher's value would be equal to some percentage of the historical cost of providing services to beneficiaries with the same actuarially determined characteristics. Setting the voucher value below the average per capita charges for such services

would encourage beneficiaries to become more cost-conscious and, possibly, result in an immediate savings for the Medicare program (U.S. Congress, Senate, Comm. on Finance 1984a).

- Pros:
  a. This option could help promote competition in the health care industry by promoting incentives to use cost-effective services.
  b. Voluntary vouchers would provide the beneficiary with a reasonable degree of certainty regarding the extent of out-of-pocket expenses for medical services.
- Cons:
  a. Start-up costs for this program would be high ($50 million estimate).
  b. Administrative costs would also be significant (for example, for enrollee entrances, withdrawals, monitoring health care delivery systems, and so on).
  c. Unless safeguards are provided, there could be discrimination regarding those whom the health care delivery systems choose to serve.
- Social Security Advisory Council recommendation: Approval.
- Dollar impact on Medicare: Unknown.

Options Affecting Outlays through Changes in Provider Reimbursements

18. *Annual adjustments to hospital payment rates.* Under this option (which took effect in 1986) hospital payments are made under a prospective payment system (PPS), based on diagnostic related groups (DRG). This is intended to hold hospital cost increases down, since payments are predetermined based on diagnosis and the hospital's geographic area. Any expenses hospitals incur above the payment may not be reimbursed unless special provisions are made for outliers.

    - Pros:
      a. Competition and cost-efficiencies will be promoted in the inpatient service market.
      b. Rising medical costs will be constrained to some degree by this system, which will help reduce Medicare's future outlays.
    - Cons:
      a. Some hospitals may be forced to close if they are unable to provide services efficiently, creating employment and medical service losses in some communities.

b. Although this system attempts to control inpatient costs, it does not go far enough, in that outpatient and other medical service costs are not similarly controlled.

- Social Security Advisory Council recommendation: Support, but with recommendation that annual adjustment formula be changed from use of the present Hospital Input Price Index (HIPI) plus one percent to just use of the HIPI (U.S. Congress, House 1984).
- Dollar impact on Medicare: $157 billion in expected savings from 1986 to 1995 under the present formula (HIPI plus one percent). Additional savings if the formula is changed to use of HIPI only for annual adjustment. If implemented in 1988, savings from this change would be $34.52 billion through 1995 (U.S. Congress, Senate, Comm. on Finance 1984a).

19. *Medical education expenses.* Under this proposal, Medicare would no longer reimburse hospitals for training such medical personnel as residents, nurses, and other health care workers. Such expenditures are not considered appropriate for a program that was designed to provide medical insurance for the elderly.

- Pros:
  a. With the elimination of this outlay, cost savings would be significant.
  b. It is not logical to include medical education expenses under the Medicare program since it was not designed for that purpose.
- Cons:
  a. Medical education is an important need of the health care delivery system as a way of enhancing and protecting service delivery quality and availability. Medicare coverage of it could not be eliminated without creating severe problems.
  b. It would be difficult to transfer this expense to other areas of the federal budget due to the present government's fiscal problems.
  c. It is difficult to measure the true cost of medical education, since the personnel to whom this training is provided also provide substantial services to the hospital during training.
- Social Security Advisory Council recommendation: Further study should be given this option.
- Dollar impact on Medicare: If Medicare support for medical education expenses is withdrawn, beginning in 1987, savings to the HI trust fund would be $140.8 billion through 1995 (U.S. Congress, Senate, Comm. on Finance 1984a).

20. *Fee schedules for physicians.* Under this proposal, the present method for reimbursing physicians, based on the "reasonable charge method,"

would be changed to a system based on fee schedules, adjusted for cost-of-living increases and price changes in maintaining a practice on a yearly basis.

- Pros:
  a. Fee schedules would be effective in controlling physician costs.
  b. Competition and cost-effective use of services would be encouraged through use of this system.
  c. Payment equity would be encouraged under the system.
- Cons:
  a. Physicians may reject this procedure, and many may withdraw from the Medicare system.
  b. If physicians begin to refuse to accept Medicare as payment, beneficiaries' physician choices may become severely limited; and those physicians who do agree to accept Medicare may be unable to provide services as quickly as before, due to increased demand.
- Social Security Advisory Council recommendation: Approval.
- Dollar impact on Medicare: The impact on the SMI trust fund is unknown.

21. *Creating assignment incentives for physicians.* Under this proposal, physicians would be provided incentives to accept assignments on all services to Medicare patients. The incentives would be new policies to promote streamlined billing and payment procedures and free advertising in annually published local directories of participating physicians.

- Pros:
  a. More physicians would be expected to accept Medicare assignments, based on the incentives offered, thus increasing beneficiary physician choices.
  b. Beneficiaries would experience lower out-of-pocket expenses, assuming they choose a physician who accepts assignment.
  c. Beneficiaries would benefit from the annual physician directory, since they would be able to determine assignment physicians more easily.
- Cons:
  a. Those physicians who refuse to join the assignment system would be excluded from accepting Medicare. Thus, the beneficiaries would be left to pay the entire bill until Medicare makes direct repayment to them.
  b. Administrative costs may increase as beneficiaries begin to increase their applications for repayment. Form accuracy would probably be reduced, and more effort would be required in processing claims.

Also, costs would be incurred with more rapid billing, repayment efforts, and local directory publishings.
- Social Security Advisory Council recommendation: Approval.
- Dollar impact on Medicare: Proposal should be cost-neutral.

Miscellaneous Options

22. *Encourage medical technology.* Under this proposal, all new medical technology would be evaluated, using three factors, before it is approved for reimbursement. The factors would be (1) the initial cost, (2) the technology's contribution to lower treatment costs, and (3) the value of the technology in terms of improved care delivery to the elderly. If the new technology meets reasonable standards for these factors, the Health Care Financing Administration would approve it for reimbursement, using methods that allow the developer to recover the costs of its technological innovation in a reasonable period of time.
    - Pros:
        a. The evaluation criteria proposed would place greater weight on the financial aspects of new medical technology than on its medical merits.
        b. The Medicare trust would benefit from the savings incurred through the promotion of cost-effective medical technologies.
    - Cons:
        a. Medical innovations that have significant merit in terms of their treatment advances may be rejected on cost-efficient factors, thus hindering improvements in the delivery of health care.
        b. New medical technology accounted for only 20.8 percent of the growth in hospital expenditures in the period 1970–1981 (U.S. Congress, Senate, Comm. on Finance 1984a). Thus, limitations imposed in this area would not substantially reduce Medicare outlays on their own.
    - Social Security Advisory Council recommendation: Approval.
    - Dollar impact on Medicare: Unknown.
23. *"Advanced directives" or "living wills."* Under this proposal, beneficiaries would be encouraged to consider preparation of "advanced directives" or "living wills." These would document the type of care a person wants to receive if and when they need medical services but are unable to make their own decisions based on sound mental functioning. For example, persons could specify that they do not want to be placed upon life-sustaining equipment, even if death is inevitable without it. Also,

they could specify the type of custodial long-term care they desired in the event of future need. If persons chose less costly options, such as home health care, Medicare would save money.

- Pro: Eleven percent of Medicare expenditures are spent in the last 40 days of life, and some 25 percent of Medicare expenditures are incurred by patients in the last year of life (U.S. Congress, Senate, Comm. on Finance 1984b). Thus, if widely used and promoted, advanced directives or living wills would save Medicare significant amounts.
- Con: At this time, advanced directives have been legally upheld in courts in only 14 states and the District of Columbia. Thus, Medicare would have a difficult time realizing substantial savings from this option, since large segments of the population could not presently be covered.
- Social Security Advisory Council recommendation: Approval.
- Dollar impact on Medicare: Unknown.

24. *Improved management of Medicare.* Under this proposal, the Health Care Financing Administration (HCFA), which manages Medicare, would be encouraged to find better management techniques in three areas: (1) improved cash management of funds, (2) improved operational management of programs, and (3) elimination of fraud, abuse, and waste.

- Pros:
    a. Since federal programs the size of Medicare are generally prone to mismanagement, safeguards need to be taken to ensure that trust monies are appropriately handled.
    b. In 1982, of the $36.1 billion in HI disbursements, $35.6 billion was for benefit payments, while the remaining $0.5 billion was spent on administration expenses (U.S. Congress, Senate, Comm. on Finance 1984a). Of the $15.6 billion in SMI disbursement, $14.8 billion was for benefit payments, while the remaining $0.8 billion was spent for administrative expenses (U.S. Department of Health and Human Services 1987). Thus, in 1982, a total of $1.3 billion was spent in administering Medicare. Given this enormous amount, improved management techniques could save millions.
- Con: Although the concept of better management efforts is a good one, this proposal does little to spell out the specifics of how better management would be accomplished. In government, the word reform is often used, but it usually ends up accomplishing very little. This proposal could end the same way.
- Social Security Advisory Council recommendation: Approval.
- Dollar impact on Medicare: Unknown.

25. *Develop health care IRAs.* Under this proposal, a long-term restructuring of the Medicare program would be designed to encourage individuals to save during their working years in order to purchase health care coverage in their retirement years. The savings would be exempted from taxation and Medicare would be modified to complement individual spending. Eventually (over a 30-year period), Medicare's deductibles will become so high that the program will be of help only for catastrophic care (defined on an individual basis according to income). Under this option, future Medicare tax rates would be frozen at present levels.

- Pros:
  a. The proposed system would help reduce the government's role in providing elderly medical insurance protection.
  b. This system would place greater insurance control in the hands of the individual, allowing for greater discretion in arranging protection in retirement years.

- Cons:
  a. This program would create a drain on federal and state tax revenues by providing tax exemptions for the savings involved.
  b. If greater discretion is given individuals in providing for their retirement medical protection, greater financial hardships will result for many who did not save enough to cover heavy medical costs in their retirement years.
  c. Although Medicare's role is seen as a shrinking one, this may not actually be the case. Thus, this option could lead to larger deficits if the health care IRAs do not become as popular as hoped.

- Social Security Advisory Council recommendation: Approval of further study of the plan.

- Dollar impact on Medicare: Unknown.

26. *Improved information to beneficiaries.* Under this proposal, beneficiaries would be provided better information about Medicare so that they would better understand its benefits, their rights and responsibilities, and other aspects of the program. Surveys indicate that presently, there is a substantial degree of misunderstanding in the beneficiary population about the program.

- Pros:
  a. Beneficiaries who contribute substantial amounts to the Medicare programs have a right to know more about it.
  b. Better-educated beneficiaries would be able to utilize Medicare's services more effectively and with less apprehension in terms of their cost responsibilities. Also, better-educated beneficiaries would be more cost-conscious as consumers of medical services.

- Con: Money will be needed to improve beneficiaries' understanding of Medicare, and the program may have difficulty establishing the initial financing.
- Social Security Advisory Council recommendation: Approval.
- Dollar impact on Medicare: Unknown.

27. *Expanded Medicare as secondary payer.* Under this proposal, Medicare would be expanded as a secondary payer to the employed elderly's spouses. Under current law, although an elderly employee must be offered the same group health plan provided to other employees (with Medicare becoming secondary payer), if the employer has more than 20 employees, their spouses, if over 69 years old, are not entitled to group plan coverage. The 69-year limit would be removed under this option.

  - Pro: Since many employees are continuing to work beyond age 65, this option could save millions of dollars in Medicare outlays for the spouses of employed elderly who are over 69.
  - Con: This proposal could cost employers of the elderly extra medical insurance premiums on their group plans, which could lead to further discrimination against the elderly, as well as higher health insurance premium costs for all the workers in the organization.
  - Social Security Advisory Council recommendation: Further study is needed.
  - Dollar impact on Medicare: Unknown.

POLICY OPTION EVALUATION

At this point, we shall try to select out those option choices proposed by the Advisory Council on Social Security that have the greatest potential for restoring the Medicare trust fund's financial stability. In the selection process, we shall use the following criteria to evaluate each of the 27 options developed by the council:

1. *Cost competition.* To what degree, if any, does the option promote cost competition in the medical service market? Competition is important in holding down costs and promoting and making available a range of service alternatives to the consumer. Health care delivery systems and the consumers should be given greater incentives to use cost-effective services.
2. *Distributive equity.* How evenly and fairly are the option's costs and benefits distributed among those directly (beneficiaries) and indirectly (contributors) affected by the Medicare system? It appears reasonable to assume that the greater its distributive equity, the easier it will be to sell the option

to the general public. Broad public acceptance is vital for the option to survive politically and to justify the fairness and continued existence of the Medicare system.

3. *Administrative ease/minimal compliance costs.* What is the degree of difficulty and expense associated with establishing and maintaining the option in the Medicare framework? The higher the degree of administrative ease and the lower the compliance cost, the greater will be the value of the option.

4. *Revenue/expense certainty and stability.* What is the degree of certainty and stability offered by the option in terms of its revenue/expense projections over the long term? If the option has a high degree of financial certainty and stability, it is more desirable than one that offers less certainty or the potential for instability. Financial uncertainty and instability can lead to trust fund insolvency in the future, as demonstrated by the current problems with which the Medicare system is confronted.

The following simple scale can be used to indicate the degree level for each of the above criteria:

- *High*, indicating a substantial number of positive elements in the option.
- *Medium*, indicating some positive elements in the option, but also some degree of uncertainty or concern.
- *Low*, indicating a substantial number of negative elements in the option.
- *Not applicable*, meaning that the evaluation criterion cannot be applied to the option.

Finally, the following point system is used to weight the above degree levels: high—40 points, medium—20 points, low—0 points. No weight is assigned when the criterion is not applicable.

The final evaluation score for each option is calculated by adding the points assigned to all criteria applied to the option and then dividing that total by the number of criteria (1 to 3) applicable to that option. The resulting average point score is the basis for ranking the 27 options. Those with the highest average point scores are given the top ranking (1), while those with the lowest average point scores are given the lowest ranking (9). Options receiving rankings of 7 to 9 should be eliminated from consideration or, at best, receive further study; those with rankings of 1 to 3 may be regarded as those with the highest potential for successful implementation. The resulting scores and rankings for each of the 27 options on each of the four criteria are presented in Table 19-3.

This evaluation model involves, of course, a considerable degree of subjectivity. This is particularly true when the criterion has multiple facets that may apply in different ways to various options. For example, when distributive equity

Table 19-3 Evaluation of Policy Options Proposed by the Advisory Council on Social Security

Policy Option	Cost Competition		Distributive Equity		Administrative Ease/ Minimal Compliance Costs		Revenue/Expenditure Certainty and Stability		Average Points	Rank
1. Index deductible	High	40	High	40	High	40	High	40	40	1
2. Increase age of eligibility	N/A		Low	0	Medium	20	High	40	20	6
3. Apply means test	High	40	Medium	20	Low	0	High	40	25	5
4. Do not extend coverage to specific diseases and treatments	N/A		High	40	High	40	High	40	40	1
5. Increase reliance on general revenue	Low	0	Medium	20	High	40	Low	0	15	7
6. Increase scheduled payroll tax	Low	0	Medium	20	High	40	High	40	25	5
7. Interfund borrowing	Low	0	Medium	20	High	40	Low	0	15	7
8. Reallocate OASI tax rate to HI	Low	0	Medium	20	High	40	Low	0	15	7
9. Tax on health insurance fringe benefits	High	40	Medium	20	Medium	20	Medium	20	25	5
10. Excise taxes on alcohol and tobacco	Low	0	Medium	20	Medium	20	Medium	20	20	6
11. Extend covered employment	Low	0	High	40	High	40	High	40	30	3
12. Restructure HI	High	40	High	40	High	40	High	40	40	1
13. Optional Part A benefit improvements	Low	0	Medium	20	Low	0	Low	0	5	9
14. Optional Part B benefit improvements	Low	0	Medium	20	Low	0	Low	0	5	9

Table 19-3 (continued)

Policy Option	Cost Competition	Distributive Equity	Administrative Ease/ Minimal Compliance Costs	Revenue/Expenditure Certainty and Stability	Average Points	Rank
15. Targeted long-term care benefits (assumes implementation)	Medium 20	Medium 20	Low 0	Low 0	10	8
16. Preventive service benefits	Low 0	High 40	Medium 20	Low 0	15	7
17. Voluntary vouchers	High 40	High 40	Medium 20	Low 0	25	5
18. Annual adjustment to hospital payment rates	High 40	High 40	High 40	High 40	40	1
19. Medical education costs (discontinue)	N/A	High 40	High 40	High 40	40	1
20. Fee schedules for physicians	High 40	Medium 20	Low 0	Medium 20	20	6
21. Assignment incentives	High 40	High 40	Low 0	Medium 20	25	5
22. Encourage medical technology (based on cost-reducing criteria)	High 40	High 40	High 40	Medium 20	35	2
23. Promote living wills	High 40	Medium 20	High 40	Low 0	25	5
24. Improve Medicare management	High 40	High 40	Medium 20	Low 0	25	5
25. Develop health care IRAs (assumes implementation)	High 40	Low 0	Low 0	Low 0	10	8
26. Improve information to beneficiaries	Medium 20	High 40	Medium 20	N/A	27	4
27. Expand Medicare as secondary payer	Medium 20	Medium 20	Medium 20	Medium 20	20	6

is applied to the option for increased reliance on general revenues, it must be applied separately to each aspect of equity involved: contributor/beneficiary equity, beneficiary/beneficiary equity, and contributor/contributor equity. Thus, when so applied, it reveals a low degree of contributor/beneficiary equity (contributor pays, beneficiary receives), a low degree of beneficiary/beneficiary equity (beneficiaries with incomes contribute while those without incomes do not), and a medium degree of contributor/contributor equity (although income tax rates are progressive, actual taxes paid are regressive to total income). Since, on this criterion, the option had two low aspects and one medium, it was given an overall low degree level on the criterion.

Also, it may be argued that the evaluation procedure stresses financial considerations over quality considerations. In fact, this bias is intentional. It was felt that, since there is already a high level of quality in this nation's health marketplace, quality aspects should be considered secondary to financial aspects. On the one hand, the United States leads the world in medical technology and in health care delivery excellence. On the other, large annual increases in health care costs can no longer be tolerated without creating significant hardships in other areas of human need (shelter, food, defense, and so on) and eventually excluding large segments of the population from proper medical treatment.

With these limitations in mind, our evaluation tool should be regarded, not as a definitive basis for option selection, but as a starting point for option review. Once an option has gone through this basic evaluation process, it may be further scrutinized in terms of other factors, using other forms of evaluations appropriate to the specific option. Only after it has been examined carefully in this larger evaluation process should the final decision, to implement or not to implement, be made.

CONCLUSION

Serious problems are looming for Medicare and the Social Security system. The 27 options designed to maintain the financial viability of the Health Insurance trust fund require urgent consideration. Some tough decisions will have to be made by Congress if we are to avoid seeing the HI trust fund depleted or in arrears. Already, the proposed expansion of Medicare through catastrophic illness coverage is receiving considerable opposition because of the precarious financial position of the HI trust fund (Davidson and Birnbaum 1987).

Individual congressmen have in fact voiced their concern; but, collectively, Congress has not been able to accomplish much to alleviate the crisis.

Elsewhere, three different, but complementary, approaches to the Social Security problem have been proposed: Pete Dupont, former governor of Delaware and a presidential candidate, proposed an individual account system to supplement the present system. Newt Gingrich, a Georgia congressman, proposed a value-added tax to provide improved liquidity for the Social Security system. And former governor Bruce Babbitt of Arizona proposed a means test to identify the elderly who were really in need and those who could pay for at least a portion of their health care, thus relieving Medicare of some of its burden ("Addressing the Unassailable" 1980).

In short, Congress must re-examine the 27 options as presented and evaluated in this chapter and identify the specific ways to raise funds and/or reduce spending while simultaneously maintaining the quality and integrity of the Medicare program.

REFERENCES

"Addressing the Unassailable in U.S. Politics." *Wall Street Journal,* 15 December 1980.

Davidson, J., and Birnbaum, J.H. "Bipartisan Backing to Expand Medicare to Cover Catastrophic Illnesses May Fade if Price Fog Soars." *Wall Street Journal,* 6 May 1987.

U.S. Congress. Congressional Budget Office. *Changing the Structure of Medicare Benefits: Issues and Options.* Washington, D.C.: U.S. GPO, 1983.

U.S. Congress. House. Committee on Ways and Means. *Proceedings of the Conference on the Future of Medicare.* 98th Cong., 2nd sess., 1984.

———. *Description of the Administration's Fiscal Year 1986 Budget Recommendations Under the Jurisdiction of the Committee on Ways and Means.* 99th Cong., 1st sess, 1985a.

———. *Medicare, Health Care Expenditures, and the Elderly.* 99th Cong., 1st sess., 1985b.

U.S. Congress. House. Select Committee on Aging. *Medicare Options for 1985: Hearing.* 99th Cong., 1st sess., 1985.

U.S. Congress. Senate. Committee on Finance. *Background Material Related to Medicare Financing Issues.* 98th Cong., 2nd sess., 1984a.

———. *Social Security Advisory Council Recommendations on Medicare Trust Solvency: Hearing.* 98th Cong., 2nd sess., 1984b.

U.S. Congress. Senate. Special Committee on Aging. *Prospects for Medicare's Hospital Insurance Trust Fund.* 98th Cong., 1st sess., 1983.

———. *Medicare and the Health Costs of Older Americans: The Extent and Effects of Cost Sharing.* 98th Cong., 2nd sess., 1984.

U.S. Department of Health and Human Services. *What You Should Know About Medicare.* SSA Publication no. 05-10043. Washington, D.C.: U.S. GPO, 1987.

Chapter 20

Prospective Payment Systems Based on Diagnostic Related Groups*

INTRODUCTION

On 1 October 1984, Medicare reimbursement to hospitals changed from a retrospective mechanism, which was based on the actual costs incurred by the hospital, to a prospective payment system (PPS) in which diagnostic related groups (DRGs) are used by Medicare to determine the amount of hospital reimbursement. Congress had approved this plan for most inpatient services in March 1983 as a part of the Social Security Amendments, which President Reagan signed into law on 20 April 1983. The new policy was based on the assumption that, in any given transaction, the way in which medical care is delivered and priced depends on the economic incentives at work. Thus, health care is viewed more as an economic product than as a social good. In the old cost-based reimbursement system, in contrast, hospitals were paid essentially for whatever they spent; there was no incentive for them to operate more efficiently, since all allowable costs were fully reimbursed.

CASE CLASSIFICATION SYSTEM

The case classification system of DRGs was developed in 1975 under the leadership of John D. Thompson, head of the Yale School of Medicine's Division of Health Services Administration. The purpose was to develop an inpatient classification system that differentiated the amount of hospital resources required to provide particular types of care. The resulting system assumes that hospital

---

*Much of this chapter is based on two papers entitled ''Diagnostic Related Groups'' by Peter Storey and ''Prospective Pricing: An Impact Analysis'' by Mark J. Stramaglia, School of Management, SUNY/Buffalo, 1985.

cases can be classified into clinically coherent groups that are reasonably similar in resource consumption, cost, and length of stay.

The International Classification of Diseases (ICD), a coding source used by all hospitals, was the basis of the groupings. Diagnoses were divided into 23 major diagnostic categories, corresponding to the various organ systems and medical specialties. The principal diagnosis, which is the diagnosis after admission and investigation or the principal reason for the admission to the hospital, places the patient in a major diagnostic category (MDC). The first partition in most MDCs is the presence or absence of a surgical procedure.

In developing the DRG system, the operating room procedures in each major diagnostic category were arranged in a hierarchy from most resource intensive to least resource intensive (Mullin 1983). Some of the first groupings were further subdivided in terms of the presence or absence of malignancy, substantial comorbidity, or substantial complication. Age 70 was found to be the significant point for the older groups and age 17 for the younger groups (Keith 1983). The distinctive groupings were created by a computer program based on the greatest reduction in variance in length of stay. The initial groups were then reviewed by clinicians, and reassignments were made for clinical coherence.

From this process, 383 mutually exclusive groups were developed. The Health Care Financing Administration modified the classifications to fit the kind of cases that typify elderly patients. In the final classification, there were 467 groups of DRGs (Vladeck 1982).

In using the DRG system, patients are assigned to a DRG by a computer program that looks at the principal diagnosis, secondary diagnosis, surgical procedures, age, sex, and discharge status. Trim points (high and low lengths of stay) are applicable to each DRG. Patients falling outside these points are called outliers. This permits separate consideration of the small group of truly different patients who cannot be neatly categorized by a specific DRG.

Payment to hospitals is based on a per diem rate, which is subject to the following adjustments before a final payment rate is determined:

- *Penalties.* Facilities are grouped together with other facilities of like characteristics, as determined by a seed-cluster grouping methodology. Cost ceiling limits are then developed. Any facility that experiences costs in excess of the ceiling will not be reimbursed for those excessive costs.
- *Case mix.* This refers to change in the intensity of services offered, as determined by comparing the rate year to the base year.
- *Volume.* This concerns changes in case load or length of stay, as determined by comparing the rate year to the base year.
- *Service.* This refers to the addition or deletion of patient services.
- *Intensity by payer.* This involves changes in the intensity of services provided by payers.

- *Trend factor revisions*. These are determined by the direction of the economy during the course of the year (Strategic Plan 1984).

The use of DRGs is a relatively straightforward management technique. Inherent in any such grouping or averaging mechanism is some disregard for the characteristics of individual cases. This insensitivity to individual cases is, however, necessary if the technique is to be of value as a management tool. Indeed, if one made the technique sensitive to every variation in case characteristics, it would cease to be useful as a standard by which meaningful comparisons could be made.

PROFESSIONAL STANDARD REVIEW ORGANIZATIONS

Under the DRG system, hospitals must contract with independent Professional Review Organizations (PROs). The PRO quality review system relies on a utilization review coordinator in each institution who is provided with PRO criteria of standards based on the intensity of service being provided in the care of patients, the severity of illnesses, and the dischargeability of patients at any point. The utilization review coordinators are nurses who are given the authority to approve cases in accordance with these criteria (Yoder and Connor 1982).

Under the DRG system, hospital management has an incentive to control costs because it knows in advance how much it will be paid for treating a patient. For example, the cost of treating a heart attack patient might average $1,500 at one hospital and $9,000 at another. Yet, because both hospitals are paid the same DRG rate, the more efficient hospital would be able to retain any surplus over cost in the Medicare payment for that treatment ("Roll the DRGs" 1983).

THE NEW JERSEY EXPERIMENT

In 1978, the New Jersey legislature established the framework for a statewide prospective payment system. In this federally sponsored demonstration, which included 26 New Jersey hospitals, the state set payment levels for all private, as well as public, payers. It thus provided a useful state laboratory to test the application of PPS using DRGs.

At the time, the rate of increase in costs for all New Jersey hospitals was approximately five percent below the rate of increase for all hospitals in the country. In 1980, the 26 hospitals that were paid on the basis of DRGs increased their costs by 13.1 percent, compared with a rate of increase of 13.8 percent for all other hospitals in New Jersey (Iglehart 1982). This is not a statistically significant difference. Interestingly, of the hospitals being paid under the DRG system, those that made money in 1979 increased their costs by an average 14.1

percent in 1980, while those that lost money in 1979 increased their costs by only 10.1 percent in 1980. Thus, though the DRG system does contain incentives for cost cutting, the incentives appear to operate much more strongly in hospitals experiencing financial problems than in those that are not.

The biggest backers of New Jersey's prospective payment system are urban hospitals that have had huge uncompensated care burdens. For these hospitals, the system spreads the cost of the care burden to all payers. Thus, for St. Joseph's Hospital and Medical Center in Paterson, an operating loss of $1 million on 10 percent uncompensated care in 1979 was turned into a $2.1 million profit by 1982 (Diggs 1982). In sum, most administrators and some physicians agree that the overall results have been positive and that New Jersey hospitals continue to provide quality care to their patients.

POTENTIAL PROBLEMS

Because hospitals now receive less money per case under the DRG system, they can still boost reimbursement in two ways—by cost shifting or through "DRG creep."

With the first method, astute hospital administrators may shift costs from patients reimbursed under Medicare to those with private insurance, as they are doing presently with Medicare or Medicaid. This means overpricing services to the people paying billed charges. The increase in revenue from such nonregulated sources is then used to subsidize losses suffered in the provision of care to regulated patients.

A typical procedure employed by hospitals to shift costs is to increase selectively the charges for services rendered to the group of patients to whom costs are to be transferred. That is, the charges for services used most often by the former group are marked up. It is expected that such transfers will be more commonly used in suburban hospitals, which typically have the greatest percentage of revenue derived from private payers, than in inner-city hospitals, which typically have the smallest percentage of such revenue (Thompson 1982).

The second method, "DRG creep," can provide windfall profits for hospitals (Finley 1981). This method involves systematic optimization of the discharge summary. For example, at the University of California at San Francisco, a computer program was written to determine the DRG of each patient as originally reported, and then to redetermine the DRG by reversing the first and second listed diagnoses. By selecting the costlier of these two possible DRGs for each discharge, it was determined that the cost of the case-mix index would have increased by 14 percent during the year. Moreover, although such "DRG creep" increases the number of incorrectly reported principal diagnoses, that increase may go unnoticed in view of the fact that the baseline error rate in the identification of principal diagnoses is as high as 35 percent in many hospitals. Thus, both the cost-shifting and "DRG-creep" methods may end up increasing the cost of health care, or at least keeping it at its present level.

There are other potential problems associated with the establishment of PPS using DRGs. Research involving Medicare and Medicaid data has demonstrated that DRGs and other case-mix grouping procedures do not produce groups that are homogeneous with respect to resource utilization. The reason is that many DRGs are based on a length-of-stay measure. One possible solution is to include a severity-of-illness measure in the grouping. For example, to assess severity properly, a classification system based on five key patient attributes has been developed. The attributes were age of the patient, systems involved in the disease, stage of the disease, complications, and response to therapy. When DRGs were developed experimentally on the basis of severity of illness, using this classification scheme rather than length of stay, the result was more homogenous groupings (Horn 1982).

IMPACT OF THE PROSPECTIVE PAYMENT SYSTEM

The prospective payment system, as represented by the use of DRGs, is an attempt at health care cost reduction and control that affects all aspects of hospital services to patients. The effects are complex, yet observable, and are being felt particularly by physicians, nurses, and medical records personnel and in the areas of medical technology and education. They are also being felt in such areas as clinical nutrition, and even, at least potentially, in the field of nursing home care. In this section, we explore the impact of PPS in each of these areas.

Impact on Physicians

The impact of PPS on physicians is both direct and indirect. That is, the system does not currently set physicians' fees based on DRGs. However, it does establish physicians as the key gatekeepers to health care cost reduction.

The main concern facing physicians as a result of PPS involves the legal and ethical implications of "DRG dumping" ("DRG Dumping" 1985). One might expect that physicians who succumb to pressures to shorten lengths of stay might become more vulnerable to malpractice lawsuits. It has been established that length of stay (LOS) may be shortened without increasing patient complications, but does it increase the potential for lawsuits? Given the high risks of malpractice suits today, the lawsuit potential could be a strong disincentive for physicians to accept PPS.

Besides the lawsuit disincentive, DRGs also represent a threat to physician reimbursement rates. Currently, legislators have been trying to decide how to incorporate physician payments in PPS. The alternatives being considered include (1) direct payment to the physician and hospital; (2) direct payment to the hospital, which then pays the physician part of the fee; or (3) direct payment to the physician, who then pays the hospital out of the total fee. The various alternatives proposed will probably be topics of much controversy in the years ahead. Eventually, however, physicians' fees will find their way into the PPS.

Beyond the above proposals, since physicians are obviously the key to the success of the PPS, perhaps more direct methods to enlist physician cooperation will be considered. If the present hospital-physician relationship does not provide enough incentive for physicians to accept PPS, some hospitals that are on the verge of insolvency because of reduced income might well decide to pinpoint publicly those physicians who are noncooperative, thereby hoping to force them to join the system.

Physicians are already running into problems in gaining sufficient reimbursement for most cost-effective treatments, that is, in cases where the hospital cost is higher, but the total cost of therapy (including posthospital therapy) is lower (Saksena, Greenburg, and Ferguson 1985). These cases point to a need for a mechanism to allow physicians to petition for additional DRGs by which total reimbursement costs can be increased. Indeed, this type of physician involvement in the PPS process might also provide additional incentives for physicians to work actively with the PPS to lower health care costs.

If physicians try to take advantage of DRGs instead of following standard therapies, the result could be increases in elective surgery and higher health care costs (Neuhauser and Pine 1985). This could lead to physician attempts to discredit the system rather than join it. As a possibly viable alternative, they might point to the system of global budgeting used in Canada, which may be more successful than DRGs in reducing hospital costs (Wennberg, McPherson, and Caper 1984).

Clearly, for physicians, PPS is still a highly volatile issue, and their objections may well limit its success. Because they are the focal point of PPS viability, perhaps what is needed is a more carefully structured balance of pressures and incentives to win their support.

Impact on Nurses

Since the PPS is aimed at shortening patient LOS and reducing treatment costs, one of the first places that hospitals might look for support of the system is their nursing staff. Indeed, New Jersey's experience shows that PPS can have a positive effect on the nursing profession (Lee 1984). Nurses in New Jersey have been the least affected by cutbacks as a result of PPS. Elsewhere, however, many nurses have been displaced from hospitals that have been forced to the brink of bankruptcy. In this situation, the nursing profession has decided to play a key role in reducing costs and patient LOS. For example, the following cost-containment suggestions have been made:

- Avoid expensive packaged kits and trays.
- Change from disposable to reusable items, or vice versa, depending on cost.
- Base purchasing decisions on price rather than individual preferences.

Still, nurses today are confronted with the reality that fewer filled hospital beds are supporting fewer nursing jobs. This is testing nurses' ability to adapt to new kinds of positions that are emerging from PPS. Nursing home care services, home health care services, free-standing emergency centers, surgicenters, and other care facilities are all expected to grow as a result of reduced LOS in acute care hospitals. And this is expected to provide a much broader range of career opportunities for nurses. Those nurses who adapt and seize these opportunities will help to ensure nursing's continuing leadership in providing health care.

Within the hospital, the method of nursing care has a direct impact in reducing costs under PPS. For example, it has been shown that the use of primary nursing systems is more cost-effective and patient-acceptable (leading to more rapid recoveries) than team nursing. This means that potential cutbacks will occur at the level of LPNs and aides (not RNs). Though the auxiliary positions of LPNs and aides initially were thought to decrease the need for expensive RNs, the additional RNs needed for primary nursing care (without LPNs and aides) have been shown to reduce total costs.

The outcomes of the combination of DRG requirements and primary nursing care have been shown to be (van Servallen and Mowry 1985):

- shortened hospital stay
- early patient assessment and care planning (including discharge planning)
- efficiency in intervention
- effectiveness in achievement of nursing care outcomes

Thus, overall, it would appear that the PPS and the use of DRGs will both improve nursing care and help nurses achieve greater recognition for their key role in health care.

Impact on Medical Records Personnel

The PPS reimburses hospitals according to the DRG rates that are reported at the end of the patient's stay. If a hospital is to maintain sufficient cash flows, timely and correctly billed DRGs need to be prepared regularly for Medicare. Additionally, PROs are dependent on such records as a basis for identifying any improper uses of DRGs. All of this places new pressure on the medical records function.

According to Ryckman and Sourapas (1985), a well-managed hospital medical records system should include the following:

- receipt of the medical record within 24 hours of discharge
- record assembly within two days of discharge
- review of the record for completeness of information
- coding/abstracting/DRG grouping within three days of discharge
- physician attestation of all Medicare cases within four days of discharge
- correction of any preliminary data (if an on-line abstracting system is used) within 24 hours of data entry and prior to the submission of codes to billing
- submission of codes and other data to the hospital's business office within five days of discharge

These various functions require continuous improvement and updating of medical record procedures. They also require close interdepartmental communication and cooperation. This is especially true in working with physicians to ensure correct DRG coding so that the hospital does not lose any more money than absolutely necessary through the use of DRGs.

To deal with these various requirements, a six-step strategy has been suggested (Ryckman and Sourapas 1985):

1. Conduct a medical records operational review.
2. Develop a PPS action plan based on the findings of the operational review.
3. Identify a focal point (PPS steering committee) for monitoring follow-up responsibilities in the action plan.
4. Create a single point of administrative responsibility for key PPS-related functions.
5. Develop a PPS key-factor reporting system.
6. Conduct tailored training sessions.

Such a strategy is particularly appropriate in view of the fact that medical records have become the hospital's key to survival under PPS. With such procedures, the entire medical records staff can be mobilized to implement the cooperation and controls necessary to survive and prosper under PPS.

Impact on Medical Technology and Education

The impact of PPS on further innovation in technology and training is another major concern. In the area of education, even though teaching hospitals are scheduled to receive additional reimbursement for residents in training, the PPS cost-cutting hatchet may well cut out many of these teaching opportunities (Greenberg 1985). Even short of removing these residencies, there is concern that cost-cutting requirements will erode the quality of learning available.

In the area of technology, in radiology and other laboratories, there are PPS-induced pressures to operate more efficiently and to coordinate more effectively with physicians. Across the board, the need for new and better cost-cutting technology is apparent (Alessi 1985). In some cases, the requisite equipment may not be available due to a lack of capital. In other cases, equipment that was acceptable because it could improve the quality of patient care now must prove its cost-effectiveness as well. Overall, the shrinking capital base for hospitals throughout the country may exacerbate the situation. All of this points to an increased need for marketing to match available technology with those hospitals that will utilize it best, that is, in terms of optimal application and cost-effectiveness.

In fact, there appears to be no immediate negative impact by the DRG system on the availability and development of new innovations and technologies in health care. Areas of recent innovative developments in technology include laser surgery, nutritional support, endoscopy, immunodiagnostic procedures, digital subtraction angiography, angioplasty, enzyme therapy, lab equipment, computerized drug formularies, dictation devices, ultrasound, wound closure devices and catheters, implantable infusion pumps, and x-ray film systems (Kuntz 1984).

Still, some believe that DRGs will eventually decimate discretionary clinical research funding in hospitals. For its part, the government maintains that clinical research should be funded by both the government and the manufacturers of new technology. Indeed, Congress has given authority to the prospective payment assessment commission and the secretary of HHS to authorize clinical trials funded under the Medicare trust funds. At the same time, however, the government has reduced its support for research and development in health care from nearly 3.0 percent to 1.5 percent of total U.S. health care spending over the past two decades (Rabkin 1984). Although industry has shown some selected support for medical R&D, it is not enough to fill the gap. Clearly, the negative impact of reduced outlays for technology must be addressed quickly by health care policy makers.

Impact on Clinical Nutrition Services

Nutrition services can affect length of stay by reducing the chance of morbidity and mortality in the hospitalized patient (Smith and Smith 1985). And, since reduced length of stay under the prospective payment system provides financial benefits to the hospital, the use of nutrition services to achieve lower average lengths of stays is particularly desirable.

However, the literature suggests that programs that address problems of pro-tein-calorie malnutrition (PCM) among hospital patients should be used cau-tiously. Despite a strong correlation between PCM and added average length of stay, it is impossible to isolate PCM as the sole cause of the added LOS. Several studies indicate that the nutritional status of most patients worsened after lengths of stay exceeding two weeks. Indeed, it has been found that 30 percent or more of hospitalized patients have PCM. And, although improved outcomes, as meas-ured by reduced average lengths of stay and reduced nosocomial infection rates, have resulted by administering nutritional support, the full potential of such support has not yet been realized.

Yet, Smith and Smith (1985) caution that reducing average lengths of stay will not necessarily produce proportionate savings to the hospital, due to the high intensity of care and more active application of nutrition therapy during the early stage of hospitalization. However, even small savings in reduced hospi-talization are important in producing a surplus or profit for the hospital.

As we have seen, reducing average lengths of stay will provide financial benefits for a hospital if it is reimbursed on a prospective payment system based on diagnostic related groups. It will also benefit hospitals that have negotiated per capita fees, as commonly used for patients from health maintenance and preferred provider organizations. However, reducing average lengths of stay for fee-for-service patients or patients reimbursed by retrospective systems would actually reduce revenues for the hospital. Of course, if a hospital prides itself on excellent care and if active nutrition therapy improves the quality of that care, as well as reduces LOS, it should be practiced regardless of the financial outcome.

Impact on Nursing Home Care

The use of a prospective payment system for skilled nursing facility care has been proposed by Hazelbaker and Zazwiecki (1985). In their proposal, which is restricted to Medicare patients in skilled nursing facilities (SNFs), they identify five basic and necessary guiding principles:

1. recognition of patient needs
2. grouping of services where appropriate
3. monitoring of separately reimbursed services
4. inclusion of profit and capital costs
5. regional variation

With respect to the recognition of patient needs, they propose that a basic reimbursement rate be provided for each of a limited number of classes of patients. The classes should be determined in terms of the number and types of activity of daily living (ADL) dependencies or, as a proxy for that, in terms of the hospital DRG available for all Medicare SNF patients.

Hazelbaker and Zazwiecki propose two types of reimbursement: One is based on the ADL class, the other is based on the special services required by patients (not necessarily all the patients) in a given class. Examples of special services would be tube feeding, IV care, physical therapy, occupational therapy, and speech therapy. These services would be reimbursed on the basis of a unit of service. To ensure that the special services reimbursement feature would not be misused, standards would need to be developed to monitor the special services.

Profit and capital costs would be folded into the basic ADL-based rate. Ideally, this reimbursement segment should be charge-based instead of cost-based, since the latter would require extensive monitoring of costs.

Since wages and salaries differ significantly by region, specific rates for each patient class and for the special services would be set for each region. These rates would take into account geographic regions and urban/rural locations; and no distinction would be made in terms of hospital ownership, size, or affiliation. Only valid differences due to regional price variations, factor prices, and the patient needs of the facility would be recognized for reimbursement purposes.

The objective of the Hazelbaker and Zazwiecki proposal is to encourage greater Medicare program participation by nursing homes and simultaneously to help constrain the growth in aggregate Medicare health program expenditures. As a result of increased nursing home participation in Medicare's SNF program, fewer patients would need to remain in acute care hospital settings because of the unavailability of nursing home beds. The proposed system would, in effect, provide incentives for nursing homes to accept post-acute care hospital patients, thus providing better care for the patient and lowering the cost to Medicare.

FUTURE IMPLICATIONS

Basic Trends

The use of DRGs becomes significant for management when the DRGs are linked with other variables, such as cost per case, and the information provided is acted upon. The result is case-oriented management. The information provided by linking DRGs with other variables is particularly significant in that it creates a bridge between the relatively isolated realm of medical practice and other relatively well-analyzed realms, such as financial management. DRGs provide a common language and statistical link between the administration and the medical staff.

Today, home care executives have only indirect, if any, authority over the medical staffs at their institutions. Payment by DRGs requires responsibility for medical practice even in the absence of such authority. The first step in coping with the new environment thus should be the installation of a costing system. Once a hospital knows its costs, it can start weeding out its money-losing services. It can also use its cost data to monitor medical personnel. By setting up profiles of physicians on the staff, hospitals can judge which physicians are incurring excessive costs in the way they practice and thus constitute a liability.

In the past, since return of expended capital was virtually assured, the risk of any venture was minimal. Under the DRG system, however, the consequences of good or bad decisions will be felt. Thus, decisions to keep or drop certain ventures should be made consciously, with full knowledge of their impact. Reports on revenue for individual DRGs, costs for individual DRGs, physician-specific profiles across DRGs, DRGs associated with particular services, particular equipment or particular demographic groups, and other composite DRG-based variables can provide the information necessary to make such decisions intelligently.

Consumers, physicians, and health care executives each exercise control over a portion of the health care system, and thus over each other. Consumers choose the provider or plan they desire. Physicians evaluate the medical needs and treat them in an effective and efficient manner. Health care executives manage institutions. These various functions overlap and interact.

Traditionally, physicians have had economic incentives to increase hospital use, with generous utilization of costly high technology. Also patients have been cost-insensitive, seeking the seemingly highest quality care, which is often the most expensive care. Thus, there is an urgent need to involve physicians in planning for this new era of limits and cost efficiency, and a correspondingly urgent need to make patients more sensitive to medical care costs in order to discourage inappropriate utilization.

In sum, the prospective payment system for Medicare based upon DRG case-mix classifications represents only one step toward an ultimate solution. To ensure major advances in providing cost-efficient care, a major restructuring of the nation's medical care system may ultimately be required.

Keys to the Future

The key to the future of the PPS health care policy will be its impact on the quality of care. In a Medicaid study of the use of PPS for long-term care, it has been shown that neither the quality nor the availability of care was impaired by the use of DRGs (Buchanan 1983). In fact, use of PPS made nursing home care more accessible to recipients. If this effect can be achieved in other health care areas, the most desirable course of our health care policy will become better understood: to apply prospective reimbursement to all providers of health care.

Indeed, it appears that third party payers have already seen the PPS as the wave of the future. A study of the impact of DRGs on Medicare, Medicaid, and Blue Cross plans suggests that, if all third party payers adopt DRGs, there would be no room for negotiation of payment rates. Although the PPS adjusts for hospital case mix differences and third party payers can be distinguished by case mix, future policy may have to address third party payer mix problems that may arise indirectly from the DRG system for Medicare. Thus the PPS provides incentives for all third party payers to adopt DRGs and prospective payment while not safeguarding hospitals from potential third party payer mix problems. Just how important this impact will be, will have to be determined over time. The finger on this pulse will have to be the PRO's recognizing such a negative trend while policy changes are still possible.

In the final analysis, a definitive assessment of the benefits of the PPS will have to be made. At present, some argue that the potential negatives of DRGs outweigh the potential positives (reducing health care costs) (Mariner 1984); yet they do not seem to have a better alternative.

In fact, it is not yet clear how well the system will serve in the long run. In particular, treatment case mixes and payer mixes may play an important role in determining its ultimate viability. The key here appears to be the peer review organization (PRO). As controller and monitor of PPS health care providers, the PRO must serve as the watchdog over system abuses, as well as the provider of data to assess the positive or negative effects on health care quality.

CONCLUSION

The PPS has the opportunity to establish standardized high quality care that is more accessible to the public and at a lower total cost. Yet, despite these potential positive impacts, concerns about its ultimate effect on our national health care system persist and will have to be addressed by policy makers.

Clearly, the commitment to high quality care through research and development must be continued, with more support from government. Without such commitment and support (especially in the area of clinical research), we may see the eventual end of significant research breakthroughs.

In the shorter term, two areas must be monitored carefully. First, the lack of positive physician incentives may create barriers to PPS acceptance and efficient use. Thus, policy concerning physician incentives must be guided by studies of ways to achieve optimum levels of physician cooperation in the utilization of the PPS.

Also, peer review organizations must be closely monitored to determine their effectiveness in deterring abuses of the PPS and in tracking PPS procedures and relevant trends throughout the nation's health care system. Finally, policy makers must be ready to make changes in the PPS as they become necessary to ensure continued quality care and reduced costs.

Even at this point, however, it appears that prospective reimbursement will prove useful in creating business efficiencies in health care and providing a wider variety of quality products (services) to benefit society. The resulting enhanced for-profit competition in health care and improved marketing arrangements to meet patients' needs can only serve to further lower health care costs.

Overall, the system of cost control and competitive incentives should add to the public good. Though the system needs additional means of providing economic incentives to physicians, it has already shown its potential, even in the absence of such incentives (for example, in New Jersey). Clearly, however, to minimize the system's vulnerability over the short term, ways must be devised to include physicians more directly in the PPS payment scheme.

PPS began with the objective of controlling Medicare spending, and it will probably achieve that goal. However, it has also opened up a Pandora's box of health care issues that will have to be resolved over the next decade or two. Whatever the final outcome, the U.S. clearly has embarked on a new health care enterprise that will have profound and lasting effects.

REFERENCES

Alessi, A.A. "The Impact of DRGs on Medical Devices: A Commentary." *Bulletin of the American College of Surgeons* (May 1985):131.

Buchanan, R.J. "Medical Cost Containment: Prospective Reimbursement for Long Term Care." *Inquiry* (Winter 1983):334–342.

Diggs, W.W. "Lack of Intensity Factor in DRGs." *Hospitals*, 16 May 1982, 54.

"DRG Dumping," *Modern Healthcare*, 15 March 1985, 5.

Finley, J.E. "DRG Creep." *New England Journal of Medicine* (15 October 1981):961–962.

Greenberg, L.A. "Diagnosis Related Groups. Their Potential Impact on Pediatric Resident Training." *American Journal of Diseases of Children* (May 1985):524–526.

Hazelbaker, R.E., and Zazwiecki, T. "Medicare SNF Prospective Reimbursement: Paradox or Panacea." *American Health Care Association* (January 1985):10–14.

Horn, S. "Severity of Illness Applied to DRGs." *Hospitals*, 16 December 1982, 37.

Iglehart, J.K. "New Jersey's Experiment with DRGs." *New England Journal of Medicine* (23 December 1982):1655–1660.

Keith, S.N. "Prospective Payment." *Journal of the National Medical Association*, June 1983, 612–614.

Kuntz, E.F. "Task Forces Scour Diagnosis, Therapy Methods for Cost-Cutting Procedures." *Modern Healthcare*, 15 February 1984, 138–142.

Lee, A.A. "How DRGs Will Affect Your Hospital—and You." *RN* (May 1984):71–81.

Mariner, W.K. "Diagnosis Related Groups: Evading Social Responsibility?" *Law, Medicine and Health Care* (December 1984):243–244.

Mullin, R.L. "DRGs: A Brief Description." *Connecticut Medicine*, May 1983, 281–282.

Neuhauser, D., and Pine, R. "DRGs and Elective Surgery—What's Best for the Provider? What's Best for the Patient?" *Medical Care* (February 1985):183–187.

Rabkin, M.T. "Will the DRG Decimate Clinical Research?" *Clinical Research* (September 1984):341–344.

"Roll the DRGs." *Forbes*, 26 September 1983, 36–38.

Ryckman, D., and Sourapas, J.K. "Medical Records: A New Challenge Under Prospective DRG Reimbursements." *Topics in Health Care Financing* (Spring 1985):47–58.

Saksena, S.; Greenburg, E.; and Ferguson, D. "Prospective Reimbursement for State of the Art Medical Practice: The Case for Invasive Electrophysiologic Evaluation." *American Journal of Cardiology* (1985):963–967.

Smith, P.E., and Smith, A.E. "Can Nutrition Services Affect Hospital Costs under PPS?" *Healthcare Financial Management* (July 1985):18–25.

Strategic Plan. Trend factor revisions based on a strategic plan developed for a local hospital. Buffalo, N.Y.: School of Management, State University of New York, August 1984.

Thompson, J.D. "One Application of the DRG Planning Model." *Topics in Health Care Finance*, Summer 1982, 51–65.

van Servallen, M.G., and Mowry, M.M. "DRGs and Primary Nursing: Are They Compatible?" *Journal of Nursing Administration* (April 1985):32–36.

Vladeck, B.C. "Diagnosis Related Groups." *Journal of the American Medical Association* (25 June 1982):3314–3315.

Wennberg, J.E.; McPherson, K.; and Caper, P. "Will Payment Based on Diagnosis Related Groups Control Hospital Costs?" *New England Journal of Medicine*, 2 August 1984, 295–300.

Yoder, J.L., and Connor, R.A. "DRGs and Quality Assurance." *Topics in Health Care Finance*, Summer 1982, 29–42.

Chapter 21

Supplementary Health Insurance

INTRODUCTION

On the average, and in the aggregate, Americans spend over 11 percent of the gross national product on health care. However, older Americans spend about 30 percent of their income for health care services. These expenditures impose a considerable burden on those elderly who are trying to make ends meet on a retirement income. When Medicare was established in the 1960s it covered most of the health care costs of the elderly. Since then, a considerable number of restrictions have been placed on what Medicare covers. As a result, the elderly incur considerable out-of-pocket expenses for their health maintenance.

In response to this situation, an entire industry has been developed to provide supplementary health insurance to the elderly. This type of insurance covers all or part of the portion that is not covered by Medicare. This chapter reviews the pitfalls and problems with this kind of health insurance.

In addition, another kind of organization has entered the supplementary health insurance market for the elderly. That organization is the health maintenance organization (HMO). The HMO not only provides supplementary health insurance but also delivers a complete range of health care services, including those covered, and paid for, by Medicare. HMOs are discussed in the next chapter.

MEDIGAP PROTECTION

Medicare and Medicaid Coverage

The Medicare and Medicaid programs have helped senior citizens carry some of their health care cost burden. Government expenditures for these two programs have increased from $9.9 billion in 1970 to about $100 billion presently. Taken together, the two programs account for about two-thirds of average per capita health care costs incurred by the elderly.

However, these are only average figures. Not all older individuals are eligible for both Medicare and Medicaid. Medicaid, which is essentially a welfare program, is available only to about one out of five senior citizens—those whose incomes fall below the poverty line. Individuals with incomes over the poverty level are generally not eligible for Medicaid. For those not covered by Medicaid, Medicare covers only about 38 percent of the average senior's yearly health care bill (Cafferata 1984).

Medicaid is generally regarded as a welfare program by most of the population. As a result, acceptance of Medicaid is a traumatic occasion for the vast majority of senior citizens who have grown up believing that one must care for oneself and not be dependent on government handouts. Interestingly, there is virtually no trauma associated with having to accept government help through Medicare. Medicare reimbursement, with all its limitations, is considered to be a civil right.

Supplemental Coverage

In order to offset the ever-escalating cost of health care, senior citizens are buying private health insurance policies to supplement their Medicare coverage. Two-thirds of all senior citizens have at least one such policy. These policies are often called "wraparound" (around Medicare) health insurance or "medigap" insurance. Some senior citizens acquire more than one such policy and often have as many as four or five. As of 1978, there were an estimated 19 million private health insurance policies in effect for the elderly (U.S. Congress, House 1978).

In 1978, seniors paid an average of $200 in annual premiums for each policy— a total expenditure of $3.8 billion. The policyholders received an estimated $1.3 billion in benefits, which amounts to less than 35 percent of premiums collected. Eight years later, in 1986, 22.4 million elderly citizens spent an estimated $6.2 billion on "medigap" policies to supplement their federally funded Medicare coverage (Spears 1987).

The low return on these health insurance policies is due in part to the fact that many elderly hold multiple policies in order to maximize protection. Yet, when they become sick, they can usually make a claim on only one policy. The real beneficiaries of this wasteful practice are the private insurance companies who reimburse claims on one policy at most. Private health insurance constitutes about 50 percent of the elderly health insurance market. Blue Cross, Blue Shield, and HMOs cover the balance. The wasteful practices described above are not attributable to the latter organizations. It is rather in the private sector, involving the private insurance companies that sell to individuals, that most problems have occurred.

LEGISLATION AND REGULATION*

A congressional investigation concluded that the root of the problem lies in the limited coverage that Medicare provides and in the inability of many older Americans to understand what in fact Medicare covers. This conclusion was reached in a study by the 1978 House Select Committee on Aging. The result was the drafting of legislation to remedy the situation.

The Baucus Amendment

Public Law 96–265, enacted in 1980, added Section 1882 to the Social Security Act. The section is also known as the Baucus amendment, named after Senator Max Baucus, its chief sponsor in the Senate. The amendment was aimed directly at correcting the many abuses in the sale of medigap insurance, as documented in hearings before the House Select Committee on Aging in 1978 (U.S. Congress, General Accounting Office 1986).

The Baucus amendment defines minimum standards for supplementary health insurance policies that must be met before insurance companies can market them as medigap policies. The standards are based on a model regulation approved by the National Association of Insurance Commissioners in 1979 and incorporated in Section 1882 by reference. The standards require:

- that medigap policies cover Medicare's coinsurance amounts within certain limits
- that purchasers of a medigap policy have a cancellation period during which they may return it for cancellation and receive a full refund of any premium paid
- that many of the terms used in policies be standardized
- that the period for which coverage may be denied for pre-existing conditions be limited
- that cancellation and termination clauses be prominently displayed

*Most of the information in this section has been drawn from *Medigap Insurance*, Report to the Subcommittee on Health, Committee on Ways and Means, House of Representatives, U.S. General Accounting Office, October 1986.

The above standards apply only to medigap policies sold to persons who qualify for Medicare by reason of age.

In addition, the Baucus amendment established loss ratio targets for medigap policies to determine the percentage of insurance premiums to be returned to policyholders in the form of benefits. The loss ratio targets were to be set so that medigap policies would have to pay benefits equal to at least 60 percent of the earned premiums for individual policies and to 75 percent for group policies.

Unfortunately, the regulations contained in the Baucus amendment are difficult to enforce because insurance regulations have historically been a state responsibility. As a result, the amendment relies primarily on the states to enforce its medigap policy standards, with the federal government's role that of determining whether the state laws and regulations do in fact meet the standards. In states that do not have the required laws and regulations, the federal government certifies medigap policies on a voluntary basis. When the Baucus amendment was enacted, only nine states had rules and regulations specifically governing medigap policies. Clearly, the above procedures do not by themselves provide much clout to force insurers to abide by the Baucus amendment standards.

The Baucus amendment also established the Supplemental Health Insurance Panel (SHIP), which has as members the secretary of Health and Human Services (HHS) and four state insurance commissioners or superintendents appointed by the president. The panel is responsible for reviewing and certifying each state's insurance regulatory program in light of the Baucus amendment. Its certification procedures are based on standards that are at least as stringent as those contained in the National Association of Insurance Commissioners (NAIC) model regulation and that meet the loss ratio requirements of the Baucus amendment. In states that do not obtain panel certification, insurers may submit their policies to the secretary of HHS for approval. As of September 1986, six years after the Baucus amendment was passed, only two insurers had submitted policies to the secretary of HHS and neither had been approved. The paucity of policies submitted appears to be another indication of the difficulty of enforcing Baucus amendment standards.

Still, by 1981 at least the framework for certification of state programs was beginning to emerge. By November 1981, the SHIP had approved ten state regulatory programs and identified other states that needed to enact legislation or adopt regulations to bring their programs into compliance with the minimum standards of the Baucus amendment. By July 1982, 30 states had been certified. As of September 1986, SHIP had certified 46 states, plus the District of Columbia and Puerto Rico; at that point, 90 percent of the U.S. population resided in jurisdictions with insurance regulatory programs that met Baucus amendment standards.

Yet, as noted earlier, enforcement of a federal law that depends on the states to ensure compliance is always problematical. Thus, as a backup for SHIP, the

Health Care Financing Administration (HCFA), as administrator of the Medicare program, has established a procedure to obtain annual updates from the states on their continued compliance with the Baucus amendment. The procedure requires a state official responsible for administering the state's insurance regulatory program to sign an attestation that no substantive changes have been made in the state's regulatory program.

State Regulation of the Insurance Industry

In the McCarran-Ferguson Act, Public Law 79–15, enacted in 1945, Congress expressed its intention that the states continue to have primary responsibility for regulating the insurance industry. Thus, within each state, insurance regulation is usually accomplished through the office of the state insurance commissioner or through the office of the state insurance superintendent. The state offices of insurance are linked through the National Association of Insurance Commissioners (NAIC) for the purpose of exchanging information on insurance companies and developing model legislative acts for adoption by the respective states.

State insurance regulatory processes and procedures generally include, as a basis for approval of policies, a review of such features as policy readability and standardization of policy terms, premium rate control, and monitoring of unfair or deceptive acts through unfair trade practice regulations. Except for their premium rates, which are not directly regulated, private health and accident insurance policies, including medigap policies, are regulated through this type of mechanism. Most states also require premium rates for health and accident policies to be filed with the state, and they can disapprove any policy whose benefits are not considered reasonable in relation to the premiums charged.

A reasonable relationship between premiums and benefits paid is provided by the loss ratio benchmark. Loss ratio is defined as the paid claims divided by premiums collected, stated as a percentage. For example, a group policy collecting $1 million of premiums and incurring claims of $600,000 has a loss ratio of 60 percent.

Minimum Standards

The minimum standards imposed by the Baucus amendment are based on the model regulations prepared by the National Association of Insurance Commissioners (NAIC). These regulations require the following (many medigap policies actually exceed these minimum requirements):

• Conditions for renewability must be stated on the first page of the policy.

- If a policy is sold as "noncancellable" or "guaranteed renewable," it must, if premiums continue to be paid, provide coverage for the insured's spouse after coverage of the insured ends.
- A policy that is terminated must continue coverage for illnesses or accidents that occurred while the policy was in force, except that such coverage may be predicated on the continuous total disability of the insured, limited to the duration of a stated benefit period, or limited to the payment of maximum benefits.
- The purchaser must be allowed a "free look" period during which the purchaser may return the policy and get a full refund of any premium paid; this period must be at least 10 days for policies sold through agents and at least 30 days for policies sold through the mail.
- The coverage in the policy must automatically change as Medicare's deductibles and coinsurance requirements change.
- The policy may not define pre-existing conditions more restrictively than conditions that were diagnosed or treated within six months prior to the effective date of the policy, and benefits may be denied for pre-existing conditions for no more than six months from the effective date of the policy.
- The policy must cover treatment for accidents and illnesses equally.
- Terms used in the policy—such as physician, hospital, sickness, and accident—may be defined within certain limits, and Medicare must also be defined in the policy.
- The policy must cover all of the Medicare Part A inpatient coinsurance for the 61st through the 90th day in the hospital, and for the 91st through the 150th day while the beneficiary uses lifetime reserve days, plus 90 percent of covered hospital inpatient expenses for a lifetime maximum of up to 365 days after the insured has exhausted Medicare benefits.
- The policy must cover the Medicare Part B coinsurance, but this may be subject to a deductible of $200 and a maximum benefit of $5,000 per year.
- The policy must cover the Parts A and B blood deductibles.
- The policy must have an outline of coverage, showing what Medicare covers, what the beneficiary is responsible for, and what the supplemental policy covers.

In addition, the NAIC standards include the requirement that insurers give beneficiaries a buyer's guide. This guide must be given to beneficiaries at the time they apply for insurance or, in the case of policies sold through the mail, at the time the policy is delivered to the beneficiary. HCFA and NAIC have jointly developed a guide that describes Medicare, medigap, and other health insurance plans (Social Security Administration 1987).

Table 21-1 shows hospital and physician benefit coverage for payments by Medicare, the amount the beneficiary is responsible for, and the minimum cov-

Table 21-1 Schedule of Benefit Coverage Provided by Medicare and by Medigap Minimum Requirements

Service	Benefit	Medicare Pays[a]	Beneficiary Is Responsible for[a]	Minimum Requirement for Medigap Insurance
Medicare (Part A)—Hospital insurance-covered services per benefit period:				
Hospitalization—semiprivate room and board, general nursing and miscellaneous hospital services, and supplies	First 60 days	All but the $520 deductible	$520	None
	61st to 90th day	All but the $130 a day coinsurance	$130 a day	$130 a day
	91st to 150th day	All but the $260 coinsurance	$260 a day	$260 a day
	Beyond 150 days	Nothing	All charges	90 percent of covered charges up to 365 days
Posthospital skilled nursing facility care—in a facility approved by Medicare if the beneficiary has been in a hospital for at least 3 days and enters the facility within 30 days after hospital discharge	First 20 days	100 percent of costs	Nothing	None
	Additional 80 days	All but $65 a day	$65 a day	None
	Beyond 100 days	Nothing	All charges	None
Home health care	Unlimited visits as medically necessary	Full cost	Nothing	None
Hospice care	Two 9-day periods and one 30-day period	All but limited coinsurance for outpatient drugs and inpatient respite care	Limited cost sharing for outpatient drugs and inpatient respite care	None
Blood	Blood	All but first 3 pints	First 3 pints	First 3 pints

continues

Medicare (Part B)—Medical insurance-covered services per calendar year:

	Medicare pays for health services in or out of the hospital		All Medicare-approved charges not covered by Medicare; benefit may be limited to $5,000 per year and may be subject to an annual deductible of $200
Health expenses—physicians' services, outpatient health services and supplies, physical and speech therapy, ambulance, etc.	80 percent of Medicare-approved amount (after $75 deductible)	$75 deductible plus 20 percent of balance of approved amount (plus any charge above approved amount on unassigned claims)	
Home health care	Full cost	Nothing	None
Outpatient hospital	80 percent of approved amount (after $75 deductible)	$75 deductible plus 20 percent of balance of approved amount (assignment is required)	Same as for health expenses
Blood	80 percent of approved amount (after $75 deductible and starting with 4th pint)	First 3 pints plus 20 percent of approved amount (after $75 deductible)	Same as for health expenses, plus first 3 pints
Clinical laboratory	Full cost (on assigned claims)	Nothing on assigned claims	Same as for health expenses (on unassigned claims)
Medicare		Difference between payment and charges on unassigned claims	

aBased on Medicare deductible and coinsurance amounts for calendar year 1987.

Source: Medigap Insurance, Report to the Subcommittee on Health, Committee on Ways and Means, House of Representatives, U.S. General Accounting Office, October 1986.

erage required of medigap insurance. As can be seen, medigap policies are not required to pay some items, such as the Medicare Part A deductible. Also under Medicare Part B, a medigap policy may have its own deductible of up to $200 per year and may limit benefits to $5,000 per year.

Thus, a person who is shopping for medigap insurance should be aware of the coverage options available. The buyer's guide jointly published by HCFA and NAIC includes a table similar to Table 21-1 and offers other helpful hints for Medicare beneficiaries. Each medigap policy must contain an outline of its coverage, in a format similar to that in Table 21-1.

The Loss Ratio in Medigap Insurance

As noted earlier, the Baucus amendment requires a minimum loss ratio of 60 percent for policies sold to individuals and a 75 percent loss ratio for group policies. The loss ratio is a useful measure of the extent to which the insured is obtaining good value for premiums paid. Since the large Blue Cross and Blue Shield plans usually have loss ratios of about 90 percent, the minimum standards imposed by the Baucus amendment appear to be quite generous to health insurance companies. If anything, one could claim that they are too generous and that they do not provide enough protection to the usually uninformed buyer of medigap health insurance.

Unfortunately, as we have seen, even these generous minimum loss ratios are subject to little or no enforcement by the states. The Department of Health and Human Services (HHS) has interpreted the Baucus amendment as not requiring state insurance regulators to monitor the actual loss ratios of medigap policies. Thus, a study by the General Accounting Office found that, of 394 individual and 4 group medigap policies, the loss ratios of 254 of them were below target. The study was based on 1984 data and included 92 commercial firms and 13 Blue Cross and Blue Shield plans. Generally, the larger-volume policies satisfied the Baucus amendment targets, while the smaller-volume policies did not. Table 21-2 shows the results of the GAO study. The total earned premiums in 1984 for the 144 policies whose loss ratios were above the loss ratio target amounted to $1.4 billion, while total earned premiums for the 254 policies whose loss ratios were below the target amounted to $650 million (U.S. Congress, General Accounting Office 1986).

CONCLUSION

Medicare was originally designed as a national health insurance program for the elderly. Financed by employers, by employee contributions, and by the

Table 21-2 Loss Ratio Experience of Selected Medigap Insurance Policies, 1984

Range of Premium	Type	Insurer	Above Target	Below Target
Over $100 million	Individual	Commercial	1	0
	Individual	Blue Cross and Blue Shield	3	0
$50–$99 million	Individual	Commercial	1	2
	Individual	Blue Cross and Blue Shield	2	0
$1–$49 million	Individual	Commercial	39	89
	Individual	Blue Cross and Blue Shield	10	2
	Group	Not available	1	1
Under $1 million	Individual	Commercial	86	158
	Individual	Blue Cross and Blue Shield	1	0
	Group	Group	0	2
Total			144	254

Source: Medigap Insurance, Report to the Subcommittee on Health, Committee on Ways and Means, House of Representatives, U.S. General Accounting Office, October 1986.

government, it was intended to enable Americans to draw on this "trust" for their health care costs when they reached age 65. In its early period of operation, Medicare paid about 50 percent of the average senior's total health care bill; but, by 1978, it paid only about 38 percent. Contributing to this reduced coverage was the decreasing number of physicians who agreed to accept what Medicare pays as full and final payment for services rendered. In 1978, only 50 percent of physicians were accepting Medicare reimbursements as full payments (as compared with 66 percent in the early days of Medicare). Physicians instead chose to charge the patient a greater amount, and then let the patient worry about being reimbursed from Medicare. Any extra charges over and above what Medicare recognized as a reasonable charge had to be paid by the patient.

To counteract this erosion of health care coverage and accessibility, a wide variety of wraparound or medigap health insurance policies emerged. Prior to the passing of the Baucus amendment in 1980, these medigap policies varied widely in coverage, price, and fairness. Since the Baucus amendment was passed, and with the increasing awareness of the nature of these policies, on the part of both insurance regulators and the public, the quality of medigap policies has increased substantially. Most of them protect the elderly from the costs of health care in excess of that being covered by Medicare. As a result, in many cases, the elderly's worries of being able to afford needed health care have been eased considerably, and medigap policies have come to play an increasingly important role in providing adequate health insurance coverage for this part of our population.

REFERENCES

Cafferata, G.L. *Private Health Insurance Coverage of the Medicare Population.* Data Preview 18, NCHSR National Health Care Expenditures Study. Washington, D.C.: U.S. Department of Health and Human Services, 1984.

Social Security Administration. *Guide to Health Insurance for People with Medicare.* Washington, D.C.: U.S. Department of Health and Human Services, 1987.

Spears, G. "Study Faults Insurance Policies Intended to Supplement Medicare." *Buffalo News,* 8 November 1987.

U.S. Congress. General Accounting Office. *Medigap Insurance.* Report to the Subcommittee on Health of the Committee on Ways and Means, House of Representatives. Washington, D.C.: U.S. GPO, 1986.

U.S. Congress. House. Select Committee on Aging. *Abuses in the Sale of Health Insurance to the Elderly in Supplementation of Medicare: A National Scandal.* A Staff Study by the Select Committee on Aging. 95th Cong., 2d sess., 1978.

Chapter 22

Health Maintenance Organizations

INTRODUCTION

The lack of knowledge about health maintenance organizations (HMOs) among the elderly population is probably the main reason why participation by the elderly in HMOs is still limited.

HMOs were established to provide improved access to health care and cost containment and competition in the health care field. When the development of HMOs was being encouraged and funded by the federal government in the 1970s, the focus was largely on employed workers and their families. In fact, the only people who could enroll in HMOs then were employees of corporations or other large organizations who joined the HMO as a group. Virtually all newly developed HMOs excluded individuals as enrollees because they were considered, and actually were, too risky in terms of the financial survival of the new HMOs. As a result, the idea of the elderly joining HMOs was not even considered. The only people in both Medicare and HMOs at that time were people who were already in HMOs prior to their eligibility for Medicare.

The other barrier to Medicare enrollees joining HMOs was the refusal of the Health Care Financing Administration (HCFA), the administrator of Medicare, to establish contractual agreements with HMOs whereby HMOs would be reimbursed on a capitation basis for services rendered to Medicare enrollees. This barrier was not lifted until the mid-1980s; HMO membership is now available to Medicare enrollees.

There are basically two types of HMOs. The traditional type is called the closed panel HMO. This type of HMO provides ambulatory care through relatively large medical centers or clinics where a comprehensive range of services is provided. It therefore provides a form of one-stop health care. Most medical centers have complete laboratory, x-ray, pharmacy, optical, specialist, and other ancillary services, so that usually there is no need for referral to other locations. The closed panel HMO is therefore ideal for someone who is dependent on others

215

for transportation. However, because of the considerable investment required to build and organize ambulatory medical centers, the growth of the closed panel HMO has been rather limited.

A second type of HMO is the open panel or independent practitioner association (IPA) HMO. The open panel HMO contracts with associations of individual physicians to provide medical services to its members on a tightly controlled fee-for-service basis. The physicians practice in their own offices and also continue to provide fee-for-service medical care to non-HMO patients. The growth of the open panel HMO has been much more rapid than that of the closed panel HMO because no investment for new medical centers is required. From the Medicare enrollee point of view, services are the same in both types of HMOs. However, more travel may be required by enrollees in open panel HMOs because individual practitioners usually do not provide the wide array of services that are available in a closed panel ambulatory care medical center.

BACKGROUND

Definitions

How does the HMO differ from traditional health insurance? The HMO has been described as "an organization which accepts contractual responsibility to assure the delivery of a stated range of health services, including at least ambulatory and in-hospital care to a voluntarily enrolled population in exchange for an advance capitation payment where the organization assumes at least part of the financial risk or shares in the surplus associated with the delivery of medical services" (McNeil and Schlenker 1975, 195).

In contrast, traditional health insurance is dominated by an "exclusion mentality." That is, certain types of services are excluded, and many other services are usually restricted in the treatment of illnesses. For example, preventive care and routine medical check-ups are seldom included, and the individual must actually be ill before medical assistance can be reimbursed.

Another, more subtle, difference between HMO and traditional health care insurance is in the delivery of health care. The HMO delivers health care for a prepaid fee, whereas traditional health insurance reimburses only if a claim is filed by or on behalf of the insured individual.

Both HMOs and health insurers would benefit if the public were better informed about healthful living. Yet, the HMO, by promoting preventive health maintenance, has been the more active of the two in educating its membership about the benefits of proper nutrition and the dangers of alcohol, tobacco, and stressful living.

History

Organizations that provide a broad range of medical services for a prepaid monthly fee have in fact been around for a long time. Around the turn of the century, a group that provided prepaid health care was established in San Francisco. However, the major movement for prepaid health care in America can be said to have begun with the Kaiser Foundation Health Plan, more commonly known as Kaiser Permanente. In the 1930s the Kaiser organization, a small group of doctors, were retained to provide health care to Kaiser employees who were working on a large-scale construction project in the Mojave Desert. The plan gradually expanded to cover workers at other Kaiser locations and was opened to the public after World War II. At present, the Kaiser Foundation Health Plan is still the largest HMO, with locations not only in California but also in such places as Cleveland, Dallas, and Denver.

In recent years, the growth of HMOs has been especially dramatic, with numerous new HMOs springing up, many of them owned by such for-profit organizations as commercial insurance companies, hospital chains, and, most recently, HMO chains. Enrollment growth has also been dramatic, rising from about 9 million in 1980 to about 15 million in 1985 ("The Hot and Healthy Glow of HMOs" 1985). In 1987, the enrollment was over 20 million, a figure reflecting an estimated annual growth of 20 percent (Brown 1983).

In recent years, the government has encouraged the establishment of traditional HMOs, such as the Kaiser Foundation Health Plan, as well as independent practitioner association HMOs. This encouragement has been stimulated by increasing health care costs, by employers' interest in finding new methods of financing health care, and by health care competition.

The Kaiser plan gives its physicians and providers salaries with supplemental incentive reimbursement programs that discourage unnecessary use of health care. Most HMO plans have in fact achieved lower costs through lower hospitalization rates than the traditional fee-for-service health care system. Though ambulatory care use is higher in HMO plans, surveys indicate that only a relatively small proportion of such use is thought to be unnecessary (Barr 1983). HMO plans schedule patients so that longer waiting times are incurred for low-priority problems and access is assured for emergency problems.

In HMOs, hospitals and medical groups are usually organizationally separated from the plan's administration. Hospitals can be owned by the plan but can also be affiliated contractually. IPA HMOs allow the physicians to remain in practice privately; but the IPA, which is a corporation controlled by the physicians, contracts with the central HMO corporation, which handles enrollments, premium collections, and so on.

In the period 1970–1980, there was a poor fit between HMO policy strategy and the government's structural characteristics (Brown 1983). Under the Reagan administration, while direct federal support for HMOs has diminished, restrictions on HMOs have been lifted. As a result, the growth of for-profit HMOs has been dramatic. Indeed, most of future HMO enrollment growth will probably be in for-profit HMOs because of their ability to attract new capital for expansion purposes.

Recent Developments

The successful functioning of at least one HMO in an urban area has usually led to the formation of other HMOs in the area. And, although they compete against one another, the presence of several HMOs provides competition for the major health insurers in that area. This, in turn, creates considerable economic pressure to keep the costs of hospital and other health services at a competitive level.

Just how HMOs can control costs is demonstrated by examining the specific differences between their procedures and services compared with those of traditional health insurance carriers. Traditional health insurance reimburses the insured for health care costs incurred. The insurance carriers usually have little control over costs and the utilization of health care services. As a result, traditional health insurance is largely a payment mechanism to finance health care, especially hospital-based health care. HMOs, on the other hand, not only provide health insurance but also arrange for the provision of the health care services. Also, they usually provide much more comprehensive coverage of health services than the typical health insurance carrier.

Thus, since HMOs provide more comprehensive coverage and at the same time compete with traditional health insurance, they have a particularly strong incentive to contain costs. Specifically, their cost containment is achieved by lower hospital utilization rates for their members. The savings obtained from lower hospital utilization are then available to provide more comprehensive health care in such areas as ambulatory care, drug therapy, and physical therapy.

In 1985, a survey revealed that, in that year, HMO inpatient hospital days were 427 per 1,000 HMO members. This compared with 920 inpatient days per 1,000 population in the entire country. Similarly, the average length of hospital stays for HMO members in 1985 was 4.7 days, while the national average was 6.5 days. Clearly, because of lower hospitalization costs, HMOs can provide more extensive and comprehensive ambulatory care services than traditional carriers.

HMOs AND THE ELDERLY

An Attractive Alternative

HMOs, especially those that provide all ambulatory care services under one roof, offer certain health care services that make them an especially attractive alternative for the elderly. First, HMOs bring various medical specialists together in one location. Because elderly people are likely to suffer from multiple symptoms and various interrelated disabilities, HMOs thus reduce the transportation costs of medical care and the bother and frustrations that often go along with such costs. Second, many elderly people feel uncomfortable about seeking a second opinion on a medical problem. When dealing with HMOs, there is no need to seek a second opinion because medical histories are regularly brought to the attention of other physicians at staff meetings. Third, when older persons move, they must find a new physician. Through HMO membership, the availability of physicians is assured, and their qualifications are under continuous review by their peers. Finally, there is the issue of cost, which is probably the central factor that makes the elderly opt for this type of health care delivery. The vast majority of today's elderly live on fixed incomes. With its procedures for prepayment, the HMO enables older people to budget their expenses and be protected against the threat of catastrophic illness. Alleviating this threat can in turn alleviate the fears and anxiety that can contribute to other illnesses.

Most of the elderly who join HMOs do so as an alternative to buying medigap insurance. In the HMO, they are provided a package of services that includes both those services that are covered by Medicare and those that are typically covered by a medigap policy. Thus, for the elderly HMO member, there is no distinction between health care provided covered by Medicare or that covered by a medigap policy. The HMO provides the entire package of care in one location. For these reasons, HMO membership is particularly attractive to the elderly, provided, of course, that they can afford the somewhat higher monthly premium than that charged by the typical medigap insurance policy.

Accessibility

One of the problems for the elderly HMO member remains the accessibility of the facility. Transportation is frequently a difficult chore for the elderly; and HMOs, with their own comprehensive medical centers, are not always built in locations where the elderly reside. Still, in most cases, the problem is probably no worse than that for a patient who has to travel to a personal fee-for-service physician. It is nevertheless a point the elderly person should consider when joining an HMO. Especially when there are several HMOs in a community, it makes sense to choose one that has ambulatory locations close to the older person's place of residence.

Another problem faced by the elderly living in small towns or rural areas is that there may not be any HMO available to them. However, this situation is rapidly changing. In many of the large cities, several HMOs frequently are competing with one another. It can thus be expected that some of them will soon begin to extend their operations to rural areas and small towns that are not now served by HMOs.

Despite these various problems, enrollment of the elderly in HMOs continues to climb. In 1985, the average enrollment in HMOs among people over age 65 grew by 71 percent (HMO Survey 1987). In 1987, Medicare enrollees served by HMOs were estimated to number close to one million. This large enrollment clearly reflects a substantial interest in HMOs among the elderly, now that they have that option through Medicare.

CONCLUSION

One of the closest approximations to total health care coverage is offered by the closed panel HMO. Especially in the better HMOs with low copayments, the elderly know that their HMO physician and support staff are ready to treat them as necessary. For an elderly person, who on average consumes three to five times as much health care as a younger person, the accompanying feeling of comfort and security is quite important. Thus, membership in an HMO can take a lot of pressure away from the elderly person as far as health care availability and health care financing are concerned.

The remarkable growth of HMOs in both number and enrollment in recent years can be attributed to several factors. First, in the 1970s the federal government provided considerable encouragement and start-up funding for HMOs. Specifically, there was strong federal government encouragement to the for-profit sector, with its ability to attract investment capital, to enter the HMO field. Complementing this was a strong corporate interest to lower health care premiums through control of health care utilization—a goal that could be implemented successfully by HMO-style health service organizations.

It now appears that a combination of Medicare and HMO-type health care coverage can effectively supply health services to those elderly who are able to afford the HMO premiums for coverage. Others, of course, will continue to use medigap policies. Those who cannot afford HMO or medigap coverage must, at present, survive without such coverage, though they will probably eventually be covered by Medicaid, or possibly by a type of catastrophic insurance extension of Medicare.

REFERENCES

Barr, J.K. "Physicians' Views of Patients in Prepaid Group Practice: Reasons for Visits to HMOs." *Journal of Health and Social Behavior* 24 (September 1983):244–245.

Brown, L.D. "Politics and Health Care Organization—HMOs as Federal Policy." *Medical Care Review* 40 (Fall 1983):239.

"The Hot and Healthy Glow of HMOs." *Fortune*, 15 April 1985, 28.

McNeil, R., Jr., and Schlenker, R.E. "HMOs, Competition and Government." *Millbank Memorial Fund Quarterly/Health and Society*, Spring 1975, 195–224.

"New Survey Shows HMO Trends." *Medical Benefits* 4 (30 April 1987):2.

Chapter 23

Quality Control and Cost Containment: The PSRO and the PRO*

INTRODUCTION

In its partial coverage of the costs of medical care for the elderly, the expenditures of the Medicare program increased from $6.2 billion in 1970 to $76 billion in 1986. In 1980, Medicare payments, totaling $37 billion, made up about 38 percent of all government expenditures for health services and supplies. About 92 percent of that was spent for hospital care and physician services (Health Care Financing Administration 1984a).

The government and the taxpayer need to be assured that the money being spent for health care through Medicare is being used to provide quality care in a cost-effective manner. However, there is considerable variation in per capita expenditures in different regions of the country. There is also significant variation in the criteria for length of stay in different areas of the country, even among institutions within the same area (Health Care Financing Administration 1984b).

To minimize these variations, the federal government obviously needed some sort of review system. The idea of such review had been debated at the time Medicare and Medicaid were established, but it was not implemented. Finally, four years after Medicare was introduced, the government began to set up a system for review of the cost and quality of health care. In this chapter, we summarize the basis for and the implementation of that system and its reviewing entity, the Professional Standards Review Organization (PSRO) and discuss why it was not an effective system. We then examine the current review system, the Professional Review Organization (PRO), and consider how it differs from the PSRO.

---

*This chapter is based on a paper entitled "The Review of the Cost and Quality of Medical Care" by C.M. Twarog Carter, School of Management, SUNY/Buffalo, December 1985.

BACKGROUND

The federal government began its involvement in the field of social services during the Great Depression. Its first significant step was in the support of welfare programs for the indigent. Shortly after this, in 1935, President Roosevelt signed legislation that created the Social Security system. At that time, however, and for the next thirty years, financial support for medical care was not included.

In 1965, the Medicare system was introduced, providing medical care to all Social Security recipients. Two years later, in 1967, the Medicaid program was signed into law, extending medical services to the poor. Included in both programs was the concept of the review of the quality of care. All services provided by hospitals to those persons covered under either system were subject to review. However, the laws did not specify the organization that was to do the review.

Prior to Medicare and Medicaid, the physician-patient relationship was a two-way process. Physicians were accountable to patients for the care they provided; and, in return, patients were accountable to physicians for payment for the services rendered. As health insurance systems and the federal health care systems developed, a new entrant, the third party, became concerned that the services that were being paid for were both medically necessary and at an appropriate level of quality.

In 1970, the federal government, based on American Medical Association guidelines, proposed a federally financed review system for the medical services provided under Medicare and Medicaid. The system was to be based on a peer review organization (PRO). The PRO was intended to review only those services provided directly by the physician. It was to be administered by the secretary of the Department of Health, Education and Welfare (DHEW) through a contract with each state medical society, which was to establish a local peer review organization. The review process was to be done only in response to a complaint. No criteria were established to guide the review process.

THE PROFESSIONAL STANDARDS REVIEW ORGANIZATION

The 1970 proposal for a PRO was never put into effect, but it subsequently became the basis for the Bennett Amendment, which created the Professional Standards Review Organization (PSRO) (Bureau of Quality Assurance 1977).

The Bennett Amendment

The Bennett Amendment, sponsored by Senator Bennett of Utah, was aimed at reducing the multimillion dollar cost overruns in the Medicare and Medicaid programs. These excessive costs were partly the result of the enormous infusion of new money into a health system that was already overburdened, with a fragmented organization and control mechanism.

The Bennett Amendment stipulated several changes in the original PRO concept. The first change was that all services, not only physician services, rendered to the patient would be subject to review. The second change was in the organization of the peer review system. The secretary of the DHEW was to designate the local review areas. This contrasted with the original PRO idea of contracting with the various state medical societies. Control was to be retained by the secretary.

The third change encouraged local physicians to organize themselves into independent PSROs. Then, as a group, they could apply to the secretary for the right to conduct reviews. The fourth change permitted each PSRO to develop its own norms and standards against which to judge the quality of medical care.

The fifth change gave the local PSRO the authority to take disciplinary action and send related recommendations to the secretary. Also, details of the disciplinary actions that could be used against physicians were to be specified.

A last change ensured that there would be no denial of appropriate access to records. This would allow the PSRO to bring physicians to courts for due cause.

The Bennett Amendment was introduced on August 20, 1970. It was approved by a Senate-House conference on October 17, 1972 and became Public Law 92–6032 on October 30, 1972 (Congressional Budget Office 1981).

Resistance to the PSRO

The PSRO did not receive overwhelming support. Many different groups opposed it. Aside from this resistance, there were problems with its implementation. One of these was that there was no pool of knowledgeable people to serve as managers of the program, either at the federal level or at the local level. Another problem, often found in government programs, was that administrative responsibilities were split among the several agencies in the DHEW, which administers Medicare and Medicaid. There was controversy over funding of the hospital review costs. In 1975, three years after it was signed into law, another amendment allowed PSRO funding through the Social Security Trust Fund. This was to be managed by the Bureau of Quality Assurance (BQA) in the Health Services Administration of the Public Health Service (Bussman and Davidson 1981).

Resistance to the PSRO came from four distinct groups: physicians, hospitals, state agencies, and the DHEW (Goldfarb 1978).

Physician Resistance

Obviously, for a peer review system to work and be successful, it must be supported by the majority of those who are to be reviewed. But with the PSRO, there was neither broad commitment nor participation among physicians. Many actively opposed the PSRO and organized efforts to repeal the legislation. Lawsuits challenged the constitutionality of the program. On local levels, the PSRO often had support from only a handful of physicians.

Hospital Resistance

Hospitals were also critical of PSROs, and this added to the atmosphere of conflict. The hospitals' major concern was that an external organization, the local PSRO, was determining matters that they previously had controlled. Frequently, hospitals delayed the signing of working agreements, and some even refused to cooperate at all.

State Agency Resistance

The state Medicaid agencies were also creating problems. Some of them had already implemented and were working with their own utilization review systems. They saw the PSRO as an unnecessary duplication of their own efforts. Generally, the states did not approve of the physician-run organizations. With the rising expenditures for Medicaid, they saw federal dollars for such organizations being used inefficiently. Many states refused to negotiate or delayed in negotiating the necessary agreements.

DHEW Resistance

Perhaps most important resistance, the one with the most effect, was that coming from the DHEW in the early phases of the program. There was internal tension between the DHEW and the Social Security Administration, which administers Medicare, and also between the DHEW and the Social and Rehabilitative Service, which administers Medicaid. This internal resistance emerged during the critical stages of program implementation. The resulting atmosphere of tension within the government created problems with outside agencies; state Medicaid agencies and Blue Cross organizations were reluctant to aid in effecting a smooth introduction of the PSRO.

Goals of the PSRO Program

The PSRO system was enacted as a multipurpose program. It was intended to affect two areas: (1) the cost of medical care and (2) the quality of medical care. It had three major objectives (Bureau of Quality Assurance 1977; Bussman and Davidson 1981).

1. Elimination of inappropriate and unnecessary health care. This would free up scarce resources that could be used to deal with other unmet needs.

2. Improvement in the quality of health services. This would make quality services more uniformly available and raise the overall level of performance.

3. Assistance in the identification and, where necessary, correction of the small minority of providers whose practices are harmful to the health and safety of patients. This was to be followed up by making necessary referrals of such individuals and institutions to the appropriate agencies for investigation.

Two specific goals for the program were also stipulated:

1. To reduce variation in hospital use and thus bring hospital rates nationwide closer to levels achieved in the more efficient prepaid and fee-for-service sectors.

2. To reduce the variation of ancillary services utilization. This was to be accomplished by the elimination of unnecessary tests and procedures and the shifting of services from inappropriately intense levels of care to lesser ones. At the time the PSRO program was enacted, the achievement of this goal was considered to be coupled with reimbursement.

There was also considerable controversy regarding the dual role of the PSRO. Many critics insisted that the review system must be oriented either toward cost containment or toward quality control. These two roles, they said, were mutually exclusive and incompatible. It was, however, agreed that, in a specific situation where cost and quality were at odds, the PSROs would always put quality ahead of cost. There would, of course, be many instances where quality enhancement would have little effect on cost. But there also would be situations where quality improvement could be brought about only through the addition of services, thus increasing costs. In all of these situations, it was important to consider all factors and use clinical judgment to ensure that realizable benefits were not being lost in cost-containment efforts.

Overall, the PSROs should have given top priority to reviewing activities that could maintain or improve quality while decreasing inappropriate and/or unnecessary use of services.

Components of the PSRO Review System

The PSRO review system was designed with three components:

1. concurrent review of individual cases
2. medical care evaluation (MCE) studies
3. profile analyses of health care practitioners, institutions, and patients

The first of these components was implemented on a case-by-case basis, while the health services were being delivered. The second and third components were designed to study patterns of practice after the health services had been delivered.

Concurrent Review

Concurrent review of the individual cases was based on prespecified criteria. The objective was to assess the medical need for admission to or continued stay at a hospital or for specific procedures or ancillary services. The review staff for these screenings were generally not physicians. The criteria for the reviews were developed primarily by physicians. Cases that did not meet the criteria were referred to a physician advisor or a peer of the practitioner whose practice was under review.

Medical Care Evaluation Studies

The purpose of the medical care evaluation (MCE) studies was to identify and correct deficiencies in the quality of care. These studies were often called quality review studies. The criteria for them were designed to meet the purposes of the particular study and were therefore more specific than those used in concurrent review. The criteria were used to identify the extent and precise cause of problems that were previously detected during concurrent review of individual cases. Of equal importance was the need to identify the extent and precise cause of problems that were previously detected during concurrent review of individual cases. Of equal importance was the need to identify the degree to which these problems could be corrected through concurrent and preadmission review, continuing medical education, or other interventions. MCE studies could also be used to detect and correct problems in the quality of hospital services other than the specific one under review.

Profile Analysis

The objective of the profile analysis was to aggregate large amounts of data as a basis for examining patterns in physician practices, institutions, diagnoses, and health services. Patterns of similar providers were compared with previous patterns to identify natural tendencies, trends, and exceptional patterns. Aside from detecting potential problems, profile analysis was also used to monitor the effects of interventions in correcting previously detected problems. As problems were detected, they were referred to the second component of the PSRO, a MCE study, for follow-up. Practitioners and hospitals whose profiles showed good performance would be exempt from concurrent review.

A national PSRO reporting system of comparative profiles was established, based on a uniform hospital discharge data set developed and reported by each PSRO. This allowed for rapid comparisons from the national to the local level and for easy observation of trends.

This profile analysis was the backbone of the PSRO hospital review objective of eliminating excess hospital use. Profiles were examined at the national level to identify a nationwide average performance and range of variation. The analysis then moved to the regional level, then to the state level, and finally to the local PSRO area. Within each area, the profile analysis was done by examining statistics from the hospitals within the area and then by the practitioners within the hospitals. This was useful in detecting where local practice patterns differed significantly from regional or national norms. Also, comparative analysis of hospitals across a PSRO area allowed for a comparison of hospitals by type (teaching, public, or proprietary).

Problems with the PSRO System

There were many problems with the PSRO program. These problems were found in two major areas: technical and political (Bussman and Davidson 1981; Goldfarb 1978; Goram 1979; Kellogg 1978).

Technical Problems

The first technical problem arose from limitations in the type of knowledge and techniques that were to be applied. The idea of a program with problem-oriented review and cost-effectiveness analysis was a totally new concept. Thus, knowledge about the best way to put the system into use was limited. The result was that, as obstacles were encountered, solutions to the problems raised required experimentation and the development of new approaches.

The second technical problem involved the lack of expertise. Formal educational programs in the areas to be addressed were just in the development stage. Physicians involved in peer review had little relevant experience to rely upon and often sought advice and assistance. Nonphysician staff experienced similar problems and had to learn many aspects of the program by working on the job.

The third technical problem concerned the data collected by the PSROs. Data quality is an essential prerequisite in producing accurate profiles. But the classification, coding, and statistical analysis of the PSRO data were not always valid and reliable. There was no assurance that similar patient groups were being compared. Specific problems arose in the classification of primary diagnoses and multiple conditions and in distinguishing primary from secondary diagnoses. There also were problems as a result of a failure to adjust for patient distribution by age and sex. The sample size of cases used in the analysis of patterns was small, thus making it difficult to draw valid conclusions. Improvements in the clustering of patients included the use of diagnostic related groups.

The fourth technical problem stemmed from the lack of uniformity among PSROs. There was wide variability in commitment, level of effort, and performance. The local organizations varied in their ability to detect and correct the problems that required action. At the outset, improvements in hospital review were implemented in only a small number of successful PSROs.

The fifth technical problem arose from the difficulties in changing practice behavior. PSROs were able to detect problems in the quality and utilization of hospital services; but, once these problems were detected, correction was not easy. It was not yet known which corrective measures worked best to solve the difficult problems.

The final technical problem involved the dependence on external bodies. Certain factors affecting the program were outside the control of the PSRO. Examples of such external factors were the shortages of alternatives to hospital care and an excess supply of hospital beds. Improvements in these factors would have involved the cooperation of a number of agencies. The result was to limit the effectiveness of the PSROs.

Political Problems

Aside from the many technical problems, there were also political problems. One of the most important of these was posed by the lack of time needed to accomplish change. Due to the concern with controlling health care costs, the PSRO program was under intense pressure to eliminate quickly unnecessary and inappropriate hospital care and services. In order to receive continued funding, the PSRO program was expected to provide evidence that unnecessary services had been eliminated. The survival of the entire program was therefore called into question each year. A related problem was that PSROs were subject to unrealistic and inappropriate expectations; they were under intense pressure to demonstrate savings directly attributable to review.

The third political problem was that agreed-upon measures of success were lacking. There were three distinct areas in which disagreements arose concerning what constituted success. The first area concerned the means to determine measurable objectives; the second concerned the amount of change, over what period of time, that would constitute success; the third area concerned those measures of accomplishment over which the PSROs had no control.

The fourth political problem stemmed from the lack of adequate funding. Because of the controversy surrounding the PSROs, the program was faced with the prospect of not receiving the funding necessary to support successful performance.

The final problem arose from the lack of willingness of the medical profession to cooperate and devote enough time and energy to make the program work. Physicians were frustrated with the governmental process and often lost interest and stopped participating.

THE PROFESSIONAL REVIEW ORGANIZATION

The Peer Review Improvement Act

In December 1980, with all the controversy surrounding the PSRO program, the American Medical Association's House of Delegates called for the repeal of the program. Shortly after this, in 1981, the Reagan administration announced that it intended to eliminate the PSRO program, in line with its stated objective of reducing burdensome, unnecessary, and inefficient government regulation. The administration stated that it would advocate competition in health care as a means of encouraging private enterprise to promote quality medical care at low cost.

In the spring of 1982, Congress passed the Tax Equity and Fiscal Responsibility Act, commonly referred to as TEFRA, to address the issue of review of the quality and cost of health care. It allowed existing PSROs to operate until the secretary of the Department of Health and Human Services (HHS) could designate a new review organization.

TEFRA called for the replacement of the PSRO with utilization and quality control peer review organizations (UQCPROs). The secretary of HHS was to contract with these UQCPROs for the purpose of promoting the efficient and economic delivery of health care services and ensuring the quality of services covered under Medicare. The review process was to be similar to that of the PSRO, but it was to be intensified. The emphasis for review under the UQCPRO program would be on admissions, quality of care, DRG assignment, and outlier cases (Grimaldi and Micheletti 1985; Mikalski 1984).

A major change in the review system for UQCPRO, compared with that of the PSRO, was that specific criteria for review contracts were to be negotiated individually with each UQCPRO; the criteria for the PSRO were mandated nationwide. Also, it was no longer required that the review organizations be nonprofit. Medical societies were permitted to contract as a UQCPRO, although physician groups were to be given priority. Finally, whereas the PSRO had a stated minimum requirement that the review group be composed of a substantial number of practicing physicians (about 25 percent), the minimum number of physicians needed to make up a UQCPRO was to be 5 to 10 percent.

The number of review areas was decreased under the new system. Under the PSRO program, 194 review areas were formed; under the new law, each state was designated as a UQCPRO area, thus decreasing the number of areas to 50.

The new law clearly stated that UQCPROs would be exempt from the Freedom of Information Act (FOIA). This would aid the organization in maintaining the confidentiality of medical information. Whereas, PSROs were subject to the FOIA because they were federal agencies, UQCPROs were now excluded from FOIA responsibilities because of their contractor status.

There was also a difference in the funding of the two programs. The PSROs were funded by federal grants. The UQCPROs would be paid directly by HHS through negotiated two-year contracts. Their funding was to be allocated directly from the Medicare Trust Fund as hospital costs under Part A.

One final difference between the two review organizations was that, unlike PSROs, the UQCPROs would be required to make their resources available for contracting with public or private payers to facilitate private review by the organization. It should be noted that the UQCPRO was not required to enter into contracts for private review, it was required merely to make its resources available.

PRO Functions, Criteria, and Objectives

Functions

The UQCPRO is commonly referred to as the Peer Review Organization (PRO). The Social Security Amendments of 1983 stipulated specific requirements for the new PROs. For example, they required that hospitals receiving Medicare payments under the prospective payment system contract with a PRO before October 1, 1984, in order to continue to receive reimbursement (this date was later extended to November 15, 1984).

The functions of the PRO are threefold (Grimaldi and Micheletti 1985; Mikalski 1984).

1. to determine whether the services furnished to Medicare patients are reasonable and medically necessary
2. to determine whether the quality of services furnished meets professionally recognized standards
3. to determine whether the services furnished could be effectively provided on an outpatient basis or in a different type of health care facility

The major difference in PRO functions, compared to those of the PSRO, is the specification that outpatient care or a different type of health care facility can be used. Also, the scope of the review function is expanded to include evaluation of the appropriateness of admissions and discharges and the validity of diagnostic information. The PRO is authorized to make conclusive determinations on the quality of care. It is the responsibility of the PRO to notify the practitioner or provider of claim disapproval and then to provide an opportunity to discuss the negative determination. The case may be brought up for appeal if necessary.

The PRO is authorized to review any and all services covered under Medicare. This review can be preadmission, concurrent, or retrospective. As with PSROs, the review is to include examination of the records of the providers or practitioners where the review is taking place and inspection of the facilities where the services are being provided.

In the extreme case, a PRO may bar a provider or practitioner from the Medicare program. The provider or practitioner then has the right to an appeal and a judicial hearing. Unlike the PSRO legislation, the new laws extend civil and criminal immunity to individuals who provide information to a PRO in situations where the information is related to the performance of the review and is true to the best of the individual's knowledge.

Criteria

The criteria for review also differ in the two review programs. Under the PSRO system, the criteria were mandated nationwide. This led to problems, in that practice patterns and the types of medical care required differed in different areas of the country. The specific objectives of a PRO's review activities are stated in its contract with HHS.

Four basic types of review are included in the objectives of each PRO:

1. admission review
2. invasive diagnostic and therapeutic procedure review
3. outlier review
4. DRG validation

In admission review, the objective is to decide whether the services were delivered in the most appropriate setting. The outcome of this review forms the basis for deciding whether DRG payments are to be approved or disapproved. Admission patterns are monitored by a random sampling of at least 5 percent of hospital admissions. The PRO attempts to reduce admissions for procedures that could be adequately provided in an ambulatory surgical setting or on an outpatient basis. After review of these admissions, if the number of unnecessary admissions is greater than 2.5 percent of the sample for one calendar year quarter, all Medicare admissions in the next quarter are reviewed. Specific attention is given to transfers to psychiatric and rehabilitation units and to acute care beds that are to be used as long-term care beds (psychiatric and rehabilitation units and "swing" beds are exempt from the prospective payment system). All patient transfers are monitored to make sure they are justified. Admission review also includes the checking of any readmission of a patient made within 7 days of that patient's discharge from the hospital. The review organization will want to make sure that the patient was not discharged prematurely and readmitted to boost payment.

The second type of review deals with invasive diagnostic and therapeutic procedures. These procedures may affect the classification of a patient in a DRG that results in an increase in hospital payment. The HHS wants these procedures monitored to detect patterns of abuse. The PRO also reviews every permanent cardiac pacemaker implantation or reimplantation; payment will be denied for any case where such treatment was unnecessary.

The third type of review is that for outliers. Outliers are those patients whose length of treatment, by length of stay (LOS), or by total cost of care, is extraordinarily high. Eligibility for outliers is automatic once the person's LOS exceeds a prespecified limit. The eligibility for most other outliers is determined by the review organization.

The fourth type of review is for DRG validation. In this type of review, a random sample of discharges is screened every quarter. The reviewer checks to ensure that the medical records substantiate the diagnostic and procedural codes used by the hospitals. These codes are used as the basis for classifying patients in a DRG and, thus, for determining the hospital's payment rate.

Objectives

There are five quality objectives that the federal government requires of PROs:

1. to reduce unnecessary readmissions due to substandard care during the prior admissions
2. to ensure the provision of medical services that, if not performed, would create a significant potential for serious patient complications
3. to reduce unavoidable deaths
4. to reduce unnecessary surgery or other invasive procedures
5. to reduce avoidable postoperative and other complications

CONCLUSION

The review system of the PRO is an improvement over that of its predecessor, the PSRO. It directly addresses issues that the PSRO failed to address. One very important advantage it enjoys is that it replaces a review system already in place. The PRO is able to use the mistakes of the PSROs as learning tools. It thus will be able to avoid many of the problems that the PSRO was forced to face because of its inexperience.

Practitioners and providers must work with the PRO system. The choice is not whether or not there will be a review of the cost and quality of health care; the choice now is who will perform the review.

When the Medicare program was originally devised, it was projected that it would cost about $9 billion annually by 1990. In 1986, the program cost about $76 billion. The estimates have accordingly been revised to project a cost of more than $100 billion for 1990. Faced with this enormous expenditure of federal funds, Congress must be assured that every attempt is made to deliver the services at the lowest possible cost. If physicians do not use the PRO to prove that they are the group best qualified to be accountable for cost-effectiveness, the task will be given to a private agency or an insurance company. However, enactment of the Peer Review Improvement Act reflects the confidence of Congress in the ability of physician-sponsored organizations to conduct peer review. In effect, the act gives physicians the authority to develop standards and to certify payment for medically necessary services.

The criteria for review is much more specific for the PRO, compared with the PSRO. The criteria of the PSRO were often vague and ambiguous, and PSRO objectives often projected using such uncertain terms as abnormal, excessive, or significant. This led to problems in deciding how abnormal or excessive a situation should be before action is taken. In contrast, the objectives of the PRO are much more specific, using statistics for clarification, thereby eliminating the loopholes in the early program.

The PSRO was a very costly program. In terms of cost-benefit ratios and based on 1978 data for concurrent review, it was estimated that, overall, only $2.27 was saved for every dollar spent. The highest cost-benefit ratio was observed in the northeast ($3.38 saved for every dollar spent), and the lowest was observed in the south ($1.91 saved for every dollar spent). In contrast, Health Care Financing Administration experts expect that, for every dollar spent, a PRO saves Medicare five dollars, through its procedures for reporting unnecessary hospital admissions and exposing other abuses of the reimbursement system.

There is still some concern by hospital administrators and practitioners that the PRO program will increase the threat of medical malpractice suits. If a PRO determines that hospital care was unnecessary, the service will not be reimbursed. However, the identification of medical malpractice problems can lead to the development of effective quality assurance programs. Also, PRO's quality criteria can be used as a set of medical standards as a basis for developing treatment plans. This may help in resolving legal problems.

In any event, the need for a quality review program is indisputable. This need is underscored by an uncertain economy, the rising cost of labor and medical technology, and the increasing number of elderly in the United States. Private industry has amply demonstrated the advantages of economies of scale and the cost savings associated with standardization. The PRO has the potential to increase standardization in medical practice and to reduce the costs associated with overutilization.

Medical personnel support, participation, and commitment are, however, essential for the PRO program to be successful. If physicians show a lack of interest and choose not to be involved in the peer review program, the concept of peer review will not be abandoned. But it would probably be changed to a nonpeer review program, and physicians would then have to adjust to the idea of others reviewing and making recommendations on the cost and quality of the care they provide.

REFERENCES

Bureau of Quality Assurance. *PRO Program Manual.* Washington, D.C.: Bureau of Quality Assurance, Health Services Administration, Department of Health, Education and Welfare, 1977.

Bussman, J.W., and Davidson, S.V. *PSRO: The Promise, Perspective and Potential.* Menlo Park, Calif.: Addison Wesley, 1981.

Goldfarb, N., ed. *Public Control of Medical Care: History, Practice and Problems of the Federal PSRO.* Series 13, no. 2. Hampstead, N.Y.: Hofstra University, 1978.

Goram, M.J. "The Evolution of the PSRO Hospital Review System." *Medical Care*, supplement, vol. 17, no. 5 (1979).

Grimaldi, P.L., and Micheletti, J.A. "PRO Objectives and Quality Criteria." *Hospitals* 59 (1 February 1985):64–67.

Health Care Financing Administration. *Health Care Financing Review*, Winter 1984a.

———. *Medicare Program Statistics, Selected State Data, 1978–1982*, Washington, D.C.: U.S. GPO, 1984b.

Mikalski, E.J. "The New Era of Utilization and Quality Control: PRO." *Bulletin of New York Academy of Medicine* 60 (January/February 1984):48–53.

U.S. Congress. Congressional Budget Office. *Impact of PSROs on Healthcare Costs: Update of CBO's 1979 Evaluation.* Washington, D.C.: U.S. GPO, 1981.

W.K. Kellogg Foundation. *Private Initiative in PSROs.* Ann Arbor, Mich.: Health Administration Press, 1978.

Chapter 24

Vision, Speech, Hearing, and Dental Care

INTRODUCTION

In September 1976, the U.S. House of Representatives' Subcommittee on Health and Long-Term Care of the Select Committee on Aging published a report titled *Medical Appliances and the Elderly: Unmet Needs and Excessive Costs for Eyeglasses, Hearing Aids, Dentures and Other Devices* (U.S. Congress 1976). The report documented the fact that the well-being of virtually all of the 22.4 million elderly (in 1975) was dependent on one or more medical appliances. It also found that the elderly's needs in this area were not being met for two reasons: First, there was a lack of federal assistance to help the elderly obtain the needed devices. Many of the elderly could not afford the devices, and public and private health benefit programs provided only limited help in this area. Second, there was a lack of adequate safeguards to protect the elderly from abuses in purchasing health aids. Those elderly who could afford them or that sacrificed other things to acquire them frequently were victims of overpricing and unnecessary goods or services.

Today, in the area of vision care, about 90 percent of the elderly require and wear eyeglasses. However, over five million elderly are wearing eyeglasses that need correction. In cases where there may be a conflict of interest (for example, in the case of an optometrist who provides both the eye examination and the eyeglasses), there is a high incidence of unnecessary prescriptions. Also, overpricing has been discovered in numerous surveys conducted in various parts of the country.

Not as many of the elderly have hearing problems as have vision problems. However, about 50 percent of the elderly have some hearing impairment, and about 8 percent have severe hearing problems. Conflicts of interest are also common in the hearing aid industry. Although it is generally recommended that persons with hearing problems consult an otolaryngologist or an otologist (both physicians), frequently hearing aids are purchased without such medical intervention. Frequently, the hearing aid dealer selects the hearing aid for the customer, possibly providing an unnecessary or inappropriate device. Overpricing is also a common problem in the hearing aid industry.

In the mid-1970s, over half of those over 65 had no natural teeth. Over five percent of those elderly without teeth had no dentures, and many of those with dentures had problems with them that needed correction. Yet, the cost of acquiring, replacing, or repairing dentures is considerable. The elderly on limited budgets therefore often forgo dental care rather than commit more than they can afford to take care of their needs.

In all of these cases, little or no financial assistance is available from private or public health benefit programs. In some states, Medicaid covers some of the unmet needs, but only for those elderly who are eligible under that program.

SPECIFIC CARE PROBLEMS

In this section, we summarize some of the findings and conclusions reported by the House Subcommittee on Health and Long-Term Care regarding vision, hearing, communication, and dental problems of the elderly (U.S. Congress 1976).

Vision Care

Vision care, including the prescription and acquisition of eyeglasses, is a need that virtually all elderly share. Next to arthritis, chronic vision impairment is the most common ailment of the elderly. Also, vision deteriorates with age; as a result, there are more eye problems among the elderly than among any other segment of the population. About 25 percent of the elderly need new corrective lenses because their present eyeglasses do not help their sight, and in some cases may actually impair it. Many other elderly persons need eyeglasses but currently do not have them.

Many of the eye problems the elderly have need early and constant attention to avoid blindness. In particular, glaucoma and senile cataracts should be diagnosed early so that proper treatments can be prescribed to avoid severe and nonreversible vision impairment. The rate of blindness in those over 65 is over 12 percent, and the blindness is frequently caused by untreated glaucoma and cataract conditions.

About 12 percent of the elderly are legally blind, but an additional 8 percent have chronic vision impairments. In many of these cases, the vision impairment can be corrected, but the costs of vision care and eyeglasses often inhibit the elderly from seeking such care. Medicare and private insurance generally do not provide coverage for eyeglasses and vision check-ups. Only under Medicaid, and then only in some states, are vision care and eyeglasses covered benefits.

The cost of vision care to the elderly is inflated for two reasons: (1) prescription of the wrong lenses, and (2) excessive cost for eyeglasses. For example, extensive investigations by the New York Department of Consumer Affairs revealed that optometrists frequently prescribe the wrong lenses, or they prescribe eyeglasses in cases where they are not required. It was found that many of the wrong prescriptions were not intentional but were the result of poor or inadequate conditions in the optometrist's office. Poor lighting and improperly focused eye charts frequently contributed to poor conditions.

There is in fact evidence that overpricing of eyeglasses is rampant. Price variations of 200 percent, and occasionally as high as 300 percent, are common. Such price variations clearly cannot be justified on the basis of differences in overhead costs. The only conclusion is that serious overpricing exists. Unsuspecting elderly clients often are the victims of this overpricing. Usually, they do not discover they have been victimized until it is too late.

How can the elderly avoid becoming victims of such practices? More and better information dissemination is probably the best approach. If the elderly knew which optometrists were unqualified or tended to overprice, they could avoid them. The question is, Who will gather such information and disseminate it? The logical agency to do this is the local office or department of the aging. Another possibility involves the elderly themselves. Through senior citizen centers, the elderly could develop lists of vision care providers who are qualified and trustworthy. Without such an organized system to disseminate relevant information, the elderly will continue to be victims of overpricing, which in turn will inhibit many of them from searching for much-needed vision care in the future.

Hearing Care

According to the Federal Council on the Aging and the American Speech and Hearing Association, about 10 percent of those 65 and over suffer from serious hearing impairment, that is, they are unable to hear words that are spoken at a normal voice level. The solution in these cases is a suitable hearing aid. Unfortunately, hearing aids are expensive, and few health benefit programs cover the acquisition and fitting of such aids. As a result, for those unable to afford the aid, the only alternative is to forgo it. In such cases, the lack of a hearing aid can create other problems, including feelings of isolation, loneliness, or shame.

Hearing impairment takes a variety of forms. The first is an inability to hear speech and other sounds at normal volume levels. This is referred to as a ''loss in hearing sensitivity," or simply "hearing loss." A second form of hearing impairment is an inability to hear speech and other sounds clearly, even though the sounds are sufficiently loud. This is referred to as "speech discrimination."

The likelihood of having a serious hearing impairment rises sharply with increased age. Only about 2.6 percent of persons between 12 and 24 years of age have serious hearing problems; in the 45-to-64 age bracket, the percentage increases to 10.0 percent; in those 65 and over, about 10 percent have serious hearing impairments. According to a National Health Survey conducted in the mid-1970s, slightly over a million of those in the last group were using hearing aids.

Because of the high cost of hearing aids, the hearing aid delivery system has been the subject of numerous investigations. Among others, the Retired Professional Action Group (RPAG), a nonprofit consumer advisory group, and the Senate Special Committee on Aging's Subcommittee on Consumer Interests of the Elderly have conducted or prompted such investigations. In 1973, the RPAG published *Paying through the Ear: A Report on Hearing Health Care Problems*. The report of the Senate Subcommittee was titled *Hearing Aids and Older Americans*. These two reports in turn prompted a DHEW investigation that resulted in a 1975 document on "hearing aid health care." In all of these investigations, serious abuses were found in the way hearing aids are sold. In each case, the final report urged that these abuses be corrected.

Overselling was the most serious problem uncovered. Because it is the primary interest of the dealer to make a sale, hearing aids frequently are sold to people who do not really need them. Though, in a sense, this is not a health care problem, but an economic or legal fraud problem, the Senate subcommittee proposed requiring a medical examination before a hearing aid could be sold. However, although this would provide some degree of protection, it would also increase the cost of acquiring a hearing aid. Thus, a compromise solution was reached, whereby patients would be permitted to waive a medical examination if there were no obvious medical problems present.

There have also been numerous questions raised about the competency of hearing aid dealers. An instructional home study course consisting of 20 lessons for hearing aid dealers was developed in the mid-1970s by the National Hearing Aid Society (NHAS). However, the Veterans Administration, the American Council of Otolaryngology, and the American Speech and Hearing Association all severely criticized the course as being inadequate, too technical for most participants, and superficial.

There were also questions about pricing. Retail costs of hearing aids were found to be up to two and one-half times the wholesale costs. The National Hearing Aid Society has defended these high costs on the basis of the mark-ups required to cover the costs of such services as audiological tests, fitting, counseling about hearing aid use, and postdelivery services.

What about economies of scale? Could the cost of hearing aids be reduced through larger delivery centers? At present, the hearing aid delivery system at the retail level is largely a "cottage industry." Entry of nonprofit corporations into the market or large scale national franchising might very well lower costs considerably. But there is little indication at present that such moves are about to take place.

Care for Communication Problems

Approximately 25 percent, or 6 million, of the 24 million people 65 and over have hearing disorders resulting from degenerative changes in the auditory pathway (Diggs 1980). Speech and language problems resulting from degenerative changes in the cortex (senile dementia) or from cerebrovascular accidents (dysphesia, dysarthia) are also prevalent among the elderly (National Center 1975). A study on institutionalized demented patients revealed that only five percent of demented patients have adequate communication (Ferm 1975). Speech and language problems are in fact quite common among the elderly, especially the institutionalized elderly. A 1978 study revealed that 25 percent of nursing home patients have speech problems and 36 percent have impaired hearing (Administration on Aging 1978). The extent of communication disorders in our society may actually be greater than indicated in these studies. Hearing impairment is not readily apparent, and only the more advanced cases of hearing impairment are clearly identified.

Dancer and Drummond (1985) have developed a questionnaire instrument to discover to what extent senior centers and nursing homes provide speech and hearing services to the elderly population. The questionnaire was relatively simple and easy to complete by directors of senior centers or nursing homes. The questions covered four major categories: availability of professional services, speech services, hearing services, and further services and training.

Of the 415 questionnaires sent out, 137 were completed and returned. The returned questionnaires contained data from 73 nursing homes, 58 senior centers, and 6 other organizations. Of the 73 nursing homes, 16 had speech services and 31 had audiology services; of the 58 senior centers, 8 had speech services and 28 had audiology services. These differences are not surprising, since nursing home clients are patients and senior centers usually cater to healthy people.

The responding directors of nursing homes and senior centers indicated that they recognized the communication problems of their clients. But their perception of the extent of communication problems in their facilities was quite low. This was especially true for nursing homes, where other studies have generally reported a much higher incidence of communication problems.

Unfortunately, the Dancer and Drummond study involved a sampling of only one state (Arkansas) and thus has limited generalizability. Still, the findings (summarized in Table 24-1) suggest the need for more in-service training of both nursing home and senior center staff in the identification of communication disorders and in the ways they can better serve clients with such disorders. Trained speech therapists and audiologists would of course be required in such training programs, assuming appropriate funding were available.

Dental Care

As recently as the mid-1970s, one-half of the U.S. population over 65 was edentulous (without any natural teeth). A majority of these people had dentures. However, for the older person on a limited budget, the cost of acquiring dentures can be a considerable economic barrier. Very few health benefit programs cover dental care; in virtually all cases the individual must cover the acquisition costs.

The reason for the high rate of edentulousness among the elderly can be traced to the fact that this age group grew up in a period when the benefits of fluoridation and other preventive measures were unknown. Extraction of teeth was common in the absence of alternative tooth-saving procedures. Today, extraction is a last resort in most cases. In fact, many of the acute dental problems common to elderly Americans declined significantly between 1958 and 1971. For those between 65 and 74, edentulousness declined by 10.0 percent; for those 75, it declined by 7.5 percent.

There is considerable evidence that the rate of edentulousness is still on a steady decline. In a 1960 survey, the American Dental Association found that

---

Table 24-1 Responses by Directors of Nursing Homes and Senior Centers Concerning Clients' Communication Problems

	Number of Facilities	
Recognition of Speech and Hearing Problems	*Speech*	*Hearing*
Nursing homes	90	89
Senior centers	38	64

	Percentage	
Perceived Incidence of Speech and Hearing Problems	*Speech*	*Hearing*
Nursing homes	7.2	17.0
Senior centers	0.5	4.6

Source: Nursing Homes, pp. 26–29, Centaur & Company, © May–June 1985.

31 percent of people between the ages of 30 and 39 were wearing dentures or bridges. A similar survey done in 1975 on the same age group revealed that the rate had declined to 11 percent.

Despite the declining rate of edentulousness generally, the conditions of the edentulous elderly continued to be precarious. In 1970, of the 11.4 million elderly, 0.6 million were without any teeth at all—dentures or natural teeth. Another 3.4 million had dentures that needed to be replaced or refitted. Indeed, it was found that about 1.3 million people over age 65 had so much difficulty wearing inadequate dentures that they never used them or wore them only part of the time.

It is thus particularly important that people who have had their teeth removed be fitted with dentures quickly. If too much time elapses between the teeth removal and the denture fitting, it becomes extremely difficult for the person to adjust to the dentures. Among the elderly, the importance of dentures is frequently not fully understood. The nonuse of dentures or the use of faulty dentures often means that the elderly person is forced to choose foods that are easier to chew but lower in nutritional value. The edentulous elderly tend to avoid foods like meat, raw vegetables, and fresh fruits because these foods are difficult to chew.

Clearly, large numbers of the elderly continue to be in need of dental care—care of their own natural teeth or of the dentures or bridges they are wearing. These dental care needs, the result of years of inadequate care, are much more serious than those found among the younger population. Yet the elderly use considerably fewer dental services than do younger segments of the population.

Dental care, including the fitting of dentures, is expensive; and this factor frequently inhibits the elderly from obtaining adequate dental care. The cost of obtaining dentures—including extraction, x-rays, the making of impressions, and the purchase of the dentures from the laboratory—can vary from $500 to $1,000 (these costs are estimates from the mid-1970s and are clearly higher now).

If the elderly person is fortunate enough to live near a dental clinic that specializes in dentures, costs can be reduced substantially. For example, in the mid-1970s, the Seaton Clinic in Florence, South Carolina, provided dentures for substantially less than the average cost of $500–$1,000. Although the South Carolina Dental Association reported numerous complaints from patients of the clinic, the clinic's tremendous volume of business indicates that there must also be a large group of satisfied clients. To cite another example, the dental clinics in Canada's province of Ontario are visited by many Americans from border cities like Buffalo and Detroit because the cost of obtaining dentures through those clinics is frequently only a fraction of the cost of dentures obtained from a local American dentist.

All of this suggests that there is a considerable potential for economies of scale in providing dentures to people. The economies of scale are achievable not merely as a result of the higher volume of a clinic versus a dentist office. It appears that, in fact, the fitting of a denture, including adjustments to the denture, can be handled more cost-efficiently by the laboratory technician than by the dentist. The dentist's time is considered more valuable; as a result, the dentist's professional fee is higher. Dental technicians, on the other hand, are probably more skilled in fitting and adjusting dentures, since that is their specialty, yet the cost of their time is less. (These conclusions are based on considerable evidence but have not yet been proven.)

It is not clear from the evidence whether economies of scale are also achievable in providing routine dental services to those people who still have all of their teeth, but experience suggests they are not. It is difficult to improve the efficiency of the personal services of a dentist, especially if that dentist is already utilizing dental assistants, dental hygienists, and administrative and clerical support staff. This suggests that the elderly can expect to gain little in reduced costs if they still have all their teeth and are determined to maintain their teeth. They must seek out the appropriate dental care and pay the prevailing prices. If, on the other hand, the elderly need dentures, there are, as we have seen, ways of obtaining services at lower cost, for example, at clinics like the ones described earlier. In communities where such clinics do not yet exist, there will undoubtedly be increasing pressure to develop them.

RECOMMENDATIONS FOR COST CONTAINMENT

The Subcommittee on Health and Long-Term Care made numerous suggestions as to how consumers can avoid overpricing and unnecessary services. In general, it recommended that, to ensure that consumers obtain the highest possible quality at the lowest possible price, government at all levels should make efforts, where appropriate and feasible, to disseminate relevant information to enable them to make correct decisions.

Specifically, in the area of vision care, the consumer was urged to ensure that the eye examination by the optometrist or opthalmologist is thorough. The consumer should insist that the health professional take a complete case history and that tests for near, distance, depth, peripheral, color, coordination, and unaided vision be conducted. It is also important that eye charts are well placed and that adequate lighting is available.

Following the eye examination, the client should not simply accept what is suggested but should ask questions. The client who already has eyeglasses should ask about the difference between the present glasses and the suggested ones. If no change is recommended, a second opinion may not be necessary. If it is recommended that new eyeglasses be acquired, the client should take the prescription and shop around, since there is considerable variation in the cost of eyeglasses.

Similar guidelines apply in the case of a hearing examination. Before acquiring a hearing aid, clients should have their hearing tested by an otolaryngologist or an otologist. Both are physicians and can provide an unbiased opinion regarding the need for a hearing aid. If a hearing aid is needed, the consumer should shop around among the many hearing aid dealers, checking in particular on the product guarantees; some dealers offer money-back guarantees if a customer is not satisfied. Also comparisons among hearing aids can be checked with such organizations as Consumers' Union, the publishers of *Consumer Reports*. In using the hearing aid, the consumer should follow the manufacturer's instructions. As with any external device, it takes time to get used to it, and maximum value is obtained only after one has become accustomed to using it.

The subcommittee also recommended that consumers shop around for dental care, especially with regard to price. Although there is usually uniform pricing among dentists in a community, there are always those who price their services higher or lower than the norm. The consumer should not be afraid to call a dentist and ask how much a given procedure will cost. Price is particularly important in the case of dentures. A local dentist should be consulted first. But the wise consumer will also check dental clinics (independent or associated with dental schools) that might provide dentures at a lower cost. Before making a final decision on complete or partial dentures, the consumer should be sure that everything is spelled out as far as cost, payment, and delivery time is concerned.

CONCLUSION

Although service systems for vision, speech, hearing, and dental care and delivery systems for eyeglasses, hearing aids, and dentures are used by all age groups, it is the elderly who particularly need these services and products as means of at least partially alleviating existing disabilities.

Cost is the big barrier to acquiring such products and services. None of them are fully covered by Medicare, and private health insurance also typically does not provide coverage. Thus, though Medicaid may cover some of these products and services in some states, generally the elderly must pay for them out of their current budgets. Unfortunately, many people over 65 cannot afford the extensive costs involved in the acquisition of eyeglasses, dentures, or hearing aids. So acquisition is postponed or does not occur at all. As a result, their quality of life is severely reduced, and many of them suffer from feelings of loneliness, shame, or inferiority.

There are two possible solutions to this situation: (1) develop delivery systems for eyeglasses, hearing aids, and dentures that will cause costs to be reduced substantially, to a level that all elderly could afford; and (2) provide at least partial coverage for these products and services under Medicare.

REFERENCES

Administration on Aging. *Facts About Older Americans*. OHDS-79-2006. Washington, D.C.: Administration on Aging, 1978.

Dancer, J., and Drummond, S.S. "Communications Problems of the Elderly: A Survey." *Nursing Homes*. May/June 1985, 26–29.

Diggs, C. "ASHA Recognizes Needs of Older Persons." American Speech and Hearing Association 22 (1980):401–403.

Ferm, L. "Behavioral Activities in Demented Geriatric Patients." *Gerontology* 16 (1975):195.

National Center for Health Statistics, Health Resources Administration. *Prevalence of Selected Impairments, United States, 1971*. HRA–75–1527. Washington, D.C.: U.S. GPO, 1975.

U.S. Congress. House. Select Committee on Aging. Subcommittee on Health and Long-Term Care. *Medical Appliances and the Elderly: Unmet Needs and Excessive Costs for Eyeglasses, Hearing Aids, Dentures, and Other Devices*. 94th Cong., 2d sess., 1976.

Abuse and Neglect

INTRODUCTION

The problem of elder abuse and neglect is not a new one. During the 1970s, however, the issue of abuse and neglect in the nation's nursing homes became a subject of national concern. Today, reports of abuse and neglect of the elderly in the home setting as well are expanding the area of popular concern.

It is probably correct to emphasize the noninstitutional environment as the focus of concern, for several reasons. First, the nursing homes are generally open facilities and abuse or neglect is usually difficult to hide in such settings. Second, with the increase and stress on home health care, the elderly patient at home is in particular need of protection from abuse and neglect. Third, the prospective payment system for Medicare patients is resulting in many of them being discharged from hospitals much earlier than before. They then continue their recuperation in a home setting where they are usually cared for by a family member and occasionally visited by a health care provider, usually a home health agency nurse. In such a setting, again, the chances for abuse and neglect are probably increasing.

In this chapter, we first attempt to define the nature of elder abuse and neglect in the context of relevant state statutes. Next we review a study of health care providers regarding the issues of diagnosing and intervening in cases of elder abuse. Finally we look at the potential for health care neglect in this area, in the light of Medicare reimbursement policies for home health care patients, that is, patients who have been discharged early from the hospital because of the incentives provided by the Medicare prospective payment system.

DEFINITIONS

Elder abuse usually refers to physical injury not caused by accident. Elder neglect usually refers to the failure to provide goods and services necessary to sustain life and health. Thobaben and Anderson (1985) provide considerable detail on how various state laws define abuse and neglect. Their study focused specifically on the requirements for health care providers to report abuse when it is observed. They found that two states, Alabama and California, consider elder abuse and neglect a misdemeanor, with a fine of up to $1,000 if a health care provider fails to report observed cases of such abuse or neglect. Other states have no specific penalties, but most of them require health care providers to report elder abuse. Indeed, state legislatures generally view elder abuse and neglect as a serious issue and have enacted laws to protect the elderly in this area. Though these laws vary widely, they usually stipulate that a health care provider's failure to report occurrences of elder abuse or neglect is either a misdemeanor or a violation of mandatory requirements to report such information to authorities.

DIAGNOSIS AND INTERVENTION IN CASES OF ELDER ABUSE

Defining elder abuse may be considerably easier than diagnosing it, particularly in the home setting. With the increasing emphasis on home health care, more and more of the elderly are remaining in a home environment instead of moving to an institutional setting, such as a nursing home. And, though the home environment is usually associated with a friendly and more acceptable setting for an elderly resident who requires health care and other services, it is so only if there is a willing and able care giver around to provide the necessary services. Thus, the quality of such care in a home environment varies widely. Much of it is indeed characterized by a warm, friendly, and caring atmosphere. There are, however, also situations in which it is characterized by abuse and neglect. Such situations must be brought to the attention of the proper authorities. But a precondition for that is the proper identification and diagnosis of the abuse or neglect by the care giver involved.

Phillips and Rempusheskie (1985) have developed a conceptual model for diagnosing and intervening in elder abuse and neglect, based on four research questions:

1. How do health care providers giving advice and care to the elderly in the community conceptualize elder abuse and neglect?
2. How do health care providers translate their definitions of elder abuse and neglect into decisions about abused and/or neglected elders?
3. What are the social phenomena that surround the health care providers' decision-making processes for elder abuse and neglect?
4. What other characteristics of elders and care givers enhance or inhibit the health care provider's decisions regarding the presence or absence of elder abuse and neglect?

In their study, Phillips and Rempusheskie obtained answers to these questions in a closely controlled interview process. The interviewers consisted of 16 nurses and 13 social workers employed by home health agencies or community service agencies. Based on the information generated, a conceptual model was developed, showing that health care providers assess the quality of care-giving situations but not the quality of elder-caregiver relationships when making decisions about abuse and neglect.

Although this conceptual model is too complex to describe here in detail, we can briefly summarize five paths that it projects. Path A is characterized by the health care provider formulating a diagnostic decision based on structural factors and the performance of the role of the elderly patient's care giver. The health care provider then surveys the intervention options available and makes the intervention decision. Although this would appear to be the most desirable way for health care providers to behave in situations where elder abuse is suspected, use of this path was the least commonly reported by the health care providers in the sample.

Path B is characterized by the health care provider formulating both a diagnostic decision and a value decision, which then results in vacillation between the two decisions. A final decision usually is not made until more definitive evidence is obtained. The vacillation cycle results in active worry by the health care providers, together with expressions of self-doubt and guilt about being unable to decide.

Path C is characterized by the health care provider making a diagnostic decision and a value decision but then choosing not to intervene because of excess weight given the value decision. The value decision in this case is heavily weighted because of the health care provider's empathy with the care giver's actions which led to the elder abuse.

Path D is characterized by the health care provider surveying the available intervention options, their perceived constraints, and their perceived consequences, but then not making an intervention decision. In this case, the health care provider attributes importance to the perceived lack of intervention options, the possible consequences, and the perceived constraints. In this situation, the health care provider expresses hopelessness, helplessness, and powerlessness.

Finally, Path E is characterized by the health care provider arriving at one or more intervention decisions, consisting of a variety of therapeutic or self-protective strategies. Extreme intervention amounts to removal of the patient from the home environment, while a mild intervention consists of educating the family of the patient.

Based on their findings, Phillips and Rempusheskie conclude that intervention strategies for elder abuse are not easily developed. They found that the association between the diagnostic decision and the intervention decision is quite low. In a number of cases, the type of intervention strategy chosen did not match the diagnostic decision. In other cases, the strength of the intervention strategy selected did not match the diagnostic decision. Explanations for the lack of association between intervention and diagnosis lie in the relative importance that health care providers attribute to factors other than the diagnosis and intervention options.

THE IMPACT OF FEDERAL POLICIES

With the introduction of prospective payments for hospitalization of the elderly under Medicare, the issue of health care neglect because of early hospital discharges has become a matter of concern. The home health care industry has been able to intercept those patients who need posthospitalization services, but the question remains, To what degree can the home health care industry cope with the situation?

Indeed, Taylor (1986) questions whether the Medicare prospective payment system has introduced forces that undermine the ability of home health providers to meet the needs of elderly patients. Taylor points out that regulatory restrictions in home health eligibility under Medicare and the prospect of reduced cost limits for home health services jeopardize home health agencies' ability to respond to the new demand.

Under the prospective payment system (PPS) for Medicare hospital payments, based on the DRG classification scheme, hospitals receive a predetermined amount, depending on the diagnosis of the patient. If the hospital's cost is less than the DRG rate, the hospital retains the difference; if the actual costs are higher, the hospital must absorb the additional costs.

Because of the PPS monetary incentives, hospitals seek to discharge patients once their medical conditions have become stabilized. However, many of these patients require continued nursing care during the recuperative period—care that is typically provided by home health agencies. As a result, the workload on home health agencies has increased considerably. In addition, the types of services provided by home health agencies now include high technology services, such as intravenous therapies, respiratory therapies, and chemotherapy. This is increasing the complexity of home health care. So far, home health agencies have been able to cope with this situation, but Medicare's efforts to control costs in home health care are putting increasing pressure to contain the rates home health agencies can charge.

Taylor (1986) notes that the increased pressure to control Medicare reimbursement rates in home health care for the early discharged Medicare patient has, in turn, put increasing pressure on home health agencies to consider case-mix factors. And the use of case-mix factors may very well limit the amount of time home health agencies are able to devote to the elderly Medicare patient.

As a result home health care may become rationed and the potential for health care neglect may grow. Thus, the tightened reimbursement rates threaten most directly the people who are being discharged from hospitals in compliance with PPS incentives. Medicare's restrictions on home health care reimbursements are especially surprising since there is no evidence of excessive growth in costs of home health services (Taylor 1986).

The homebound elderly ill are uniquely vulnerable. They are the ones who are least able to defend themselves when services are cut back. Thus, current Medicare policies on home health agency reimbursement represent a growing potential for creating conditions of elder neglect.

CONCLUSION

There is no disagreement about the importance of reporting elder abuse or neglect when these conditions are observed by health care providers. Yet, as we have seen, though most states have elder abuse statutes on their books, only two have misdemeanor penalties for the nonreporting of elder abuse when observed.

In our examination of the behavior of home health and community service personnel in diagnosing and intervening in cases of apparent and alleged abuse, the finding of widespread reluctance to report elderly patient abuse was somewhat surprising. Yet, the cost and risks presently associated with the reporting of alleged elderly abuse makes the behavior of these health care providers understandable.

Finally, the possible adverse effects of Medicare's efforts to reduce reimbursements for posthospitalization home health services to the nation's elderly should be cause for concern. The fact that such cost-saving efforts may actually have a serious negative impact on the provision of necessary services to the elderly after they have been discharged by hospitals should prompt policy reconsideration of the way the prospective payment mechanism is currently being applied.

REFERENCES

Phillips, L.R., and Rempusheskie, V.R. "A Decision-Making Model for Diagnosing and Intervening in Elder Abuse and Neglect." *Nursing Research* 34 (May/June 1985):134–139.

Taylor, M.B. "Contradictions in Federal Policies Put Elderly at Risk of Health Care Neglect." *Home Health Care Services Quarterly* 7 (Summer 1986):5–12.

Thobaben, M., and Anderson, L. "Reporting Elder Abuse: It's the Law." *American Journal of Nursing*, April 1985, 371–374.

Chapter 26

Terminal Care: The Hospice Movement*

INTRODUCTION

The hospice concept of care has been evolving for several centuries, starting with the places of comfort and shelter offered to pilgrims of the Middle Ages. The modern hospice provides palliative care and support to terminally ill patients and their families when it is decided that curative treatment is no longer appropriate. Hospice care has grown rapidly since the first program opened in the United States in 1974. Today, approximately 1,500 programs call themselves hospices.

The hospice model can take several forms. The most common are the hospital-based scattered bed, the hospital-based autonomous, the community-based or free-standing, and the home-care-based. The hospital-based scattered bed hospice either has undesignated beds on medical-surgical units of one or more hospitals or has specially designated rooms on given units in the hospital. The hospital-based autonomous hospice has specially designated rooms on a hospital unit and provides inpatient hospice care with its own hospice staff. The hospice staff does not provide care to other patients in the hospital. The community-based or free-standing hospice has its own inpatient facility and is not part of a hospital. The home-care-based hospice provides counseling services and other home care services to the terminally ill patient in the patient's home. At this time, no single model of care or organizational structure dominates hospice care. However, enactment of Section 112 of the Tax Equity and Fiscal Responsibility Act of 1982, which provides for Medicare reimbursement of hospice care, is having a significant impact on the formation of hospices across the country.

---

*This chapter is based on a paper entitled "Hospice Movement" by Linda Tryka, School of Management, SUNY/Buffalo, 1985.

This chapter reviews the concept of hospice care for the terminally ill and examines the cost-effectiveness of hospice care as distinguished from conventional care. The review includes examination of studies done on the federal, state, and local level.

BACKGROUND

History of Hospice Care

Dr. Cicely Saunders founded the contemporary hospice movement with the opening of St. Christopher's Hospice in England in the summer of 1967 (Koff 1978). Originally a social worker, Dr. Saunders enrolled in medical school, trained at an established hospice in London, and refined techniques for controlling the pain associated with terminal disease (Stoddard 1978). In 1959, she began to plan for the opening of St. Christopher's, and in 1967 St. Christopher's received its first patient (Saunders 1977).

Although St. Christopher's Hospice was the first to combine all of the elements of a modern hospice program, it was not the first institution to specialize in care for the dying person, nor was it the first to be called a hospice. The roots of the modern hospice stretch back to the hospices, hospitals, and hotels of medieval times (Stoddard 1978). Even earlier examples of hospices can be found, such as the Syrian hospice of 475 A.D.

Even before St. Christopher's Hospice opened, Dr. Saunders had begun to sow the seed of the modern hospice idea, and she found fertile ground in the United States. Her visit to New Haven, Connecticut, in 1963, introduced her to a group of clergy, nurses, doctors, and social workers who were eager to learn about the philosophy and models of hospice care. The end result of this visit was the planning of a hospice in Connecticut, the institution that was to be the forerunner of the hospice movement in the United States.

The Connecticut group incorporated in 1971 as Hospice, Inc. Several foundations provided grants for community education and development, and the medical director of St. Christopher's Hospice in England agreed to come to Connecticut as medical director of Hospice, Inc., and to provide much-needed experience. The medical director's first duty was to seek a demonstration grant from the National Cancer Institute. A three-year grant was eventually obtained, and Hospice, Inc., began offering home care to its first patients in March of 1974 (Lack 1978). A 44-bed inpatient facility was opened in 1980.

As Hospice, Inc., was getting off the ground, other hospice models were developing in various parts of the North American continent. A 12-bed unit within the Royal Victoria Hospital in Montreal, Canada, was opened in 1975. On the other side of the continent, the Hospice of Marin in Marin County,

California, received a license as a home health agency and began serving patients in early 1976 (Lamers 1978). The first complete, free-standing hospice in North America was Hillhaven Hospice of Tucson, Arizona. This full-service, 39-bed hospice opened in April 1977 under the sponsorship of the Hillhaven Foundation of Tacoma, Washington.

Philosophy of Hospice Care

Up to 1976, the hospice concept was understood by only a few people in the United States. As of November 1985, however, it was estimated that 1,500 hospice programs were in existence in this country. These hospices provide comprehensive programs of care for those persons with terminal illness and for whom active therapeutic treatment is no longer appropriate or being pursued. Thus, its emphasis is on care rather than cure, on comfort rather than rehabilitation.

Hospice care involves the patient and family as the unit of care, with emphasis on control of symptoms, under medical direction. The care extends through the bereavement period. In this sense, hospice is a concept, not an institution; and the services offered by hospice programs vary. Some hospice programs offer only counseling services, to patients in hospitals, at home, in nursing homes, or other settings. Other programs provide a hospice team in an existing hospital or nursing home. The main thrust at this time is toward home-care programs offering a full range of services, including 24-hour on-call service and bereavement services (Koff 1978).

The U.S. health care system may be roughly classified into acute and chronic care. Traditionally acute care is provided in the hospital, and chronic care is provided in the nursing home or by home health care staff. The difference between acute and chronic care is not based on the number of days of care needed as much as the expectations of the patient using either form of care. A hospital patient expects life-saving techniques and restored health. A chronically ill patient often anticipates neither cure nor total improvement. The hospice patient has still a different set of expectations. This patient requires palliative care and management of symptoms. Indeed, it is now recognized that the needs and expectations of the dying patient deserve the same considerations as those of the acutely and chronically ill. These needs and expectations are in fact defining a third level of care—hospice care—to complement acute and chronic care.

ASSESSMENTS OF HOSPICE CARE

In this section, we address the following questions: (1) What is the cost of hospice care and how do costs compare with conventional care? (2) Are patients and family satisfied with the care being provided in the hospice setting? (3) What are the utilization rates associated with hospice care?

Evaluation of Cost

The Federal Role

In the 1970s, the growth of the hospice movement and the public recognition it received catalyzed advocacy of federal support for hospice services. In 1979, Congress responded by mandating a study to examine the implications of including hospice services in the Medicare program. The Health Care Financing Administration (HCFA) selected 25 hospices (from an experimental applicant pool of 233) to participate in a two-year program. These hospice demonstration sites received reimbursement for services to Medicare beneficiaries that would not otherwise be available under current regulations. The special reimbursement provisions went into effect in October 1980. In the spring of 1980, the Robert Wood Johnson Foundation and the John A. Hartford Foundation joined with HCFA in soliciting proposals for a national evaluation of hospice care as a basis for future federal fiscal policy and legislation in this area. Brown University was selected as the evaluation center in a competitive process, and the grant was awarded on September 30, 1980.

The resulting evaluation was a quasi-experimental process in which the impact of hospice care (with and without reimbursement) on the quality of life was compared with that of nonhospice (conventional) terminal care. Costs of the two types of care were also compared. The relevant data were collected over an 18-month period from approximately 4,000 patients receiving terminal care in 25 hospice sites and 12 conventional terminal care sites. Analysis of different outcomes was performed using standard linear multiple regression and logistic multiple regression, with separate models for each comparison group (Green et al. 1983).

The National Hospice Study

The National Hospice Study (NHS) was designed to answer explicit questions about the costs of hospice care and its potential for reducing costs. It also examined the impact of the hospice setting on the type of care provided and on the quality of life of patients and families. The NHS was based on the two-year evaluation demonstration program sponsored by the HCFA. Its findings were used extensively by the HCFA in preparation of its TEFRA hospice regulations and reimbursement rates, as discussed in a subsequent section.

Initial exploratory analysis of the NHS data emphasized the importance of distinguishing between hospices with beds, either as part of a hospital or free-standing organization with its own inpatient beds, and hospices without direct control over inpatient beds. The former are referred to here as hospital-based (HB), the latter as home-care-based (HCB). The NHS analysis included 11 HB and 14 HCB hospices. In addition, it included 12 conventional care (CC) sites located in different areas and representing good quality (nonhospice) oncological care, in the opinion of knowledgeable area physicians (Birnbaum and Kidder 1984).

Data on the characteristics of the 2,746 HCB and 1,143 HB hospice patients at the time of their admission into the hospice are presented in Table 26-1. Ninety percent of the sample was 65 years or over, as would be expected from a sample of Medicare beneficiaries. Males and females were approximately equal in number, and most patients were married at time of admission.

The NHS results suggest that the average HB hospice day costs Medicare 44 percent more than the average HCB day ($95 versus $66). Since the HCB patients stayed longer in the hospice program than the HB patients, the average cost per patient in the two groups showed less of a difference. Total cost per patient for HB enrollment was $5,890, 24 percent more than the $4,758 cost per HCB patient. There was considerable variation in cost among hospice patients. Most of this variation was at the extremes of the cost distribution curve. The cost distribution of HCB patients is skewed more toward less costly patients than it is for HB patients, with 17.9 percent of HCB patients having total costs of $500 or less, compared with 9.4 percent of HB patients (Birnbaum and Kidder 1984).

The average length of stay (LOS) was longer in HCB than in HB hospices. The sample distribution of LOS for both types of care was extremely skewed, with median LOS (37.1 days and 33.0 days for HCB and HB, respectively) being about one-half of the mean LOS. Most patients remained in the hospice program about one month, but 7.8 percent of HCB patients and 6.0 percent of HB patients exceeded 210 days (Birnbaum and Kidder 1984).

The major determinant of cost of care in both the HCB- and HB-style hospices was the utilization of inpatient hospital care. HB patients received 3.5 times the number of patient days of care that HCB patients received. The mean number of patient days was 5.2 days for HCB and 18.2 days for HB, as shown in Table 26-2. HCB patients received almost twice as much home care, but this care was less expensive than hospital inpatient care.

A surprising finding was that almost ten percent of the patients with a terminal diagnosis were discharged from the hospice alive. This ten percent had higher costs than those patients who died in the hospice. Data were not available to determine whether the former patients left because of discontent or remission or because they moved out of the area. Noncancer patients and patients who lived alone also stayed in the hospice program longer and had a higher cost.

In another approach, the cost of care for hospice cancer patients was compared with the cost of conventional care for cancer patients. The findings showed that

Table 26-1 National Hospice Survey: Patient Characteristics of Hospital Cost Sample

Demographic and Diagnostic Variables	Home Care (N = 2746) (Percent)	Hospital-Based (N = 1143) (Percent)
Age		
21–64	10.7	8.2
65–74	54.9	58.3
75 +	34.4	33.7
Sex		
Male	51.4	52.5
Female	48.6	47.5
Marital status		
Currently married	62.9	54.7
Not currently married	37.1	45.3
Family income		
$0–9,999	60.4	58.3
10–49,999	38.4	41.0
50,000 +	1.2	.7
Patient living arrangement		
Alone	8.9	16.5
Not alone	91.1	83.2
Primary care person (PCP) relationship[a]		
Spouse	56.0	49.8
Child	28.1	34.3
Other	15.9	15.9
Race		
White	94.3	94.9
Other	5.7	5.2
Diagnosis		
Cancer	92.6	93.0
Noncancer	7.4	7.0

[a]The National Hospice Study required that all patients have a primary care person. This is not a requirement for Medicare reimbursement.

Source: Journal of Chronic Diseases, Vol. 36, pp. 737–780, Pergamon Press, Ltd., © 1983.

while HCB hospices seemed invariably to produce savings, HB hospices showed cost increases for patients with stays longer than two months (Birnbaum and Kidder 1984).

Traditionally, the common belief has been that hospice care costs less than conventional treatments of terminal illness. There are two reasons given for this belief. One reason is that the hospice presumably substitutes home care for more expensive hospital care. The other reason is that the hospice patient would appear to require less aggressive treatment, permitting the hospice to free itself from

Table 26-2 Utilization of Hospice Service

Utilization Units Per Hospice Patient	Home Care Hospice	Hospital-Based Hospice
Inpatient days (hospice and hospital)		
Mean	5.2 days	18.2 days
Median	0.4 days	9.0 days
Home services hours		
Mean (excluding continuous care)	108.4 hours	59.3 hours
Median	38.6 hours	9.4 hours
Continuous home respite care hours		
Mean	11.9 hours	0.5 hours
Median	0.1 hours	.005 hours

Source: Journal of Chronic Diseases, Vol. 36, pp. 737–780, Pergamon Press, Ltd., © 1983.

intensive use of expensive ancillary services (radiation, chemotherapy, diagnostic tests, and so on). However, from the data gathered on the HB style of hospice, it appears that costs can actually increase when home care is provided as a supplement to inpatient care rather than as a substitute.

Medicare Reimbursement for Hospice Patients

A direct result of the National Hospice Study was the enactment of Section 122 of the Equity and Fiscal Responsibility Act of 1982 (TEFRA), providing the hospice Medicare benefit. It was stipulated that the hospice benefit would be available for four years, after which time it would be reviewed. Based on NHS findings, however, significant limitations and restrictions were placed on hospice care reimbursement. The main limitations were:

- The 80/20 ratio, that is, the aggregate number of home care days must be at least 80 percent of total days, and aggregate inpatient days can be no more than 20 percent of total days.
- A $6,500 cap, the maximum reimbursement for any eligible hospice patient.
- The stipulation that Medicare reimbursement is available for up to 210 days of care. A patient in the program after 210 days cannot be discharged by the hospice; however, the hospice will not be reimbursed for the care.

The Health Care Financing Administration has developed a cost-based prospective payment system consisting of four levels of care to be reimbursed, and regionally adjusted, in the following manner:

Routine home care	$ 53.17/day
Inpatient hospice care	$217.00/day
Continuous home care	$358.67/24 hour (paid in 8-hour increments)
Respite care	$ 55.33/day

The routine home care is the backbone of this reimbursement system because it accounts for 80 percent of care. It should be noted that the $53.17/day rate for such care represents a hard-fought increase (as of October 1984) from the $46.25/day rate allowed in the rule implemented in 1982. Many certified hospices are reporting that it costs $70.47/day for routine home care. Included in the home care rate is reimbursement for the professional services of registered nurses, social workers, physical therapists, occupational therapists, physicians, and home health aides; for drugs, equipment, and supplies; and for homemaker and outpatient services (Tehan 1985). Continuous care means the presence of hospice staff on a continuous basis. Respite care is patient care provided to a patient to relieve the primary care giver for short periods of time.

Evaluation of Satisfaction with Care

In New York State, legislative recognition of the hospice concept is embodied in Chapter 718 of the state Laws of 1978 (Hannan and O'Donnell 1984). Chapter 718 authorized the New York State Public Health Council to establish a hospice demonstration program to evaluate the use of hospice care within the health care system of the state and aid in the establishment of regulations governing the certification and operation of hospices.

As a result of this legislation, 15 hospices were chosen for the New York State Hospice Demonstration Program. Of these, 12 were fully operational, including 2 that were part of the federal demonstration program. All 12 hospices were in urban areas of New York.

Chapter 718 initially mandated three hospice models based on inpatient bed arrangements: scattered bed, autonomous unit, and free-standing. The two hospices that were originally designated as free-standing did not operate their own inpatient units during the demonstration program. Therefore, the categories were reclassified as follows: community-based, hospital-based scattered bed, and hospital-based autonomous unit. In each category, there were four hospices.

The New York study evaluated the 12 hospices in four areas:

1. assessment of hospice utilization and charges
2. comparison of costs of hospice care and conventional nonhospice care for terminal patients
3. assessment of the satisfaction with hospice care
4. estimation of the impact of volunteers

Also, the study was to provide the basis for recommendations on the advisability of hospice legislation and regulations in New York State. In early 1983, the final report on the study was sent to the speaker of the Assembly and president of the Senate of New York State.

Several types of information were gathered in the study. Each hospice submitted two program profiles, each covering a six-month period. In January 1982, the hospices began submitting patient histories for each patient discharged. At the time of evaluation, 800 complete histories were available, covering discharges up to August 31, 1982. These histories included patient statistics and cost information. Interviews were conducted with primary care persons, in conjunction with questionnaires, to determine the levels of satisfaction with hospice care.

Satisfaction with hospice care was measured in terms of the enhancement of the physical and emotional quality of life of the patient and the extent of emotional support and assistance to the patient's primary care person and family. Satisfaction of the primary care person was very high with all models, ranging from 95 percent to 98 percent. The responses concerning the impact on the patient's emotional and physical quality of life were more mixed, but they still revealed high satisfaction levels, ranging from 84 percent to 94 percent.

Evaluation of Utilization Rates

Service Profiles

The New York State study revealed wide variation in the number of patients who died at home, depending on the hospice model with which they were associated. Considerably more community-based hospice patients died at home (66 percent) than patients in the hospital-based scattered bed (31 percent) or hospital-based autonomous unit models. These differences are not surprising in view of the inpatient orientation of the latter two models. It should also be noted that, in 1981, 14 percent of all cancer-related deaths occurred at home; thus, all hospice models had higher percentages of at-home deaths (Hannan and O'Donnell 1984).

The average charge per patient ranged from a low of $2,939 for community-based programs to a high of $8,792 for hospital-based scattered bed programs. A major reason for these differences was the average length of enrollment. The community-based model had an average enrollment of 38.7 days, followed by the hospital-based autonomous unit model with 59.4 days, and the hospital-based scattered bed model with 76.2 days.

Inpatient Utilization

The percentage of hospice patients who received inpatient care varied tremendously among the models in the New York study. The community-based model had the lowest utilization percentage, 43.1 percent, with 77.1 percent for the hospital-based scattered bed model and 83.6 percent for the hospital-based autonomous unit model. The average number of inpatient days also varied significantly. The average for the community-based model was 9.0 days, whereas it was 17.6 days for the hospital-based scattered bed model and 15.6 days for the hospital-based autonomous unit model. The low average for the community-based model was caused partially by an exceedingly low figure of 0.8 days for one of the four programs in that model category.

The average percentages of inpatient days used in each model category were 23.3 percent for the community-based model, 23.2 percent for the hospital-based scattered bed model, and 26.6 percent for the hospital-based autonomous unit model. These figures are somewhat misleading, however, because the community-based programs had a much shorter enrollment period than the hospital-based programs.

A general conclusion from the study regarding inpatient utilization is that community-based programs are much less inclined to hospitalize their patients than are hospital-based programs. This is probably the result of hospital-based programs' tendency to make use of their inpatient beds.

With respect to charges, the average charge per patient for inpatient care in the New York study ranged from a low of $1,671 for community-based programs to $6,459 for the hospital-based scattered bed program. The average charge per day for the hospital-based scattered bed programs was $366.70, nearly $100 more than the average for the hospital-based autonomous unit programs and $22 more than the average for the community-based programs. A higher level of diagnostic activity and use of ancillary services occurred in the hospital-based programs. This was probably due to the fact that, in those programs, hospice patients were treated more like other patients in the same hospital, with less emphasis on palliative care. The costs of treatment and drugs were also considerably higher in the hospital-based scattered bed model (Hannan and O'Donnell 1984).

Home Care Utilization

For the purpose of the New York study, home care days were defined as the total number of enrollment days minus the number of days in inpatient care. Data were not available for the number of days that patients actually received home care services, that is, received visits from hospice staff personnel or volunteers.

The figures in Table 26-3 show percentage of patients with at least one day of home care, the average and median number of home care days, and the average charge per home care day. Differences in these variables among the models cannot be attributed entirely to the models' varying commitment to home

Table 26-3 NYS Hospice Demonstration Program: Hospice Utilization and Charges

Utilization Measures	Community-Based	Hospital-Based Scattered Bed	Hospital-Based Autonomous Unit
Charges and Length of Enrollment			
Total number of patients	248.0	192.0	360.0
Average length of enrollment (days)	38.7	76.2	59.4
Median length of enrollment (days)	17.4	36.5	26.9
Average total program charge/patient	$2,939.00	$8,792.00	$5,254.00
Average charge per patient per day	$ 76.35	$ 115.67	$ 89.36
Summary of Inpatient Utilization			
Percent receiving inpatient care	43.1	77.1	83.6
Average number of inpatient days	9.0	17.6	15.6
Median number of inpatient days	.4	9.6	7.9
Average charge for inpatient care per enrollment period	$1,671.00	$6,459.00	$4,209.00
Average charge per inpatient day	$ 186.30	$ 366.70	$ 269.47
Summary of Home Care Utilization			
Percent with home care days	83.5	78.1	58.9
Average number of home care days	29.5	58.4	43.2
Median number of home care days	12.2	22.5	8.2
Average charge per home care day	$ 42.96	$ 39.95	$ 24.20

Source: *Inquiry*, Vol. 21, pp. 338–384, Blue Cross Association, © 1984.

care. Differences in the length of enrollment among the programs also had an effect on the statistical results.

Medicare Reimbursement

Federal legislation mandates a cap of $6,500 on reimbursement to a hospice patient. The average charge per hospice patient in the New York State Demonstration Program was $5,385 ($2,939 for community-based, $5,254 for hospital-based autonomous unit, and $8,792 for hospital-based scattered bed). Four demonstration programs exceeded the $6,500 per-patient limit. The highest cost was $11,500 per patient. It was clear that those programs that failed to meet the limit would have to lower their length of enrollment, raise their percentage of volunteers, and/or reduce the intensity of care if they wanted Medicare reimbursement to cover their costs.

With respect to utilization, federal legislation stipulates that, for hospice patients, the total number of inpatient days cannot exceed 20 percent of the total enrollment days. For the 12 hospices in the demonstration program, the average percentage of inpatient days was 24.8 percent. Seven programs exceeded the 20 percent cap, and four had more than 30 percent inpatient days.

HOSPICE BUFFALO: A CASE EXAMPLE

Hospice Buffalo was incorporated in 1976 and admitted its first patient in January 1980. Several members of the founding group of the hospice were involved with the development of the first U.S. hospice in Connecticut. Actual planning for Hospice Buffalo began in 1974; thus, the program actually took six years to become operational. It was included in the New York State Demonstration Program and was instrumental in pushing for separate hospice licensure in the state legislature.

The long period of time devoted by Hospice Buffalo to planning and education resulted in a comprehensive hospice that can be best described as a community-based or free-standing model. Hospice Buffalo admits only patients diagnosed as terminally ill cancer patients. It provides a complete range of services, including nursing, counseling, bereavement, pharmaceutical, medical, housekeeping, and home health care. The majority of these services are provided in the patient's home, with a primary care person (family member or friend) having the major responsibility for care.

Hospice Buffalo has two inpatient facilities. One is a five-bed independent hospice unit at Buffalo General Hospital that can provide acute care if necessary. This unit, staffed by hospice personnel with a ratio of four nurses to five patients, operates under the Hospice Buffalo license. The other facility is a ten-bed unit in Alden, New York, that provides respite care for Hospice Buffalo patients.

Prior to the opening of Hospice Buffalo in 1980, newspaper articles about the program brought in over 120 offers to volunteer. In 1985, the hospice had 35 paid staff members and approximately 300 volunteers. About 125 of these volunteers had been involved in active duty during the preceding six months; the other 175 were trained and awaiting assignment. The volunteers are treated as if they were paid staff; they receive a three-hour orientation, a two-hour interview, and 15–18 hours of inservice training. About a quarter of the volunteers are health professionals. Because of this screening, Hospice Buffalo is able to carry liability and malpractice insurance on both paid and volunteer staff.

Hospice Buffalo considers for admission only those cancer patients with a limited life expectancy. Approximately 65 percent of the patients in the hospice are over 65 years of age. All referrals are examined by the medical director, who then works with the patient's referring physician to provide the hospice care. Emphasis is placed on the elimination of pain and the rehabilitation of the patient to the best physical condition achievable once the pain has been controlled. Realistic goals are set by each patient, and the hospice staff and the primary care person work with the patient to achieve those goals during the patient's remaining time.

Limiting admission to cancer patients is common in hospice care because cancer is a fairly predictable disease and its symptoms frequently require special methods of pain control. Having some expectation of the course of the disease is important because of the cost and time limitations placed on hospices by Medicare reimbursement regulations.

At the present time, over 190 families are being followed by the Hospice Buffalo staff. The follow-up continues for one year after the death of the patient. Support groups are currently being established for the men, women, and teenagers involved in the lives of the patients who have died.

Hospice Buffalo receives reimbursement for its services from a number of sources, including Medicare and contracts with Blue Cross, Health Care Plan, and other private insurers. The cost of enrolling patients who are uninsured and unable to pay must be absorbed by the organization. A director of development expands Hospice Buffalo's efforts to fund itself through endowments, grants, and other contributions.

CONCLUSION

After approximately ten years of experience with hospice care in the United States, there are still many unresolved issues. Regulations and reimbursement policies are being developed for hospices, and this is resulting in a change from hospices as a movement to hospices as an industry. However, there are still unanswered questions:

1. Should hospice care be offered by for-profit agencies?
2. Is hospice care a duplication of service offered by home health care agencies?
3. How can hospice care be provided for patients without a primary care giver (relative or friend) and still be cost effective?

4. Which hospice model is best suited to care for the terminally ill patient and fulfill the hospice role?

Efforts are being made in health care generally to avoid duplication of services, as evidenced by the requirement for a certificate of need when a facility wishes to offer a service. Arguments have been made that the hospice serves merely to coordinate care obtained from existing health care providers. Advocates of the hospice point out, however, that hospice care is more than just the coordination of care from a variety of care givers. It is scrupulous attention to the physical, psychological, social, and spiritual aspects of the patient/family constellation. It is the involvement with clients from the last six months of illness through bereavement. It is the facilitation of resources to meet the concerns and needs of patient, family, and friends. And it is the catalyzing of communication and connectedness (Corr and Corr 1984).

In an effort to avoid the restrictions imposed by the Medicare Reimbursement Act, some nonprofit and for-profit agencies and institutions have resorted to offering pieces of hospice service while billing for third party reimbursement in a role other than as a hospice. There is serious doubt that this type of service can be considered true hospice care.

From the studies reviewed on the federal, state, and local levels, it appears that hospice care can be offered on a comprehensive basis. But this must be done carefully; hospice care must always be offered as a substitute for inpatient care rather than as a supplement.

Those hospice programs, usually community-based or free-standing, that adhere to the philosophy of involving patient families, utilizing volunteers, and keeping patients in their own homes are able to provide satisfactory physical and emotional support while still containing costs. In contrast, hospital-based hospice programs, while benefiting from such on-premises facilities as dietary, laundry, billing, and pharmacy, are tempted to utilize their inpatient beds and treat their hospice patients in a conventional manner, thereby increasing costs.

As a model, Hospice Buffalo appears to exemplify the best hospice care available at this time. Its community-based style and independent management allow flexibility and innovation. Costs are carefully controlled, but the needs of the individual patient always come first. Patients are not admitted unless they meet specific requirements; therefore, there is no confusion about the role the hospice is to play in the lives of the patients. Pain relief, palliative care, and emotional support are the goals of the program. Aggressive therapy and acute care do not enter the picture.

It remains to be seen whether the spirit of the hospice as envisioned by Dr. Saunders will survive, or whether the hospice movement will be absorbed and become just another indistinguishable part of the institutional package of health care in the United States.

REFERENCES

Birnbaum, H.G., and Kidder, D. "What Does Hospice Cost?" *American Journal of Public Health* 74 (1984):689–697.

Corr, C.A., and Corr, D.M. *Hospice Care: Principles and Practices*. New York: Springer Publishing, 1984.

Green, D.S.; Mor, V.; Sherwood, S.; Morris, J.N.; and Birnbaum, H. "National Hospice Study Analysis Plan." *Journal of Chronic Diseases* 36 (1983):737–780.

Hannan, E.L., and O'Donnell, J.F. "An Evaluation of Hospices in the New York State Hospice Demonstration Program." *Inquiry* 21 (1984):338–384.

Koff, T.H. *Hospice, A Caring Community*. Briarcliff Manor, N.Y.: Stein and Day, 1978.

Lack, S. "New Haven (1974), Characteristics of a Hospice Program of Care." *Death Education* 2 (Spring/Summer 1978):41–52.

Lamers, W. "Marin County (1976), Development of Hospice of Marin." *Death Education* 2 (Spring/Summer 1978):53–62.

Saunders, C. "Dying They Live: St. Christopher's Hospice." In *New Meanings of Death*, edited by H. Feifel. New York: McGraw-Hill Book Co., 1977.

Stoddard, S. *The Hospice Movement*. Briarcliff Manor, N.Y.: Stein and Day, 1978.

Tehan, C.B. "Decision 85: Is Hospice Medicare Certification Worth the Risk?" *Caring* (February 1985):41–44.

Chapter 27

Future of Health Care for the Elderly

INTRODUCTION

As emphasized in several contexts in this volume, the size of the elderly population will increase substantially during the next 50 years, both in absolute numbers and as a percentage of the total population. As a result, we will see a substantial increase in the need and utilization of health care, not only by the elderly as a group but also by the total population. Because an increasing share of the gross national product (GNP) will be used to provide this care, there will also undoubtedly be growing concern and interest in health care and in cost containment.

This final chapter explores a few areas that will have a particular impact on the health care delivery process and health care costs of the future. Some of these areas have the potential for improving the quality of health care and, indirectly, our quality of life—at some cost, of course, to the taxpayer.

RISING HEALTH CARE COSTS

As we have seen, health care costs in the United States have reached a level of over 11 percent of the GNP. We can anticipate a continuing rise in this percentage, for a variety of reasons. A major reason is that the United States has entered a service-oriented economy, and an increasing percentage of the GNP will be generated by services. Health care will have a large relative share of that percentage, and most likely an increasing share. Eventually, it will probably account for 15 percent of the GNP, though this figure may not be reached before the turn of the century.

This projected rise in health care costs, both relatively and absolutely, will be due not only to an increase in illnesses or growing demands for health care services. It will also reflect improvements, and rising costs, in diagnostic, evaluative, therapeutic, and curative techniques and technology in the coming years. In this section, we review potential changes in each of these areas and see how they are likely to add to our total health care budget.

Diagnostic Techniques

Diagnostic procedures have been expanding at a rapid rate. Multiphasic screening, CAT scanners, and other technologies have made available to the physician a growing body of data for diagnostic purposes. Indeed, the information now available frequently exceeds the physician's experience, knowledge, and ability to make accurate diagnoses. Yet, the capability to generate more diagnostic data will surely contribute to further improvements in diagnostic abilities.

In particular, the technical capabilities of diagnostic equipment will keep expanding the areas of knowledge. The explosion in expensive, highly technical equipment is frequently blamed for the rapidly escalating health care costs. To the extent that such equipment is used primarily to generate revenue rather than diagnostic data, this may be true. When such equipment is acquired without adequate demand, higher per unit costs are generated. However, increased government regulation will probably serve to reduce the number of cases where expensive, highly technical equipment is acquired by institutions for self-aggrandizement. Also, the sharing of such high-cost specialized equipment will also probably become more common in the future.

Yet, though the future will probably see a decline in outright waste through poor or unnecessary utilization of expensive equipment, the total cost of health care will undoubtedly keep rising. The new technology will provide diagnostic data that are unimaginable with today's techniques. The beneficiaries will be the ill whose treatment will improve, but the costs will be borne by all.

Evaluative Procedures

The area of physical evaluation is still very much in its infancy. When one visits a physician for a physical examination, the physician usually provides only minimal information to the client. Only in the case of a serious problem is the physician likely to provide detailed information. If there are no problems, the result of the examination is usually merely a report that everything is normal.

However, individuals are becoming more interested in using the various output measures of a physical examination to monitor their own condition. To some extent, individuals are already capable of self-evaluation. Heart rate, temperature, and blood pressure are conditions that one can monitor regularly. However, numerous other measures still require special assistance in the form of a physician or technician using a diagnostic device, such as an x-ray or chemical laboratory test. The ultimate benefits of such detailed evaluations are by no means clear in all cases. Yet, they will undoubtedly continue to be attractive, not only to younger adults but also to the elderly, particularly since many of the evaluative procedures involved fall into the category of preventive medicine. Thus, there will no doubt continue to be considerable public support for this type of physical evaluation. And, since the cost of providing such procedures will be reimbursable under most third party arrangements, this will add to health care costs.

Therapeutic Procedures

Rehabilitative therapy for mental, and especially physical, disabilities will be a rapidly growing area in health care. In the past, the physically disabled patient was usually relegated to the role of a nonproductive, or at best partially productive, citizen. Now, the increasing interest in and expansion of rehabilitative therapy is changing that situation. Although the growing resources of rehabilitative therapy will be devoted largely to younger persons who have the potential for long productive life spans, eventually, as rehabilitative resources become more extensive, the elderly will also reap the benefits.

Again, the costs of providing such rehabilitative programs will be high. In the best facilities, like a physical rehabilitation institute, a rehabilitation program for patients with low back pain now runs about $800 per day. Such costs will continue to grow for many people, adding to the overall cost of personal health care. However, no less tangible, though less easily measured, will be the benefits society derives from having the rehabilitated lead more productive lives.

Curative Procedures

Curative medicine, the kind of medicine practiced by the majority of physicians, will clearly continue to expand. To date, the fastest growth in this area has been in heart by-pass surgery. The next 50 years will witness other innovations in curative medicine that will increase the demand for physicians trained in particular specialties. In particular, the growing numbers of senior citizens will prompt increasing interest in that part of our population. The geriatrician, now a rarity, will become as common as the pediatrician.

Thus, the field of medicine will continue to expand with new curative procedures and the addition of other specialties. And, again, the cost of supporting the expanded field will add to the cost of personal health care.

THE ELDERLY AS CONTRIBUTORS TO HEALTH CARE COSTS

In 1984, those 65 years and older constituted about 12.5 percent of the total U.S. population, but they accounted for about one-third of all health care expenditures (U.S. Congress 1986). In Canada, the figures are even higher; in 1976, Canadians 65 and over accounted for 38.3 percent of Canada's personal health expenditures (Schwenger and Gross 1980). The larger Canadian percentage can be attributed to Canada's high long-term care institutionalization rate for persons 65 and over; this rate was 8.9 percent in 1976, including psychiatric patients (Hertzman and Hayes 1985). In the United States, the long-term institutionalization rate for persons 65 and over has remained fairly steady at 5.0 percent.

As we have seen, although the 65-and-over population in the United States is expected to grow from the 1984 figure of 12.5 percent to only about 13 percent in 2010, the 85-and-over group is projected to increase from 9.4 percent of all elderly in 1985 to 16.9 percent of all elderly in 2010 (U.S. Congress 1986). And, because many in this latter group reside in long-term chronic care institutions, it is also the group with the highest health care expenditures.

In 1984, life expectancy for U.S. males was 77.8 years; for females, it was 80.8 years. Since it is assumed that life expectancy overall will continue to increase, albeit at a slower rate, the life expectancy for males in 2010 is projected to be 81.1 years and for females 86.1 years (U.S. Congress 1986). As a result, personal health care expenditures for those 65 and over will probably reach about 50 percent of total personal health care expenditures by the year 2010.

In the growing debate over how we are going to pay for these projected higher health care costs for the elderly, the fact that the elderly population in 2010 is going to be more affluent than the elderly population of today is often overlooked. Between 1969 and 1984, the average income increased by 18 percent for elderly families and by 34 percent for elderly individuals, after adjusting for inflation. As a result, the overall poverty rate for the elderly was reduced from 25.3 percent in 1969 to 12.4 percent in 1984. Also in 1984, 4.0 percent of elderly families had annual incomes of $20,100 and up, and 40.0 percent of elderly individuals had annual incomes of $8,050 and up (U.S. Congress 1986).

Assuming the affluence of the elderly will continue to grow, the elderly in the aggregate may in fact soon be able to finance their own health care. What is needed in this situation is a financing scheme that would allow the cost of health care to be distributed fairly across all of the elderly, based on financial ability and need. The most promising approach would be a modified Medicare plan that would cover all health care costs for the elderly, including long-term care.

CONCLUSION

The elderly as a group will grow in numbers and in strength—politically and economically. Politically, they will inspire more respect from and greater equality with the younger population. Economically, they will be in better financial condition through improved government-financed and employer-paid retirement and health care programs. But they will continue to bear an increasing part of the economic burden through taxation (those with higher retirement incomes) and through economic participation (those able to participate in productive activities).

The elderly as a group will undergo changes. At present, all those over 65 are grouped in a single category. Soon, however, we may see the development of a special group of elderly starting at age 70. Alternatively, we may want to distinguish two types of elderly—the junior elderly, those 65 to 75, and the senior elderly, those 75 and over. Indeed, if we want to obtain accurate health care statistics in the future, we may find it particularly useful to separate the elderly into several groups. Currently, many health care statistics for the elderly are already becoming inapplicable over such a large age group that displays widely varying health care needs.

In sum, by the turn of the century, we may see the beginning of a period when health care is widely available to all, without financial constraints. The cost to society will be substantial, but in a service-oriented society such as ours, we must be willing to shoulder that burden. Yet, when health care expenditures rise to more than 15 percent of the GNP, as they probably will, we will continue to hear demands for cost containment.

However, cost containment need not be at the expense of the elderly. With their increased political and economic strength, they will be in a good position to protect their interests and ensure that high quality health care is available to all, regardless of economic condition. In this context, we will also see the enactment of some form of catastrophic health insurance, which will remove costly long-term nursing home care from the welfare (Medicaid) rolls and make it a right instead of a handout for all those who need it.

REFERENCES

Hertzman, C., and Hayes, M. "Will the Elderly Really Bankrupt Us With Increased Health Care Costs?" *Canadian Journal of Public Health* 76 (November/December 1985):373–377.

Schwenger, C.W., and Gross, M.J. "Institutional Care and Institutionalization of the Elderly in Canada." In *Aging in Canada: Social Perspectives*, edited by V.M. Marshall. Toronto, Ontario: Fitzenry and Whiteside, 1980.

U.S. Congress. General Accounting Office. *An Aging Society—Meeting the Needs of the Elderly While Responding to Rising Federal Costs.* GAO/HRD–86–135. Washington, D.C.: U.S. GPO, 1986.

Index